Practical social w

Published in conjunction with
the British Association of Social Workers
Series Editor: Jo Campling

BASW

Social work is at an important stage in its development. The profession is facing fresh challenges to work flexibly in fast-changing social and organisational environments. New requirements for training are also demanding a more critical and reflective, as well as more highly skilled, approach to practice.

The British Association of Social Workers has always been conscious of its role in setting guidelines for practice and in seeking to raise professional standards. The concept of the *Practical Social Work* series was conceived to fulfil a genuine professional need for a carefully planned, coherent series of texts that would stimulate and inform debate, thereby contributing to the development of practitioners' skills and professionalism.

Newly relaunched, the series continues to address the needs of all those who are looking to deepen and refresh their understanding and skills. It is designed for students and busy professionals alike. Each book marries practice issues and challenges with the latest theory and research in a compact and applied format. The authors represent a wide variety of experience both as educators and practitioners. Taken together, the books set a standard in their clarity, relevance and rigour.

A list of new and best-selling titles in this series follows overleaf. A comprehensive list of titles available in the series, and further details about individual books, can be found online at :
www.palgrave.com/socialworkpolicy/basw

Series standing order **ISBN 0–333–80313–2**

You can receive future titles in this series as they are published by placing a standing order. Please contact your bookseller or, in the case of difficulty, contact us at the address below with your name and address, the title of the series and the ISBN quoted above.

Customer Services Department, Macmillan Distribution Ltd, Houndmills, Basingstoke, Hampshire RG21 6XS, England

Practical social work series

New and best-selling titles

Robert Adams *Empowerment, Participation and Social Work (4th edition)* **new!**

Sarah Banks *Ethics and Values in Social Work (3rd edition)*

James G. Barber *Social Work with Addictions (2nd edition)*

Suzy Braye and Michael Preston-Shoot *Practising Social Work Law (2nd edition)*

Veronica Coulshed and Joan Orme *Social Work Practice (4th edition)*

Veronica Coulshed and Audrey Mullender with David N. Jones and Neil Thompson *Management in Social Work (3rd edition)*

Lena Dominelli *Anti-Racist Social Work (3rd edition)* **new!**

Celia Doyle *Working with Abused Children (3rd edition)*

Tony Jeffs and Mark Smith (editors) *Youth Work*

Joyce Lishman *Communication in Social Work (2nd edition)* **new!**

Paula Nicolson and Rowan Bayne and Jenny Owen *Applied Psychology for Social Workers (3rd edition)*

Judith Phillips, Mo Ray and Mary Marshall *Social Work with Older People (4th edition)*

Michael Oliver and Bob Sapey *Social Work with Disabled People (3rd edition)*

Michael Preston-Shoot *Effective Groupwork (2nd edition)* **new!**

Steven Shardlow and Mark Doel *Practice Learning and Teaching*

Neil Thompson *Anti-Discriminatory Practice (4th edition)*

Derek Tilbury *Working with Mental Illness (2nd edition)*

Alan Twelvetrees *Community Work (4th edition)* **new!**

Social Work with Addictions

Second Edition

James G. Barber

palgrave
macmillan

The author has asserted his right to be identified as the author of this work in accordance with the Copyright, Designs and Patents Act 1988.

First edition 1995
Reprinted four times
Second edition 2002

Published by
PALGRAVE MACMILLAN
Houndmills, Basingstoke, Hampshire RG21 6XS and
175 Fifth Avenue, New York, N.Y. 10010
Companies and representatives throughout the world

PALGRAVE MACMILLAN is the global academic imprint of the Palgrave Macmillan division of St Martin s Press, LLC and of Palgrave Macmillan Ltd. Macmillanfi is a registered trademark in the United States, United Kingdom and other countries. Palgrave is a registered trademark in the European Union and other countries.

ISBN 10: 0-333-98594-X
ISBN 13: 978-0-333-98594-6

This book is printed on paper suitable for recycling and made from fully managed and sustained forest sources. Logging, pulping and manufacturing processes are expected to conform to the environmental regulations of the country of origin.

A catalogue record for this book is available from the British Library.

Printed and bound in Great Britain by the MPG Books Group

Contents

v

6 Maintenance   **130**
  Level I: Interventions at the level of the individual   131
  Level II: Interventions at the level of family, work and
  social support networks   142
  Level III: Intervention at the level of social policy
  and culture   150

7 Evaluation   **160**
  The principles of programme evaluation   161
  Political issues in programme evaluation   167

References   171

Index   196

List of Figures

List of Tables

Preface

When the first edition of this book came out in 1995, the prevention of licit and illicit drug use had become one of the developed world's highest public health priorities. Breathtaking amounts of money were (and still are) being committed to crop eradication and drug interdiction by the United States in particular, and almost everywhere, it seemed, politicians were going to the polls with promises of increased public spending on policing, treatment and prevention. Seven years on and the yield from all this money and effort appears mixed. In Australia, for example, there has been little change in the lifetime and recent use of alcohol and tobacco, and illicit drug use is actually increasing, particularly among young women. In fact, in the three years after the book was released, the change in female drug-taking behaviour was largely responsible for driving up the number of Australians who had ever tried illicit substances by almost 20 per cent, and the number who had ever injected by almost 100 per cent.

In the United States and the United Kingdom, researchers and policy-makers tend to be sanguine about drug trends in their countries these days, but again, the evidence is actually mixed. Taken together, the US 'National Household' and 'Monitoring the Future' surveys reveal great regional variations in legal and illegal drug use, and suggest that while the 12–17-year age group is heeding the drug prevention message, the same is not true for the 18–25-year age group, whose use of illicit drugs is on the rise. In the UK, recent surveys suggest that the overall rate of illicit drug use among teenagers declined between 1995 and the turn of the century, but the same surveys also identified several striking regional variations and a geographically widespread rise in heroin use among both males and females.

In light of the complex picture presented by drug prevalence trends, those who claim that we are either winning or losing 'the war on drugs' are both right and wrong. Depending on country, region, class, gender, substance and age group, most countries are chalking up victories and defeats. The fact is that we humans love drugs; always have and always will. We may know that Adam and Eve 'partook' of the forbidden fruit, for example, but we don't know how. My own hunch is that they fermented it.

As professionals in the forefront of the community's efforts to ameliorate the social consequences of drug misuse and, if possible, to prevent it in the first place, social workers will find much of the discussion about drug statistics exceedingly academic. Most practitioners confront the turmoil wrought by drugs on a daily or near daily basis. This book has been written for them. More specifically, it is intended primarily for non-drug specialists who need access to brief, reliable methods for responding to drug users at every stage of change from extreme resistance, to the trials involved in staying sober or clean for life. Despite the fact that much of the research into the origins and treatment of drug misuse has been conducted by other professions, social work is particularly well-suited to the field of addictions. This is because social workers tend to encounter drug misusers before drug specialists do, and because social work's systemic approach to coping problems is consistent with the fact that all of the best predictors of treatment outcome are social factors.

In constructing this book, I have tried to maximise its utility for social workers by emphasising three characteristics. First, the book adopts social work's person-in-situation perspective so as to identify interventions at every system level, from the individual with the problem through their microsystem and eventually at the level of law reform and social policy. Second, the book devotes considerable attention to a type of drug user who is confronted more by social work than any other helping profession – the resistant type. Third, I have described brief intervention methods wherever possible because generalist social workers rarely have the luxury of dropping all their other casework responsibilities to concentrate on one individual's drug use. Rather, most practitioners require methods that can be readily incorporated into broader case plans.

The major differences between this edition and the first reflect the book's commitment to evidence-based practice. Although the structure of this edition is very similar to the first, most sections have been updated in light of the latest research findings. Research since the first edition has resulted in some new sections, such as the new material on 'pressures to change' for resistant users, and cue exposure and scheduled withdrawal for clients in treatment. In other places, it has been necessary merely to modify claims that were made in the earlier edition. As in the first edition, the book opens with a discussion of what constitutes a drug and what is the nature of addiction before moving to the model of change around which the book has been built. The rest of the book outlines methods that are appropriate at each of the stages of change described in that model. Finally, the book concludes with a discussion of the methodological and political issues involved in answering the question, 'How do you know whether or not your efforts have been worthwhile?'

Over the years, my work in various fields of practice has taught me the relevance of the principles covered in this book to many other stubborn problems confronted by social workers, such as domestic violence, gambling and various dysfunctional habits in interpersonal communication. In these and other situations, social workers will encounter the stages of 'precontemplation', 'contemplation', 'action', 'maintenance' and 'relapse' that form the subject matter of this book. It is my earnest hope, therefore, that readers will find something of value in these pages wherever they work.

Every effort has been made to contact all copyright-holders of material used in the tables and figures in this book. If anyone has been inadvertently omitted, the publishers will be pleased to make the necessary arrangement at the earliest opportunity.

JAMES G. BARBER

To the Australian Jesuits,
teachers, friends, kindred spirits

1

Drugs and Drug Addiction

Public education campaigns against drug abuse have no doubt
done a great deal to defeat old stereotypes about drugs, but the
chances are that when most of us think about 'the drug problem'
we still tend to think of kids shooting up in shabby flats or sniffing
glue behind railway stations. The truth, of course, is that just about
all of us take drugs to lift us, relax us, dampen pain or just to
escape. Heroin users and glue sniffers are no different in that
sense. In the eighteenth century coffee was considered by medical
experts to be a very dangerous drug and its use in the West was
largely restricted to the Bohemian set living in Paris at the time.
The point is that what we take to be 'the drug problem' in a given
period of history is determined by the socially acceptable standards
of the day, so the place to start in drug prevention work is by
ridding ourselves of any inaccurate myths and fears about drugs
themselves. After all, not only do illegal drugs have a similar
purpose to legal drugs, they are no more dangerous. To take just
one example, heroin creates less dependence than nicotine, is
easier to give up than alcohol for a heavy drinker and thought to
cause little long-term damage if pure and used in a controlled way.
Tobacco, on the other hand, is *the* most physically destructive drug
of all. It is more likely to produce dependence than barbiturates,
alcohol or heroin. The British Royal College of Physicians classes
smoking as a cause of death alongside the great epidemic killers,
such as typhoid, cholera and tuberculosis. We also like to place
tranquillisers, sleeping pills and analgesics in a different category
altogether from heroin or cocaine, but it has been estimated that if
tranquilliser medication were outlawed in the United Kingdom,
over 100,000 people would immediately go into full drug withdrawal symptoms (Brazier, 1984). The reasons why some drugs are

1

legal and others are illegal are rather complex but one thing is certain: it has nothing to do with dangerousness.

What is a drug?

Until relatively recently, the World Health Organisation defined a drug as 'A substance that, when taken into the living organism, may modify one or more of its functions' (WHO, 1969, p. 7). As a later WHO (1981) Expert Committee recognised, however, this definition is impossibly overinclusive. Under the definition, air and water, for example, could both be called 'drugs'! The revised WHO definition is hierarchical. At the first and most general level, a drug is said to be 'any chemical entity or mixture of entities, other than those required for the maintenance of normal health, the administration of which alters biological function and possibly structure' (WHO, 1981, p. 227). This would exclude benign substances like air, water and food, provided the amounts ingested do not interfere with normal health. At a level below this is the use to which the substance is put, and here the authors advocate the term 'non-medical use' to exclude drugs used for the alleviation of disease. Because different drugs act on different sites, WHO includes this as a third level of analysis and suggests that attention be restricted to so-called 'psychoactive drugs' which alter mood, cognition and behaviour. At the fourth and final level, the current WHO definition emphasises drugs that are both self-administered and impair health or social functioning.

Various taxonomies have been proposed for classifying substances that meet the above criteria but three approaches predominate. One approach is to classify drugs according to their mechanism of action, a second is according to their similarities in chemical structure, and a third is according to their effects on behaviour. According to Julien (2000), it is best to adopt the third of these possibilities. This is because our current understanding of the brain's physiology is too limited to permit classification according to mechanism of action, and there are too many drugs which have similar pharmacological properties but different chemical structures to classify drugs by structure. In Table 1.1 below, commonly misused drugs have been organised into four main classes according to their effect on mood and behaviour: (a) sedative–hypnotic compounds, (b) stimulants, (c) psychedelic and hallucinogenic substances, and (d) other. As the label implies, sedative–hypnotics induce behavioural depression extending from anti-anxiety through sleep to general anaesthesia, coma and, eventually, death. Depending on dosage, virtually all sedative–hypnotics can produce any of these effects. Although not exhaustive of sedative–hypnotics, Table 1.1 refers to barbiturates, benzodiazepines, Gammahydroxybutyrate (GHB), alcohol and opiate narcotics because these are the most commonly misused drugs in this class. Stimulant drugs have the opposite effect to sedative–hypnotics. Notwithstanding great differences in their molecular structures and mechanisms of action, drugs in the stimulant class act to increase behavioural activity and alertness, and elevate the mood of the user. Included under behavioural stimulants in Table 1.1 are amphetamines, cocaine, caffeine and tobacco. Third, the category 'psychedelic and hallucinogenic substances' takes in a heterogeneous set of compounds which have the common property of inducing visual, auditory or other hallucinatory experiences and which act to separate the individual from reality. The major drugs in this category are LSD, mescaline, Datura, PCP and Ecstasy, which is the most common form of 'designer drug'. Under the final category of 'other' drugs we will consider cannabis and inhalants because neither drug type fits easily within any of the other categories.

In referring to Table 1.1, it needs to be recognised that the subjective drug experience may not always conform to the generalisations proposed in the table. In the case of alcohol, for example, anthropological research (see MacAndrew and Edgerton, 1969) has shown that the social behaviour associated with drinking is so varied from culture to culture that the effects of alcohol must be mediated more strongly by social expectations than pharmacological effects. And even *within* cultures there is ample evidence to show that the precise effect of any drug on the individual can vary according to the cognitive (Marlatt *et al.*, 1973) and social (Kalin *et al.*, 1965; Pliner and Cappell, 1974) factors at work when the drug is ingested.

Table 1.1 makes frequent reference to tolerance and withdrawal effects, and a basic understanding of these terms is important to drug prevention workers. Put simply, drug users who ingest a given substance over a long period of time come to 'tolerate' that substance. This means that the dose and frequency of administration must be increased in order to obtain the original effect. As a result, users must take bigger risks with their bodies to achieve the same behavioural or mood-altering return. Cross-tolerance is said to occur where the tolerance developed for one drug works for another, as is the case with heroin and methadone. Heavy alcohol users also tend to tolerate anaesthetics and therefore frequently require a heavier dose when an anaesthetic is necessary. The notion of withdrawal effects will become clearer when we discuss the idea of an 'opponent process' in the next section; for the present it is sufficient to note that when the use of a substance is terminated, it is common for the user to suffer withdrawal symptoms which vary greatly in type and intensity according to the substance involved. As we shall see, the presence of withdrawal symptoms when the concentration of the substance in the bloodstream falls has been used as an operational definition of drug dependence itself.

Table 1.1   *Commonly misused drugs classified according to type, name and effects*

I SEDATIVE–HYPNOTICS

Barbiturates

(a) *Common type and names*

There are many different types including secobarbital (*Seconal*), amobarbital (*Amytal*), phenobarbital (*Luminal*) and pentobarbital (*Nembutal*). Street names include 'downers' or 'barbs'. Also sometimes 'reds', 'red birds', 'red devils', 'red hearts' (*Seconal*), 'blue heavens' (*Amytal*) and 'purple hearts' (*Luminal*).

(b) *Method of ingestion*

Oral.

(c) *Short-term effects*

Calmness and muscular relaxation in small doses. Larger doses usually induce sleep in quiet settings or a 'drunk' feeling in social settings. Short-term effects act quickly and last from 4 to 12 hours. Very large doses produce unconsciousness and some-times death by respiratory failure. Prescribed for anxiety, sleeplessness or sedation, although minor tranquillisers tend to be more popular.

(d) *Longer-term effects*

With prolonged use physical dependence can be very severe. Withdrawal symptoms range from intense to progressive restlessness, anxiety, insomnia and irritability through to delirium, convulsions, hallucinations and vomiting. With heavy use, tolerance also develops but more quickly in the case of sleep-inducing and intoxicating effects than to life-threatening effects such as respiratory depression. Thus, the difference between the effective and fatal dose narrows.

Benzodiazepines or 'minor tranquillisers'

(a) *Common types and names*

There are around thirty different types of benzodiazepines, but common types include: chlordiazepoxide (*Librium*), flurazepam (*Dalmane*), oxazepam (*Serepax*),

Table **1.1** – *continued*

diazepam (Valium), nitrazepam (Mogadon), temazepam (Normison), flunitrazepam (Rohypnol). Also called 'downers' or 'benzos', and sometimes 'tranx', 'rowies', 'moggies', 'vals', or 'normies', on the streets.

(b) *Method of ingestion*

Oral.

(c) *Short-term effects*

As for barbiturates but overdosage is less lethal. For this reason, they are the common agents of first choice when anti-anxiety, sedation or hypnotic (sleep-inducing) action is required. Combined with alcohol or heroin, they produce respiratory depression and impaired visual–motor performance. Overdose on benzodiazepines alone is uncommon, but injecting or combining them with other sedative–hypnotics can lead to stroke, respiratory failure and death.

(d) *Longer-term effects*

As for barbiturates. Tolerance develops quickly and withdrawal symptoms can be both severe and dangerous. Regular users are normally advised to withdraw gradually.

GHB

(a) *Common names*

GHB stands for Gammahydroxybutyrate. Its street names include: 'fantasy', 'grievous bodily harm', 'liquid e', 'liquid x'.

(b) *Method of ingestion*

Normally orally, but some instances of injection.

(c) *Short-term effects*

Technically an anaesthetic drug that also has sedative properties. Often used alongside designer drugs at dance parties and nightclubs because of its capacity to induce euphoria, relaxation, increased sociability, disinhibition and sensitivity to touch. At high doses, muscle spasms, vomiting, convulsions, respiratory failure and disorientation can also occur.

(d) *Longer-term effects*

Unclear. Tolerance and withdrawal effects similar to other sedative–hypnotics seem likely.

Alcohol

(a) *Short-term effects*

In low doses acts as a stimulant but becomes a depressant as dosage increases. Precise behavioural effects influenced by cognitive and social factors. Impairs judgement, visual-motor performance, memory and concentration.

(b) *Longer-term effects*

Long-term effects involve many different organs depending on whether the drinking is heavy or moderate. Effects of heavy use over the long term include: depression or anxiety, memory loss, premature ageing, fits of coughing and colds, infections,

Table 1.1 – *continued*

pneumonia and tuberculosis, cancer, heart attack, liver damage, diarrhoea and stomach ulcers, malnutrition, inflamed pancreas and diseased kidneys. Patterns of tolerance and dependence depend upon amount, pattern and extent of alcohol ingestion. Intermittent or moderate drinking produces little or no tolerance; regular heavy drinking produces marked tolerance and severe withdrawal effects involving rebound hyperexcitability which produces tremulousness, psychomotor agitation, confusion, disorientation, sleep disorders and sometimes even hallucinations, convulsions and death.

Opiate narcotics (such as heroin)

(a) *Common type and names*

As used here, the term 'opiate narcotic' refers to natural or synthetic drugs which behave in the body like morphine – the major active agent derived from the opium poppy. Examples include: heroin (street names include 'junk', 'skag', 'hammer', 'h', 'horse' or 'smack'), morphine, methadone, pethidine, dextromoramide (*Palfium*), codeine, paracetamol and aspirin. Opiates are prescribed mainly for pain relief; also for diarrhoea and as a cough suppressant.

(b) *Method of ingestion*

Oral, inhalation or injection.

(c) *Short-term effects*

Opiates briefly stimulate the brain but then quickly depress the activity of the central nervous system. Immediately after injecting an opiate (especially heroin) the user feels a surge or 'rush' of pleasure often compared to orgasm. This state gives way to a euphoric state of feeling replete and satisfied. Initial side effects may include restlessness, nausea and vomiting. At moderate doses the user drifts between wakefulness and drowsiness. At still higher doses, breathing is depressed and profound respiratory failure resulting in death can follow overdose.

(d) *Longer-term effects*

With regular use, tolerance develops to many of the desired effects. Nevertheless, withdrawal symptoms are reasonably mild compared with alcohol or tobacco and may include: uneasiness, yawning, tears, diarrhoea, abdominal cramps, goosebumps and running nose. Withdrawal has been compared to a dose of the flu. Besides respiratory failure, another serious risk to health involves infection (especially HIV and Hepatitis B or C from needle-sharing). Heroin is among the most commonly used opiate narcotics and it usually comes in powder form. Because heroin dealers often mix or 'cut' the powder with other substances that look similar, it is difficult to know exactly what heroin users ingest and how strong the heroin actually is. For this reason, overdose (or 'dropping') is common even among experienced users.

II BEHAVIOURAL STIMULANTS

Amphetamines

(a) *Common types and names*

Amphetamines are sold as benzedrine, dexedrine, methedrine or preludin. Street names include 'whizz', 'speed', 'uppers', 'bennies', 'dexis', 'crystal', 'sulphate', 'sulph' and

Table **1.1** *– continued*

'peaches'. Prescribed for uncontrollable sleepiness and lethargy, also for the treatment of petit mal epilepsy and for attention deficit (hyperkinesis) in children. (In hyperkinetic children amphetamines have a calming rather than stimulating effect.)

(b) *Method of ingestion*

Oral or injection.

(c) *Short-term effects*

At low doses, effects include reduction of appetite, increased breathing and heart rate, increased blood pressure, and dilation of the pupils. Behaviourally, the user feels energetic, sometimes euphoric, and capable of prolonged concentration. At higher doses, effects include dry mouth, fever, sweating, headache, blurred vision and dizziness. The user becomes talkative and restless, and frequently irritable, aggressive and grandiose as well. Heavy users are prone to sudden, violent acts of an irrational nature. Short-term effects last between 4 and 8 hours.

(d) *Longer-term effects*

With prolonged use, short-term effects are exaggerated and can result in amphetamine psychosis, impulsive violence and depression. Chronic suppression of appetite can produce malnutrition. The common practice of injecting amphetamines creates a risk of infectious diseases such as hepatitis and AIDS. Withdrawal symptoms include fatigue, long but disturbed sleep, irritability, hunger and moderate to severe depression. Tolerance also develops.

Methamphetamine

(a) *Common names*

Methamphetamine is closely related chemically to amphetamine, but the central nervous system effects are stronger. Street names include: 'speed', 'meth' and 'chalk'. Methamphetamine comes in many forms and is readily soluble in water or alcohol. In one form (methamphetamine hydrochloride), methamphetamine looks like ice and can be smoked. In this form it is known as 'ice', 'crystal' or 'glass'.

(b) *Method of ingestion*

Oral, injection, smoking, or snorting.

(c) *Short-term effects*

Generally as for amphetamine, but the precise effect on mood can depend on how it is ingested. A brief, intense 'rush' is associated with smoking or injection, while oral ingestion tends to produce a long-lasting high rather than a rush. Vascular damage, stroke and cardiovascular collapse can occur as a result of raised heart rate and blood pressure.

(d) *Longer-term effects*

As for amphetamine.

Cocaine

(a) *Common names*

'Coke', 'snow', 'c', 'flake'. A powder (hydrochloride salt) extracted from the leaves of the Erythroxylon coca bush. Crude, inexpensive and potent forms of processed cocaine known as 'crack' and 'freebase' are common in the United States.

Table 1.1 – *continued*

(b) *Method of ingestion*

Usually 'snorted' (sniffed). Sometimes applied to mucous lining of mouth, rectum or vagina, or by intravenous injection.

(c) *Short-term effects*

In low doses, produces euphoria, increased energy, enhanced mental alertness and sensory awareness. Also has local anaesthetic properties. Large doses intensify these effects, but may lead to bizarre, erratic and violent behaviours. Physical symptoms include accelerated heartbeat, increased blood pressure, respiration and body temperature. Some individuals display a toxic reaction involving overactive reflexes, tremors, delirium and muscle convulsions. Overdoses can be fatal.

(d) *Longer-term effects*

In the longer term euphoria is usually replaced by restlessness, extreme excitability, insomnia, paranoia and psychosis accompanied by hallucinations and delusions. Also blocked or running nose, damage to nasal passage and renal failure. Withdrawal symptoms are as for amphetamines. Tolerance develops.

Caffeine

(a) *Common types and names*

Coffee, tea, cocoa, cola drinks, chocolate and 'stay awake pills' such as 'no-dose'. Used as part of headache preparations and some pain relievers, and in treatment of apnoea (breathing cessation) in children.

(b) *Short-term effects*

General increase in metabolism evident as increase in activity level and/or body temperature. Delays sleep onset and reduces depth of sleep, increases performance at simple intellectual tasks and physical endurance work. Increases respiration, gastric secretions and urine excretion.

(c) *Longer-term effects*

Large doses (around 8 or 9 cups per day) over long periods produces chronic insomnia, persistent anxiety and depression, and stomach ulcers. Some suggestion of links with cancer. Tolerance develops and withdrawal effects include headache, irritability and anxiety.

Nicotine

(a) *Common types*

Tobacco, as in cigarettes, cigars and pipes.

(b) *Short-term effects*

Tobacco smoke is made up of thousands of constituents with many different effects. Short-term effects include increase in heart rate and respiration, a drop in skin temperature and stimulation of central nervous system. Despite this some smokers use tobacco to relax, which is attributable to suppression of anxiety associated with withdrawal from nicotine.

(c) *Longer-term effects*

Longer-term effects relate mainly to bronchopulmonary and cardiovascular systems: smoking is the main cause of cancer of the lung, mouth and upper respiratory tract. Also

Table **1.1** – *continued*

respiratory disease, blockages of blood vessels in heart, muscle, and limbs. Increased likelihood of stomach ulcers which are slower to heal. Dependence is very severe and withdrawal effects include: irritability, anxiety, difficulty in concentrating, restlessness, headaches, drowsiness and gastrointestinal symptoms including constipation and nausea.

III PSYCHEDELICS AND HALLUCINOGENS

Mescaline

(a) *Common names*

Commonly known as 'peyote' (the name of the cactus plant from which it is derived) or 'mescal buttons'.

(b) *Method of ingestion*

The crown of the plant is dried before being swallowed. Can also be made into cakes, tablets or powder. The powder is sometimes dissolved in water and injected.

(c) *Short-term effects*

Short-term effects last for up to 12 hours and include dilation of the pupils, increased blood pressure, heart rate and body temperature. Increased behavioural activity similar to amphetamines and visual hallucinations.

(d) *Longer-term effects*

May lead to flashback experiences (unpredictable, brief, spontaneous recurrences of the original experience) or psychotic reaction but withdrawal effects and tolerance are not normally a problem.

Datura

(a) *Common names*

There are many different species in the Datura genus. Probably the two most well-known species are: Datura inoxia (commonly known as 'devil's weed') and Datura strammonium ('jimson weed'). Datura brugmansia ('angel's trumpet') is another well-known plant that has recently been reclassified to the genus Brugmansia (Tree Datura). All of the species of Datura are leafy green plants with bright pink to white flowers.

(b) *Method of ingestion*

As for mescaline.

(c) *Short-term effects*

As for mescaline.

(d) *Longer-term effects*

As for mescaline.

Magic mushrooms

(a) *Common names*

There are dozens of species of this naturally occurring fugus which is commonly known as 'shrooms'. All species contain the psychoactive substances psilocin and psilocybin.

Table 1.1 – *continued*

(b) *Method of ingestion*

Eaten raw or cooked, or taken in solution as a tea drink.

(c) *Short-term effects*

The effects of magic mushrooms are greatly affected by dose and an individual's sensitivity to psilocybin. For some people very small amounts of psilocybin can be enough to propel them into full visionary hallucinations, unpleasant stomach cramps and other high-dose effects such as sleeplessness and tremors, lack of muscular coordination and convulsions. For other people the same amount would be barely noticeable, possibly causing a slight cold feeling.

(d) *Longer-term effects*

As for mescaline.

LSD

(a) *Common names*

LSD stands for Lysergic Acid Diethylamide. Otherwise known as 'acid'. Preparations sold as LSD are sometimes really Phencyclidine or 'PCP'.

(b) *Method of ingestion*

Normally oral but can be 'snorted' or injected.

(c) *Short-term effects*

Produces remarkable psychological changes in very small doses and with very little physiological change. Changes occur to perception, thought and mood. Users sometimes report feeling more than one mood at once or swinging rapidly from one mood to the next. At the height of the 'trip' hallucinations may occur such as feeling that parts of the body are swollen or detached from the rest. The mind may feel that it is floating, looking down at the body. The capacity to distinguish the boundaries of one object from another is impaired. The experience can be pleasant or terrifying.

(d) *Longer-term effects*

Withdrawal is not a major problem except that flashbacks can occur. Tolerance develops quickly but is lost quickly following abstinence.

PCP

(a) *Common names*

PCP stands for Phencyclidine and in its powdered form is known as 'angel dust', 'ozone', 'rocket fuel', 'love boat', 'hog' or 'superweed'. In its liquid form, PCP is commonly called 'embalming fluid', but sometimes also 'formaldehyde', 'wet', 'water' or 'amp'. PCP is a synthetic chemical which is not easily classified because of its myriad effects on the central nervous system. It is rarely sold as PCP but tends to be marketed as something else, such as LSD or as cannabis which has been dipped in liquid PCP.

(b) *Method of ingestion*

Snorted or smoked. Occasionally injected or swallowed.

Table **1.1** – *continued*

(c) *Short-term effects*

It is debatable whether PCP actually belongs in the hallucinogenic class. It is more commonly referred to in the medical literature as a 'disassociative' drug because its sedative and anaesthetic effects can be trance-like, with users sometimes reporting a feeling of being out of their bodies. At low doses (1–5 mg), PCP feels like very potent marijuana. At higher doses, the effects are much less predictable but can include: hypertension, nausea, blurred vision, dizziness, anaesthesia, muscle contractions causing bizarre body postures, seizure, depressed breathing, coma and even death.

(d) *Longer-term effects*

With repeated use, memory loss, difficulties with speech and thinking, weight loss and depression persisting for up to a year after quitting. Prolonged psychotic states have also been reported. Tolerance does not develop and withdrawal effects are mild to moderate.

Ecstasy

(a) *Common names and types*

MDMA, commonly known as 'ecstasy' or 'E', 'PMA', 'DOM', 'XTC', 'adam', 'hug' or 'love drug'.

(b) *Method of ingestion*

Normally oral but sometimes also by injection.

(c) *Short-term effects*

Ecstasy is a synthetic drug which has both stimulant and hallucinogenic properties. Although not strictly hallucinogenic at low doses, effects can include altered perception and blurred vision. Users report feelings of intense self-confidence, well-being and affection for those around them. Unpleasant side effects can include vomiting, depression, jaw spasms and irrational behaviour. Hyperthermia and dehydration are common and potentially lethal side effects. Ecstasy pills are notoriously unreliable in content, more so than most other street drugs, and commonly contain either caffeine, ephedrine, amphetamines, MDA, MDE, DXM, or – in rare cases – DOB, and do not necessarily contain MDMA or any psychoactive.

(d) *Longer-term effects*

Tolerance develops but is quickly lost and long-term use has been linked with damage to the brain (particularly to those parts involved in memory and logical thought), heart and liver.

IV OTHER

Cannabis

(a) *Common names*

Known as 'marijuana', 'hashish', 'hash', 'dope', 'weed', 'the herb', 'pot', 'THC' (after the active ingredient), 'grass', 'hemp', 'blow', 'ganja' and others.

(b) *Method of ingestion*

Smoked or eaten.

Table **1.1** – *continued*

(c) *Short-term effects*

Technically a depressant but immediate effects include a 'high' or euphoric state with a tendency to talk and laugh more than usual. Impairs short-term memory, logical thinking and psychomotor skills. These effects disappear within a few hours. In large doses, hallucinations, delusions or anxiety can result, and the user may misjudge the passage of time so that a few minutes seem like hours.

(d) *Longer-term effects*

Respiratory disorders such as chronic bronchitis, loss of energy and drive, slow confused thinking, impaired memory, diarrhoea, abdominal cramps, weight loss or gain, loss of libido. These symptoms gradually disappear when usage stops. Some suggestion of chromosome damage. Tolerance is moderate and withdrawal symptoms tend to be mild by comparison with alcohol or tobacco.

Inhalants

(a) *Common names and types*

There are four general categories of inhalants: (1) volatile solvents, such as *hexane* (plastic cement), *toluene, xylene* (glue, thinners and petrol), *acetone* (nail polish remover), *trichloroethane* (cleaning fluid), *benzene* (petrol and cleaning fluids), (2) aerosols that contain solvents and propellants (spray paints, deodorant and hair sprays, vegetable oil sprays and fabric protector sprays), (3) gases, especially *nitrous oxide* or 'laughing gas' (whipped cream dispensers, butane lighters, propane tanks and refrigerants), and (4) nitrites, such as *cyclohexyl nitrite*, (room deodorisers) and *amylnitrite* (for heart pain).

(b) *Method of ingestion*

Sniffed.

(c) *Short-term effects*

Immediate effects are similar to alcohol: euphoria characterised by lightheadedness, pleasant exhilaration, disorientation, vivid fantasies and sometimes excitement. Nausea, increased salivation, sneezing and coughing, muscular incoordination, depressed reflexes and sensitivity to light are common. These effects last from several minutes to around 12 hours. Fatalities are common, caused by cardiac arrest or asphyxiation.

(d) *Longer-term effects*

Pallor, weight loss, nosebleeds, bloodshot eyes, sores on nose and mouth. Bone marrow, kidney, liver, central nervous system, heart and brain are also damaged, and all of these effects can be irreversible. Behaviourally, long-term users report fatigue, depression, irritability, hostility and paranoia. Tolerance is uncommon, but withdrawal symptoms among chronic users can include chills, hallucinations, headaches, abdominal pains, muscular cramps and delirium.

What is addiction?

Many attempts have been made to arrive at a universally acceptable definition of addiction but the matter remains unresolved and contentious. As a result, terms which might *sound* as if they refer to much the same thing (for example, drug abuse and misuse) take on subtle shades of meaning and can lead to spirited, even acrimonious debate among drug experts.

To the lay person this will all seem rather precious and pedantic, as indeed it is, but the reason for the preoccupation with semantics is that opinion is deeply divided about such fundamental issues as when 'heavy use' becomes 'addiction', and whether the problem is primarily physical, psychological or both. As we shall see, early definitions of addiction were dominated by the physically addictive properties of certain drugs, but this approach failed to deal with craving for substances like LSD, marijuana and cocaine which are not addictive in the physical sense, nor did it explain addictions to things other than drugs, such as gambling or food. In order to deal with problems like these, the definition of addiction must incorporate non-biological factors as well. Nowadays, some drug experts prefer to think of addiction as a *behavioural* compulsion, without reference to withdrawal effects at all. To Krivanek (1982, p. 83), for example, 'Addiction will be defined as a behaviour pattern characterised by an ongoing and overwhelming preoccupation with the use of a drug and the securing of its supply'. By this definition, the addict is simply 'someone who is involved with an activity to such an extent that it is the major focus of his or her life' (McAllister *et al.*, 1991, p. 5).

Addiction as disease

Levine (1978) tells us that prior to the eighteenth century, there was little or no concept of addiction. The dominant philosophy then was that people, unlike animals, were fully responsible for their actions by virtue of reason and free will. It was assumed that people got drunk because they *wanted* to, not because they *had* to. In Levine's own words, 'alcohol did not permanently disable the will; it was not addicting, and habitual drunkenness was not regarded as a disease' (1978, p. 144). Whatever its consequences, drunkenness was a choice made for pleasure. Towards the end of the eighteenth century and certainly by the beginning of the nineteenth century, medical practitioners had started to take seriously the reports of habitual drunkards that the urge to drink was irresistible. In an effort to convey the ungovernable force of this compulsion, the American physician,

Benjamin Rush, coined the term 'disease of the will' (Rush, in Levine, 1978) and in this way hauled the problem squarely into the medical arena. As well as declaring habitual drinking to be a disease characterised by loss of control, Rush was also responsible for locating the source of the addiction *within the substance itself*. As a logical consequence, total abstinence became the only sure remedy. Rush's work gave impetus to the emergent Temperance Movement and its increasingly strident call for prohibition. In the United States, the movement for prohibition culminated in the Eighteenth Amendment to the Constitution which made the recreational use of alcohol illegal. Ironically, now that inebriety was against the law, drunkards were actually dealt with much more harshly than they had been when alcoholism was seen as sinfulness rather than illness.

Heather and Robertson (1985) have argued that the repeal of the Eighteenth Amendment in 1933 made it inevitable that the imputed source of addiction would shift from the substance to the person. The new generation of drinkers simply would not or could not tolerate the implication that *everyone* was at risk of alcoholism. On the other hand, if only an unfortunate minority were susceptible to loss of control then the majority could sit back and drink with impunity. Not surprisingly, the liquor industry has always been a strong supporter of this redefinition of alcohol addiction (Rubin, 1979; Morgan, 1988). Room (1973) explains the post-prohibition reconstruction of alcoholism as a political imperative, for it was the only way that drunkards could receive public sympathy and health and welfare provisions. If alcoholics were inherently deficient in some way, they clearly should not be blamed for their disruptive and self-destructive ways. Whatever the explanation (and there is probably some truth in both positions), the *substance* was certainly replaced by the *person* at the centre of the post-prohibition analysis of addition.

The dominance of the Temperance Movement gave way to a new but strikingly similar organisational form known as Alcoholics Anonymous (AA) which articulated the modern disease approach in a series of catchy and intuitively appealing axioms. The AA view begins with a crucial distinction between 'the alcoholic' and other types of drinker: for the alcoholic it is a case of 'one drink, one drunk', as the saying goes. In other words, craving or the compulsion to drink is the common symptom; it is the behavioural consequence of a preexistent and permanent vulnerability that alcoholics have to alcohol. Craving makes it impossible to stop. The preexistent nature of this condition is best conveyed by another of the AA axioms: 'One does not become an alcoholic, one is born an alcoholic'. Thus, alcoholics were now said to have a special vulnerability to alcohol which was present even before the first drink had been taken. Worse still, the condition is incurable or, to cite yet another AA adage, 'once an alcoholic, always an alcoholic'. This notion of irreversibility has become an essential (some would say *the* essential) element of the modern disease approach to alcoholism. Far from an act of free will, alcoholism became a progressive disease which could be arrested but never cured. After a lifetime of abstinence, the best one can hope for is to be a 'recovering alcoholic'.

From a sociological viewpoint, it is most interesting that the modern disease conception of addiction should emanate from AA, a self-help group of reformed drinkers, rather than from medical research. It could be said that medicine's ringing endorsement of AA *before* the evidence was in (and the evidence is still coming in) actually makes more sense from a marketing standpoint than from a scientific one. Indeed, it was not until the seminal work of Jellinek in 1952 (see also Jellinek, 1960), long after the publication of AA's 'Big Book' (Alcoholics Anonymous, 1939), that the modern disease approach to alcoholism began to be articulated by medicine itself. Jellinek distinguished between five 'species' of alcoholism, although he reserved the 'disease' label for only two of them: gamma and delta alcoholism. This is because only these species involve the physiopathological changes of (a) adaptation of cell metabolism, and (b) withdrawal symptoms. Alpha alcoholism is the first of Jellinek's (1960) species and it constitutes a state of psychological dependence in which the drinker relies on alcohol to relieve emotional pain; there is no physiological dependence in the sense just described. The beta alcoholic is one who suffers the presence of physical complications from excessive drinking but who nevertheless shows no signs of physical or psychological dependence. The gamma alcoholic is a 'genuine' alcohol addict. Loss of control over drinking is pathognomonic of the condition and the afflicted individual develops the symptoms of physiological dependence. Like the gamma alcoholic, the delta alcoholic is also addicted to alcohol but rather than being unable to stop, is unable to abstain. Thus, delta alcoholics may be capable of controlling their intake on any occasion of drinking, but they are unable to abstain even for a few days without developing withdrawal symptoms.

Finally, the epsilon alcoholic or dipsomaniac is the rare 'bender' alcoholic who suffers only periodic loss of control.

Nowadays, the World Health Organisation (1977, 1981) avoids the term 'disease', preferring instead to think in terms of an 'alcohol dependence syndrome'. This view originated in a paper by Edwards and Gross (1976) who admit that the idea is based more on clinical impression than scientific investigation. An important feature of the new approach is that the all-or-none categories of 'alcoholic' versus 'non-alcoholic' have been eschewed and alcohol dependence is said to fall on a continuum. There is no obvious dividing line between pathological and non-pathological drinking. The syndrome refers to the concurrence of seven clinical phenomena, not all of which need to be present or present to the same degree in all dependent individuals. The seven elements of the syndrome are as follows:

1. *Narrowing of the drinking repertoire*, such that drinking becomes more stereotyped and scheduled to achieve a target blood alcohol level.
2. *Salience of drink-seeking behaviour*, to the extent that individuals assign a higher priority to their blood alcohol level than to competing demands on their time or money.
3. *Increased tolerance to alcohol*, making it necessary to increase the dosage.
4. *Repeated withdrawal symptoms*, especially tremor, nausea, sweating and mood disturbance when the blood alcohol level falls below a certain threshold.
5. *Relief or avoidance of withdrawal symptoms by further drinking.*
6. *Subjective awareness of a compulsion to drink*, and regular or periodic loss of control when drinking occurs.
7. *Reinstatement (or relapse) after abstinence* to a pattern of drinking which is identical to that at the height of the problem.

Edwards and Gross's (1976) alcohol dependence syndrome idea has been criticised for its simultaneous acceptance of 'alcoholism' and the drinking continuum (Heather and Robertson, 1983, 1985), and clearly there is a logical problem in proposing a pathological syndrome if the condition is also said to be continuous across the population at large. There is no sense in describing a syndrome, no matter how plastic, if the continuum applies to everyone who drinks. Shaw (1979) is similarly unimpressed by Edwards and Gross's

dependence syndrome and explains the whole idea in political terms.
Bluntly, the dependence syndrome allows the disease model to
remain dominant in spite of its logical shortcomings; like Jellinek
(1960) before them, Edwards and his colleagues (Edwards and
Gross, 1976; Edwards, 1977; Edwards *et al.*, 1977a) can continue to
conceive of alcohol dependence as an irreversible state of psycho-
biological dependence in which impaired control is the leading
symptom by fudging on the issues I will come to shortly. Whether or
not we accept Shaw's critique, his more general point is certainly true
that there are vested interests in which definition of addiction will
ultimately prevail, and, sadly, much of the debate comes down to a
struggle between medicine and psychology for dominance of the field.

Before leaving the disease approach to addiction, it is necessary to
refer to the ground-breaking work which is currently under way
within the field of genetics. At least since Goodwin *et al.*'s (1973)
celebrated adoptee study, it has been widely known that there is
at least some genetic component to alcohol addiction. In that study,
55 adoptees whose biological parents had been diagnosed as alcoholic
were followed up and found to have four times the rate of alcoholism
as adoptees from non-alcoholic biological parents. A more recent
study by Cloninger and his colleagues, this time with a much larger
sample of adoptees, has since replicated Goodwin *et al.*'s basic finding. Similarly, Vaillant's (1983) 33-year follow-up study found that
having a relative with a drinking problem significantly increased the
risk of developing alcohol abuse, *irrespective of whether the individual
actually lived with the problem drinker*. On the basis of his findings,
Cloninger (1987) has proposed two types of inherited pattern of
alcohol addiction, and this view is gaining rapidly in acceptance.
'Type I' alcoholism is the milder, more common form; it is associated with later onset than 'Type II' and requires environmental
precipitants. If a Type I individual *also* has a relative with a diagnosis
of alcoholism, the chances of being diagnosed likewise increase
roughly threefold. Under Cloninger's taxonomy, Type II alcoholism
is limited to males, is highly heritable (sons of Type II alcoholic
fathers have nine times the risk of alcohol dependence as sons of
non-alcoholic fathers) and is not much influenced by environmental
factors. In fact, all that is needed for Type II alcoholism to emerge is
access to alcohol and commencement of drinking.

Consistent with Cloninger's proposal was the work of Blum and
his colleagues (Blum *et al.*, 1990) who found an association between

blind diagnosis of alcoholism and the presence of the $A1$ allele of the dopamine D_2 receptor gene. This finding was replicated in a study by a separate research team (Cloninger, 1991) and it generated considerable excitement in the field of addiction research because it appeared to prove beyond doubt that biological factors are at work in at least some alcohol addicts. Even before this breakthrough, however, numerous biological markers had been found to identify people with alcoholism *a priori*. For example, Schuckitt and Gold (1988) showed that individuals with a family history of alcoholism displayed less subjective intoxication, less body sway and less metabolic differences in response to alcohol relative to individuals without this family history. Enzyme studies have also identified biological markers. In a review of this literature, Tabakoff and Hoffman (1988) concluded that something in the order of a dozen controlled studies all converge on the conclusion that there is decreased platelet monoamine oxidase activity in alcoholics relative to controls. Finally, neurological differences have been found between the sons of alcoholic and non-alcoholic fathers (Begleiter *et al.*, 1984; Whipple *et al.*, 1988). Genetic advances like these breathed new life into the disease notion of alcohol addiction which was coming under concerted attack in the 1980s and 1990s (Jurd, 1992). However, although the most recent genetic research confirms that genetic inheritance can increase the risk of alcohol dependence (Farren and Tipton, 1999; Schuckitt, 1999), it appears that the association between alcoholism and the $A1$ allele of the dopamine D_2 receptor gene is not as clear-cut as Blum originally suggested (Foroud and Li, 1999). Indeed, research has produced equivocal results in the field of alcoholism genetics generally (Hill, 1998; Gorwood *et al.*, 2000) and Blum *et al.*'s (1990) fundamental finding has not always been replicated, particularly in cross-cultural studies (for example, Lu *et al.*, 1996; Lee *et al.*, 1997), suggesting that environmental influences cannot be easily separated from genetic ones after all.

For us, the importance of the debate surrounding the definition of addiction lies primarily in its implications for treatment. To the adherents of the modern disease approach, abstinence is the only cure for sufferers; to the opponents of the disease model this prescription is far too dogmatic and, in any case, inconsistent with the facts (Heather and Robertson, 1983, 1985). As we shall see, this clash of treatment objectives arises for two basic reasons: (i) because the modern psychological approach rejects the disease idea, and

(ii) because 'problem drinking' is seen as an instance of maladaptive learning. While it is true that most behavioural psychologists do advocate total abstinence for most severely dependent drinkers, this is usually based on a reluctant acceptance that our current psychological methods are ineffective in training very heavy drinkers to moderate their intake, *not* because these drinkers are qualitatively different from the wider community. In fact, among the most recent psychological research (Sithartan *et al.*, 1997) is the extension of 'cue exposure' techniques to heavier and heavier drinkers, in an effort to reduce the number of problem drinkers who cannot be taught to drink like the rest of us.

Addiction as learned behaviour

Social scientists in the behavioural tradition commonly object to the disease approach to drug addiction as having little clinical or scientific utility. In the first place, the 'loss of control' argument is actually circular: alcoholics cannot control their drinking because they lose control, and they lose control because they are alcoholics. Besides, the 'loss of control' concept does not withstand careful scrutiny anyway. It cannot mean that the amount consumed is not under the drinker's control because 'alcoholics' do not inevitably drink to a state of oblivion. In fact, dependent drinkers, have been shown to consume just enough to reach a very precise blood alcohol target (Mello and Mendelson, 1978). Furthermore, even if a drinker should drink to unconsciousness, there will always be *some* degree of choice involved. Certainly, it may be difficult to control the impulse, especially once drinking has begun, but a decision one way or the other is still required. This point raises a logical contradiction involved in the disease approach to treatment: alcoholics cannot control their drinking, yet the only cure for alcoholism is lifelong abstinence. This paradox can produce very curious outcomes indeed, as when hospitalised alcoholics are told that they suffer from an incurable disease, only to be excluded from treatment programmes the moment they display the symptoms of that disease! Imagine what our city streets would look like if this principle were extended to other incurable diseases such as multiple sclerosis or AIDS.

The modern psychological view is that addictive behaviour is *learned* behaviour and as such should obey the rules that govern

all learning. Thus, 'alcoholism', or 'problem drinking' as most behavioural psychologists prefer to say, is theoretically capable of being
*un*learned through the strategic application of learning theory principle (Heather and Robertson, 1985). It is worth noting, in passing,
that the behavioural or learning theory approach to addiction is not
necessarily invalidated by the evidence reviewed earlier on inborn
physiological mechanisms. In fact, it is frequently argued that social
learning theory can help to explain how these mechanisms are realised
(Babor *et al.*, 1986). After all, there is nothing to suggest that alcoholism *as such* is inherited, only an underlying vulnerability to the
development of drinking problems. Admittedly, if the existence of
the Type II sub-type of alcoholism proposed by Cloninger (1987) is
verified, it could quite properly be considered a disease of genetic
origin because it does not rely on a learned component. However,
Cloninger does not pretend that his work applies to all, or even most,
alcohol addicts.

The first behavioural theory of drug addiction was offered by the
psychiatrist Abraham Wikler (1965) who viewed addiction as the
product of operant conditioning. Drawing on the work of B. F. Skinner
(cf. 1953), Wikler proposed the conceptually straightforward theory
that each ingestion of a drug reinforces drug-seeking behaviour by
providing immediate and powerful reinforcement. Drug-seeking
behaviour is then elaborated into a complex lifestyle through the
association of secondary reinforcers with the primary reinforcer of
drive reduction. As with any other operant response, the solution is
repeated extinction trials. More recently, the motivational-learning
theorist, Richard Solomon (1977; Solomon and Corbitt, 1974), proposed an intriguing alternative model which he referred to as 'the
opponent-process theory of acquired motivation'. Basically, the theory
assumes that the brains of all mammals are organised to oppose or
suppress high levels of arousal, whether the feeling be positive or
negative. The adaptive advantage of this process is presumably to
ensure that behaviour is not disrupted by intense physiological
arousal. Thus, the primary arousal or *a* process is elicited by an
unconditioned stimulus, or follows operant reinforcement, and the
opponent or *b* process acts to suppress the *a* process. If the primary
process is pleasant and reinforcing, the opponent process will be
aversive and punishing, and vice versa. The overall affective condition of the organism will therefore depend on the subjective valence
of the *a* and *b* processes and their relative strengths at any given

Figure 1.1 *The opponent-process theory of acquired motivation*

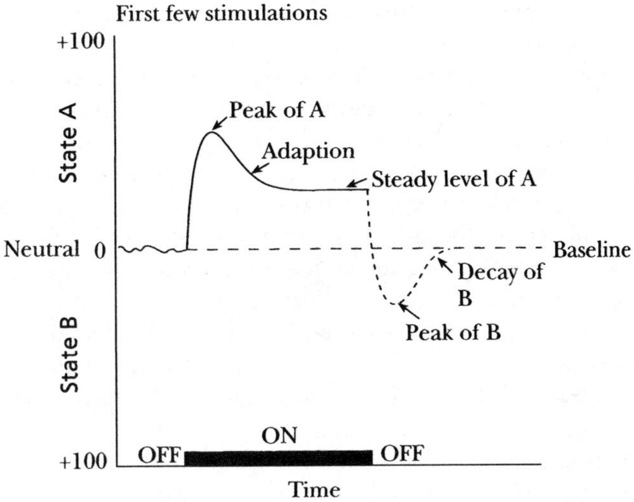

Reprinted from Solomon, R. and Corbitt, J. (1974) 'An opponent process theory of acquired motivation: I. Temporal dynamics of affect', *Psychological Review*, vol. 81, p. 120, American Psychological Association.

point in time: when *a* is greater than *b*, the organism will be in state *a*; when the *b* process is dominant, the organism will be in state *b*. Solomon's theory also proposes that the primary *a* process follows the initial stimulus closely in time and lasts a shorter period of time than the opponent *b* process. These ideas have been expressed graphically in Figure 1.1.

According to the model, then, the addict derives immediate, intense reinforcement from the drug through the *a* process. After a brief period of time, the reinforcing state is opposed by the *b* process and the person enters an unpleasant state commonly referred to as withdrawal. In order to replace the aversive *b* state with the reinforcing *a* state, the addict ingests more of the drug. Solomon's is an elegant and intuitively appealing theory which, incidentally, could be integrated quite readily with the genetic research reported earlier. However, the theory has yet to attract concerted research attention.

By far the most dominant approach to addiction from within the behavioural tradition comes from social learning theory. In their efforts to explain addictive behaviour, social learning theorists incorporate findings from classical and operant conditioning as well as from research into modelling processes. The basic claim is that through direct observation and through communications, we learn about drinking and drug-taking from parents, peers, the media and other sources. We also learn through personal experience. Our experiences lead us to expect that certain consequences will accompany drinking and drug-taking, and repeated use becomes likely when we learn that a pleasant consequence will follow or an unpleasant consequence will be avoided through drinking. The precise function of alcohol and other drugs in this regard will depend on many situational factors, including thoughts and feelings, social context and conditioned stimuli. Such factors cue the desire for the drug, while the pleasant consequences reinforce it.

According to George (1989), there are three key elements of the social learning theory of addictions. First, addictive behaviours are socially acquired and multiply determined. They are influenced by past learning, situational antecedents, biological make-up, cognitive processes and reinforcement contingencies. As we shall see in Chapter 5, situational antecedents are more often called 'high-risk situations' and they refer to factors such as time of day, places, people or emotional states which cue drug-seeking behaviour. Cognitive processes refer primarily to expectations about the likely consequences of ingesting the drug. Reinforcement contingencies refer to the rewarding aspects of alcohol and drug consumption; and the principles of behavioural reinforcement dictate that the more rewarding, the more frequent and the more proximate are the positive consequences of ingestion, the more likely it is that ingestion will recur.

A second aspect of the social learning approach is a general acceptance that addiction occurs along a continuum. As with the alcohol dependence syndrome idea, the two poles of the continuum would be total abstinence at one end and alcohol dependence at the other end. Where any given individual falls will depend on the interaction of the factors nominated above. It is important to emphasise that although the idea of a drinking continuum is similar to Edwards and Gross's (1976) alcohol dependence syndrome, social learning theorists do not necessarily accept that there is a qualitatively different, diseased group of drinkers somewhere on the continuum (see Heather and Robertson, 1985; Heather, 1992). Thus, the very same principles are used to explain the acquisition and maintenance of 'dependent' and 'non-dependent' drug use.

The third and final key element of social learning theory is the view that addictive behaviours are attempts at coping, albeit maladaptive ones. The drinker or drug-taker is trying to master, tolerate or reduce stressful internal or external demands (see also Shiffman and Wills, 1985; Sanchez-Craig *et al.*, 1987; Monti *et al.*, 1989). In the absence of healthier, more adaptive responses, the drinker uses alcohol to restore equanimity.

In all the work reviewed so far, drug addiction has been seen as an essentially clinical concept. Even within the modern psychological approach to addiction which rejects the idea of disease, drug dependence remains an interpretation of certain phenomena as constituting symptoms of an underlying behavioural disorder. The term 'problem drinker' may soften the clinical overtones but it does not remove them altogether. Yet the phenomena which the drug addiction concept seeks to organise under a clinical rubric is nothing more than repeated behaviour. Thus the intellectual function of the 'addiction' idea is to capture what the social psychologist, Robin Room (1973), calls a 'glue' holding a drug user to the behaviour. In the medical and psychological views discussed, the 'glue' of addiction has been sited in the individual's body (genes and physiopathological change) and/or in the individual's mind. It is true that clinicians in general, and social learning theorists in particular, often have a lively awareness that the cause of the complaints presented in the clinic reside outside the individual experiencing them, but even social learning theorists stop short of the possibility that the very heart of addiction might lie in forces and aggregations that transcend the individual altogether.

In the social work view, some of the phenomena covered by the term 'drug dependence' are best understood as seated at aggregate levels. As we will see in the chapter that follows, the 'glue' holding an individual to their behaviour could be a property of the social situation rather than the individual. 'Situational dependence' of this kind may be located at a number of different levels (including the level of the individual) and the extinction of dependence at one level will not necessarily cause the behaviour to disappear. In the next chapter, then, we must develop a model for undertaking social work, as opposed to purely clinical work, with alcohol and drug dependent individuals. Our approach will make use of a popular process model of change and at a number of points in the process we will appeal to cognitive-behavioural interventions like those referred to earlier; but we will also identify strategies and levels of intervention that extend well beyond the individual with the problem.

2

A Social Work Practice Model

In the previous chapter we considered the nature and aetiology of drug addiction and saw that different theoretical positions can have very different implications for treatment. In this chapter we turn our attention to social work's distinctive contribution to the field of addictions. We will find that a social work approach needs to recognise that practitioners confront drug abuse in a wide variety of settings – most of them outside specialist drug treatment agencies. It follows from this that a model of practice must prepare its adherents to deal with addicts whose disposition towards treatment can vary from violent opposition to a desperate search for help.

Moreover, a *social work* model must give expression to the dual focus on person and environment that is the hallmark of our profession (see Barber, 1991a). For social workers, it is not just the addictive process that requires assessment and understanding, it is the totality of users' lives, including all their interactions with the broader social environment. In other words, our model must look *outwards* to the social context of addictive behaviours, as well as *inwards* to the psychology of individual users. In our efforts to derive such a model we will look first at the notion of 'stages of change' as this idea helps in the crucial task of matching interventions to the user's readiness to change. In the second section we turn to social work's 'ecological perspective' before integrating this system's thinking with the stages of change literature to form a social work approach to addictions.

The stages of change

In recent times, the treatment of addictions has been dominated by the so-called 'transtheoretical model' proposed by Prochaska and

DiClemente (1982, 1983, 1984, 1988) and revised by Prochaska *et al.* (1992; 1997) and DiClemente and Prochaska (1998). This three-dimensional model emerged from the authors' painstaking follow-up research with self-changers (DiClemente and Prochaska, 1982) and clients involved in various forms of psychotherapy (Prochaska, 1979; Prochaska and DiClemente, 1982). The model is 'transtheoretical' in that it owes allegiance to no one school of therapy but seeks to provide an integrative framework capable of guiding practice irrespective of the therapist's favoured approach. After some prevarication about the precise number of stages involved (see Prochaska *et al.*, 1992), the transtheoretical model now predicts that drug misusers will pass through five stages of change on their way to resolving the problem. These five stages and the iterative manner in which they occur are presented in Figure 2.1.

The first stage of change is known as *precontemplation*. During this stage, the addict is resistant to change, normally even to the point of denying that a problem exists. After this follows a period of *contemplation* during which the user rehearses the pros and cons of change and experiences the discomfort that accompanies self-doubt and the discrepancy between one's values and one's behaviour. Eventually a point is reached where the vacillation of the contemplator gives way to *preparation* to change. Preparation is a stage which involves both intention and action. At this stage, the individual may be making some small behavioural change such as a marginal reduction in intake and is intending to make further changes in the future, but has yet to set a target level or arrive at a clear criterion for success. The *action* stage refers to the deliberate strategies that are used to modify one's drug-taking behaviour and/or environment in order to achieve a target consumption level. During the *maintenance* stage, individuals have already made significant progress but they may still be drawn to using. For this reason, vigilance is needed and the struggle against urges and temptations must continue. If maintenance efforts are unsuccessful, relapse will occur and the person will abandon change and return to the addicted life of the precontemplator. The iterative nature of the change process is conveyed by the spiral pattern in Figure 2.1. In recognition of the fact that relapse is the rule rather than the exception, the model predicts that after most people have progressed from precontemplation to the action stage, most will revert to precontemplation at least once. However, the majority of relapsers who recycle through the stages at some time in

Figure 2.1   *Prochaska and DiClemente's five stages of change model*

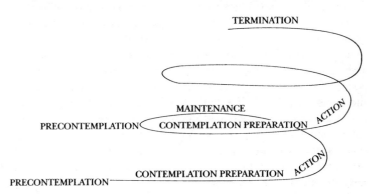

Reprinted from Prochaska, J. A., DiClemente, C. C. and Norcross, J. C. (1992) 'In search of how people change', *American Psychologist*, vol. 47, p. 1104, American Psychological Association.

the future will be wiser next time around. In other words, relapsers do not revolve in cycles endlessly but with each repetition of the process they will learn from their mistakes and try something new (DiClemente *et al.*, 1991).

Prochaska *et al.* (1992) base their separation of stages on research showing that different change processes receive differential emphasis as the addict strives to resolve the problem (Prochaska and DiClemente, 1983). This part of their work began with a comparison between 29 leading systems of therapy (Prochaska and DiClemente, 1984), resulting in the identification of the following ten basic processes:

1. Consciousness-raising
2. Self-liberation
3. Social liberation
4. Counter-conditioning
5. Stimulus control
6. Self-reevaluation
7. Environmental reevaluation
8. Contingency management
9. Dramatic relief
10. Helping relationships

1. *Consciousness-raising* refers to increasing the user's awareness of the effect drugs are having and why the drug-taking behaviour is being sustained. Thus, consciousness-raising includes both feedback (about the state of one's life) and education (about what needs to change). According to Prochaska and DiClemente (1984) consciousness-raising follows an increase in the amount, salience of or attention to information, especially with regard to the cognitive processes and structures that individuals use to avoid threatening feedback. These 'defensive processes' are manifest in all the rationalisations, denial and blind alleys so commonly traversed by resistant drug abusers. As the authors themselves put it, 'defensive processes and structures are like blinders, such as the rose-coloured glasses that some people use to selectively attend to only the positive information about themselves and society and disattend to negative input' (1984, p. 37). Thus, as awareness of past defensiveness grows, so should the pressure for change.

2. *Self-liberation* involves increases in the client's ability to choose and this flows from the belief that one can be an effective force in achieving desired outcomes.

3. *Social liberation* relates to environmental changes such as finding a job or gaining access to a new service or resource that opens up more choices and makes the drug user's life more controllable generally.

4. *Counter-conditioning* is the familiar behavioural technique of altering a conditioned response (such as drinking) to stimuli which evoke the response (such as anxiety or some cue emanating from the environment). The objective of the technique is to identify the conditioned stimulus which triggers the response and either desensitise the drug user or condition a new response which is incompatible with drug-taking behaviour.

5. *Stimulus control* seeks to deal with a conditioned drug-taking response by restructuring the environment so that the probability of the conditioned stimulus actually occurring is reduced. A simple illustration of this technique at work would be for an alcohol abuser to take another route home rather than pass by their local hostelry.

6. *Self-reevaluation* is said to be an emotional and rational appraisal of the pros and cons of overcoming substance abuse. This process is cleverly employed in Miller's 'motivational interviewing' technique

(Miller, 1983; Miller and Rollnick, 1991; Yahne and Miller, 1999) and will be elaborated on in Chapter 4 when we deal with the contemplation stage. However, the basic idea is that a user may come to see that personal values essential to their sense of self-worth are in fundamental conflict with drug-taking behaviour, and this realisation can become so aversive that behaviour change becomes imperative.

7. *Social reevaluation*, on the other hand, involves reappraising the impact that drug-taking has on significant others rather than oneself.

8. *Contingency management* looks to the consequences which follow drug-taking rather than the events which precede it, in contrast to the stimulus control strategy mentioned earlier. The intuitively obvious notion here is that by finding ways to reward periods of abstinence and/or punish drug abuse when it occurs, the overuse of the substance should be extinguished.

9. *Dramatic relief* refers to the tremendous sense of relief and regeneration (sometimes known as 'catharsis') that can accompany a new insight about oneself or an evocative scene or event such as witnessing the personal tragedy of another.

10. *Helping relationships* refers to any relationship which entices the drug user to change by conveying that they are valued and respected. This discovery was found by Prochaska and DiClemente (1984) to be capable of providing the freedom and optimism necessary to motivate change.

In summary, the above processes are intended to clarify the type of activity that is initiated or experienced by individuals in modifying their behaviour. By proposing that different processes are emphasised during particular stages of change, Prochaska and DiClemente make it at least theoretically possible to deduce the most appropriate strategy or combination of strategies to use at each stage of the client's relationship with drugs. Generally speaking, cognitive strategies should be more suited to clients in the early stages of change, and behavioural strategies should be more suited to clients at the action stage of change. During the contemplation stage, for example, addicts should be open to consciousness-raising interventions such as confrontation and interpretation. Self-reevaluation is also common at this stage. Individuals should be encouraged to examine their values and the things they hold dear and begin to make choices about what they must hold on to and what they must relinquish. These cognitive processes will be deployed in the methods to be outlined in Chapter 4. During the action stage, there is a need to acquire a sense of self-liberation and the basic principles of behaviour change also become important. Clients need to understand and draw on counter-conditioning, contingency management and stimulus control strategies in order to extinguish drug-taking behaviour and replace it with incompatible coping responses. These techniques will be developed in Chapter 5. During the action stage, clients will also be in need of supportive helping relationships to deal with the stress of radically altering their lives. Finally, successful maintenance requires a thorough-going environmental reevaluation in order to obviate relapse.

Because addictive behaviour always occurs within various and interrelated levels of human functioning, the transtheoretical model also encompasses a 'levels of change' dimension. The purpose of this concept is to direct the practitioner's attention to the possible personal and situational determinants of drug-taking behaviour that are in need of modification. The five levels which are organised hierarchically under the model are as follows:

1. Symptom/situational
2. Maladaptive cognitions
3. Current interpersonal conflicts
4. Family/systems conflicts
5. Intrapersonal conflicts

At the *symptom/situational* level, Prochaska and DiClemente (1984) have in mind the kind of situational analysis and problem definition characteristic of those behavioural approaches which concentrate only on the troublesome behaviour itself and the stimuli that immediately precede and follow it. At this level, all that matters is changing the behaviour and all that is countenanced are changes to cues and consequences. At a level below the behaviour and the immediate stimulus environment are the *maladaptive cognitions* or 'automatic thoughts' (Beck *et al.*, 1979) that accompany and sustain the behaviour. The drinker who deals with stress by getting drunk may be unaware of subconscious self-statements such as 'I can't deal with this situation by myself', but they may be influenced by such ideas none the less. At this level, therefore, alcohol abuse is likely to require quite different processes of change. At the levels of *current interpersonal conflicts* and/or *family/systems conflicts*, the problem is addressed in terms of communication difficulties and power struggles between the drug user and significant others.

Finally, *intrapersonal conflicts* refers to long-standing and subconscious inner tension as posited by psychoanalytic therapists who attempt to uncover the conflicting demands of impulses and the superego, and the ego's attempts simultaneously to defend against and gratify unconscious urges.

Under the transtheoretical model, the therapist should normally begin with the presenting problem, that is, at the symptom/situational level, both because this is the most pressing from the client's viewpoint and because change tends to occur fastest at this level. Prochaska and DiClemente (1988) acknowledge that change at one level is likely to produce change at other levels but they claim that the *primary* focus and level of intervention should be apparent at any given point in the change process. Putting all these components together we arrive at a comprehensive treatment approach involving the differential application of ten processes of change at four stages according to the problem level being addressed. Prochaska and DiClemente (1988) express all this by way of a diagram (Figure 2.2).

The transtheoretical model recognises three basic approaches to intervening across the multiple levels of change. The first is a *shifting-levels* strategy which works its way down the levels until the problem is resolved. Thus, therapy would typically focus first on the client's symptoms and the situations supporting these symptoms. If the processes could be applied effectively at the first level and the client could progress through each stage of change, therapy would be completed without shifting to a more complex level of analysis. If treating just the symptoms was ineffective, however, therapy would shift to a focus on maladaptive cognitions and the processes of change would be applied to cognitive content with the same goal of progressing through each stage of change. If therapy were unsuccessful at this level, the processes of change would then be brought to bear at the level of interpersonal conflicts, and so on through all the levels. A second possible approach is referred to by the authors as the *key-level* strategy in which therapist and client target one level only because of its crucial role in sustaining the addictive behaviour. Third, the *maximum-impact* strategy involves attacking the problem at a number of different levels simultaneously in order to establish a maximum impact for change.

Figure 2.2 *Integrating the stages, processes and levels of change*

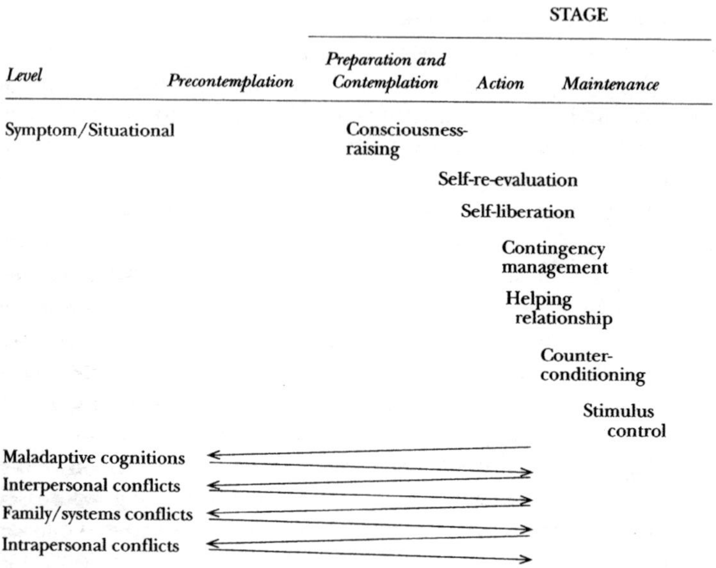

STAGE

Level	Precontemplation	Preparation and Contemplation	Action	Maintenance
Symptom/Situational		Consciousness-raising		
			Self-re-evaluation	
			Self-liberation	
			Contingency management	
			Helping relationship	
				Counter-conditioning
				Stimulus control
Maladaptive cognitions				
Interpersonal conflicts				
Family/systems conflicts				
Intrapersonal conflicts				

Reprinted from Prochaska, J. O. and DiClemente, C. C. (1988) 'Toward a comprehensive model of change', in W. R. Miller and N. Heather (eds), *Treating Addictive Behaviors*, p. 18, the Plenum Press, New York.

Despite its popularity, Prochaska and DiClemente's transtheoretical model is not without its detractors. Davidson (1992), for example, once described it as a 'bandwagon' which continues to thrive in spite of serious conceptual and empirical deficiencies. Davidson (1998) has softened his attack considerably in recent times, but his fundamental objections remain. Among these objections is that there is actually little or no evidence that people who solve an addiction problem progress in an orderly way through the stages proposed by the model. In his review article, for example, Sutton (2001) classified the evidence base for the stages into four different types: cross-sectional comparisons of people in different stages, examination of stage sequences, longitudinal predictions of stage transitions, and experimental studies of interventions that were either matched or mismatched to a stage of change. Overall, Sutton found that the evidence in support of the transtheoretical model from all four types of study was both meagre and inconsistent. Indeed Davidson (1998) and Bandura (1998) question whether the very notion of stages is helpful, with both authors preferring a continuum model of health and behaviour change. For their part, proponents of the transtheoretical model do not claim that addicts pass through the stages in the orderly fashion assumed by their critics. For example, in a study of smokers who were initially in the contemplation stage, Prochaska *et al.* (1991) reported that only 5 per cent of their sample displayed a linear change pattern over a two-year period. On the other hand, what this same study did confirm was that smokers make systematic use of the processes of change matched to each stage through which they move. Moreover, in summarising years of research on the matter, DiClemente and Prochaska (1998) claim that the weight of evidence justifies the conclusion that individuals who solve addiction problems do pass through each stage even if not in an orderly or linear fashion.

Davidson (1998) also objects that there is little or no evidence that specific treatment interventions can be matched with each stage in Prochaska and DiClemente's model to improve outcome. Indeed, the evidence from 'Project MATCH' (Project MATCH Research Group, 1997, 1998) cautions against the very idea that there exists an ideal match between client characteristics and treatment methods generally in order for intervention to be effective. In its failure to find any real link between client characteristics and three qualitatively different types of therapy, Project MATCH has weakened the argument that clients at different stages of change are likely to require qualitatively different treatment methods. We shall discuss the implications and limitations of Project MATCH further towards the end of the book (see Chapter 7) but for the present it is important to acknowledge that there is as yet no firm evidence for the idea that the processes of change identified by Prochaska and DiClemente (1998) translate into intervention methods that do or do not work according to the client's stage of change.

These criticisms of the transtheoretical model reflect the fact that it has been much more successful as a description *of* change than as a prescription *for* change. In fact, the remaining chapters of this book are an attempt to specify scientifically validated methods for advancing the user through the various stages of Prochaska and DiClemente's model, precisely because their own recommendations

about processes and levels of change are vague, difficult to oper-
ationalise and, as previously indicated, largely untested. A strength
of Prochaska and DiClemente's *trans*theoretical approach is that it
seeks to avoid dogmatic adherence to one school of thought or
another, but it does so at the cost of a coherent theory of addiction of
its own.

On this point, the general 'stages of change' model proposed by
Kanfer and Grimm (1980) and applied by Kanfer (1988) to drug
addiction is better than Prochaska and DiClemente's. Table 2.1
summarises Kanfer and Grimm's stages of change and relates each
one to its counterpart in the Prochaska and DiClemente taxonomy.
Table 2.1 also presents the basic tasks for the worker at each of the
stages proposed by Kanfer and Grimm.

***Table* 2.1**   *The self-regulation and transtheoretical stages of change*

Self-regulation phase	Worker's tasks	Transtheoretical phase
1. Role structuring and creating a therapeutic alliance	1. Facilitate the person's entry to the role of client 2. Formation of a working relationship 3. Establish motivation to work with therapist	Contemplation
2. Developing a commitment for change	1. Motivate client to consider positive consequences of change 2. Activate client towards change of status quo 3. Reduce demoralisation	Contemplation
3. The behavioural analysis	1. Refine client's problem definition 2. Identify relevant functional relationships 3. Motivate client towards specific changes	Preparation
4. Negotiating treatment	1. Seek agreement of target areas 2. Establish priorities for change programme and initiate specific procedures 3. Accept responsibility for engaging in planned therapy programme	Preparation
5. Treatment execution and motivation maintenance	1. Conduct treatment	Action

	2. Assess collateral and radiating effects of change in target behaviours	
	3. Evaluate and, if necessary, enhance motivation to change and comply with treatment requirements	
6. Monitoring and evaluating progress	1. Assess behaviour change 2. Assess client's use of general coping skills 3. Introduce new therapy objectives, if necessary 4. Motivate programme completion	Action
7. Treatment generalisation and termination	1. Evaluate and foster self-management skills for meeting future problems 2. Phase out contact with client	Maintenance

Source: Adapted from Kanfer and Grimm (1980), pp. 440–1.

Under this seven-phase 'self-regulation' or 'self-management' model of therapy, the objectives of treatment are to help the client assume responsibility for change and to provide an opportunity for learning 'survival' skills that can be applied to any problems that might arise in the future. The model gives consideration not just to the principles but also the conditions of learning. It seeks to integrate learning, motivational, and therapist–client relationship factors in a manner which gives expression to the authors' view that treatment often fails because therapists fail to establish appropriate prerequisites for change, rather than because the client's problem is insoluble.

In Phase 1, the primary focus of intervention is to establish a favourable client–therapist relationship (or rapport) which should provide the necessary motivation for the client to cooperate with the therapist. While developing this therapeutic alliance, the content of the interaction should enable therapist and client to formulate hypotheses about possible treatment goals and intervention strategies. However, Kanfer and Grimm stress that the motivation for change should not be given priority at this early stage. The authors recognise that simply entering treatment does not, in itself, imply that there is a strong desire for change. In Phase 2, therefore, the therapist is directed to help the client define their purpose in therapy. The motivation for change needs to be promoted rather than assumed and this is achieved by helping clients clarify their values and goals for the future. In other words, change must be seen in terms of planning for an end state rather than as mere escape from an aversive situation. Again, the aim is to stimulate the desire for change and not merely seek compliance with any given change strategy. The behavioural analysis that occurs in Phase 3 begins the process of formulating an action plan by assessing the addictive behaviour in relation to cues and consequences, the user's resources for change, and specific objectives for treatment. Following the behavioural analysis it becomes possible to identify small, concrete steps towards resolving the addiction. The critical task in Phase 4 is to arrive at a contract or agreement about the priority of treatment goals and the methods for arriving at them. Naturally, this process should be driven by the client. Kanfer and Grimm (1980, p. 431) state:

> By the end of this phase, several prerequisites for the change program should be soundly formed, role responsibilities should be clear, the client should view his or her problem as manageable and should be motivated to change, he or she should have a conceptual framework within which the problems and the rationale for the treatment method can be understood, and he or she should be motivated to achieve the therapeutic objectives.

As we shall see, much of what Kanfer and Grimm (1980) advocate in Phases 1 to 4 is similar in method and intent to the 'motivational interviewing' technique which has since been developed by W. R. Miller (1983, 1998; Miller and Rollnick, 1991; Yahne and Miller, 1999) (see Chapter 4).

It is only after achieving all this that Kanfer and Grimm believe that behaviour therapy can begin – in Phase 5. As well as instructing the client in behaviour change techniques (see Chapters 5 and 6), the therapist's task is to ensure that treatment is enacted appropriately and that the client keeps to their side of the treatment contract. In pursuit of these objectives, the authors point out that it is useful to emphasise to the client that this is only the acquisition stage of learning and therefore that some of the more onerous aspects of therapy are transient. For example, keeping a drink diary (see Chapter 5) will not be a lifelong requirement but will last only until the pattern of behaviour is established and understood. In Phase 6 the effectiveness of the change programme is carefully evaluated. If client and therapist fail to note progress, treatment may need to be adjusted. However, once treatment is under way and some progress has been made, therapy may begin for problems that were of secondary importance, and the therapist should assess the extent to which the skills obtained are being generalised to other problems in the client's life. Finally, in Phase 7, the objective of treatment is to facilitate the transfer and maintenance of treatment gains (see Chapter 6). According to Kanfer and Grimm, this can be approached by encouraging the client to take responsibility for accomplishing the goals of treatment (see also Goldfried and Robins, 1982), by developing coping strategies for classes of events rather than specific events (Kanfer, 1979) and by the use of guided imagery in which hypothetical problem situations are presented and planned for (see also Marlatt and Gordon, 1985).

Notwithstanding the greater clarity in Kanfer and Grimm's (1980) model about *how* to conduct treatment, their model is similar to Prochaska and DiClemente's (1982, 1983, 1984, 1988) in that both models propose commitment to change as 'the prerequisite to modification of the target behaviours and stress the reciprocal effects of intentions (and other verbal-symbolic processes) and actions' (Kanfer, 1988, p. 32). In addition, both models emphasise the recursive nature of change, the need to attend carefully to the maintenance of treatment gains, and the centrality of the client as the primary change agent. Moreover, both models are deficient for social work practice because of their limited perspective on the human condition.

The social work perspective

I have made the point in an earlier work (Barber, 1991a) that a focus on environmental factors is the most obvious and important thread running through the history of social work literature. Indeed, social work as a profession is *dedicated* to the understanding and modification of the social factors involved in client problems. One of social work's early advocates, Werner Boehm (1958), described this social work perspective in the following terms:

Social work seeks to enhance the social functioning of individuals, singularly and in groups, by activities focused on their social relationships which constitute *interaction between individuals and their environments.* These activities can be grouped into three functions: restoration of impaired capacity, provision of individual and social resources, and prevention of social dysfunction. (p. 18; my emphasis)

In a landmark treatise on the role of social work, Harriett Bartlett (1970) spoke of the profession's concern with 'social functioning', by which she too meant the relationship between people and the demands made on them by the environment. Bartlett referred to social work's 'dual focus' on person and situation this way:

> Attention is now directed primarily to what goes on between people and environment through the exchange between them. This dual focus ties them together. Thus person and situation, people and environment, are encompassed in a single concept, which requires that they be constantly reviewed together. (1970, p. 116)

It is this view of the human condition that lies at the core of social work. Many social work authors have come to embrace general systems theory as a way of giving expression to the 'holistic' perspective (for example, Janchill, 1969; Hartman, 1970; Strean, 1971; Goldstein, 1973; Pincus and Minahan, 1973; Stein, 1974; Vickery, 1974; Germain and Gitterman, 1980; Compton and Galaway, 1984). The general systems view of society is a way of thinking about the world which draws a parallel between the way society operates and the way biological systems operate. Just as biology has shown us that all living things, be they individual creatures or entire ecosystems, are a complex organisation of parts working together to survive, general systems theory conceives of the entire social world and all the regions, communities, even families and other domestic units that make up the world as interdependent parts of a much greater whole. All these parts (or subsystems) provide the conditions for the survival of the other parts. It is this *inter*dependence or *inter*-action between the parts that is the basic insight of general systems theory. Because change in any part of the system affects the system as a whole, systems can only be understood when the transactions occurring within and between subsystems is understood. The systems view ensures that people are not thought of as isolated individuals but as elements in a social system that includes but also transcends them.

The social developmental psychologist Ury Bronfenbrenner (1979) conceived of the ecological environment topologically, as a set of nested structures extending far beyond the immediate situation experienced by the person to the connection between other persons not present in the setting and their indirect influence on that person. To capture the interdependence of the various system levels, Bronfenbrenner employed a diagrammatic representation of concentric structures, each contained with the next (Figure 2.3).

At the lowest level of analysis is the individual client and social work practice will normally begin with a thorough assessment of the client's view of the problem. Beyond that is the microsystem, or the pattern of activities, roles and interpersonal relations experienced by the client in a given setting. Thus the microsystem refers to the client's immediate, phenomenological environment. It contains all individuals and settings with which the client has a direct relationship, for example, family members, the workplace, friendship networks and so on.

Figure 2.3   *The ecological environment*

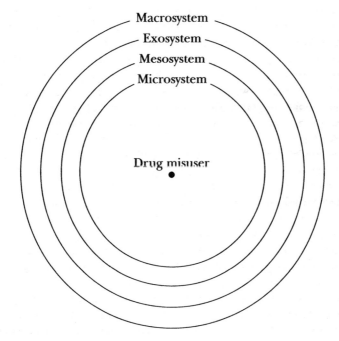

Source: Adapted from Barber (1991a), p. 6.

In order to understand a client's addiction, then, we need to understand the immediate social context within which it occurs. Beyond the microsystem is the mesosystem, or the interrelations among two or more settings in which the client actively participates. At this level of analysis, the social worker assesses relationships between the set of microsystems that comprise the client's life, such as the relationship between home and the workplace, or home and friendship networks.

At a level beyond mesosystem analysis is the exosystem, which refers to one or more settings that do not involve the client as an active participant but within which events occur that affect what happens in settings that do contain the client. Exosystem analysis in social work often involves the assessment of social policy issues impinging on the client's problem. For example, local council bylaws relating to the supply of alcohol at sporting fixtures, cultural activities and social events are known to influence the level of alcohol-related morbidity within the region (see Chapter 8). Clients and their families may never even have heard of the council members responsible for the regulations or, for that matter, the regulations themselves, but the indirect effect of the local council decisions on the client's drinking may be significant none the less. The final level in Bronfenbrenner's model is the macrosystem, or consistencies in the form or content of lower-order systems (micro-, meso- and exo-) that exist at the level of the subculture or culture. Analysis at this level relates to the norms and rituals governing drug-taking behaviour and the role of recreational drugs in society more generally. While an individual social worker and their client will be unable to exert much influence on such variables, it can be helpful at least to anticipate the pressures that exist within a given culture or subculture.

A social work approach to addictions

Despite its undoubted heuristic value, Prochaska and DiClemente's (1998) 'transtheoretical model' does contain certain weaknesses when applied to social work practice. The first concerns the authors' failure to grasp the inescapably social context within which all individuals exist. The complex systemic analysis advocated by Bronfenbrenner (1979) and generations of social work writers before and since is simply not captured by Prochaska and DiClemente's 'levels of change' dimension which looks rather superficial by comparison.

Although recognising that addictive behaviour is normally influenced by forces beyond the individual with the problem, Prochaska and DiClemente look no further than the drug misuser's interpersonal relationships. Despite laying claim to a systems view of addictive behaviour (Kanfer, 1988), the model developed by Kanfer and Grimm (1980) is similarly reductionist. Taken together, the two models show no understanding of the role of supply-side and demand-side drug prevention policies (mesosystem), or the (sub)cultural (exosystem) factors surrounding the overuse of certain drugs. If only because drug use is not randomly distributed within society, socio-cultural factors, such as socioeconomic deprivation, norms and anomie, must have explanatory and predictive utility for social work practice. For example, clients from China may be inclined to think of cannabis as a medicinal preparation, while Indian immigrants will be more likely to regard it as a ceremonial or social drug. There are strong sanctions within Asian and Jewish communities against alcohol consumption, so a level of consumption which may be less than the worker *personally* is accustomed to drinking could be condemned by the informal networks of Asian or Jewish clients. And given social work's traditional commitment to disadvantaged and marginalised sections of society, it is important for practitioners to recognise the firm evidence now linking urban slum-dwelling with a culture of illicit opiate use.

Within sociology, variations of the social deprivation hypothesis have often been advanced to account for the differential rates of drug use in various sociocultural contexts (Sadava, 1975). Basic to this approach is the idea of a set of socially structured channels of access to goals emphasised or valued by society. Where access to these goals by legitimate means is denied (or perceived to be denied) and an individual is thus blocked in seeking goal satisfactions, that person must turn to alternative behaviour. According to Merton (1957), if the individual is unable to employ illegitimate means because, for example, of internalised norms, they may turn to drug use as a means of coping with expected failure. In a similar vein, Mac-Donald (1965) views adolescent opiate addiction as a consequence of frustrated yearnings to be accepted by society, pointing out that most addicts oscillate between the 'straight' and drug cultures. Fine-stone (1964) further describes opiate use among addicts as a means of maximal differentiation of their peer group subculture from the values of the achieving society.

To the extent that these theories provide insight into the aetiology of drug addition, they also provide avenues for social work intervention that will be taken up later in the book. Whatever may be said about the social origins of illicit drug use, however, any explanation of the behaviour must also take account of the fact that it is a criminal act. The problems growing out of this critical fact are responsible for the emergence of a stringent subculture. These problems include evasion of police, maintaining sources of supply, and adjusting to the harassed role of a deviant. The cohesiveness of this subculture poses a problem which is squarely within social work's mission and mandate. The drug subculture acts to hold the user to their substance; thus social workers must position themselves to understand and manipulate the social context within which drug-taking occurs.

A second weakness of both 'stages of change' models concerns their silence when confronted with precontemplators. In the case of Kanfer and Grimm (1980), the silence is absolute, and in the case of Prochaska and DiClemente (1983, 1984), nothing of practical value is proffered. This limitation of Prochaska and DiClemente's work arises from the previously noted fact that theirs is a descriptive model of change, *not* a theory of addiction. To be sure, Prochaska and DiClemente (1984) propose that the movement from precontemplation to contemplation is due either to developmental or environmental changes but this observation is of little practical assistance. Based more on their clinical experience than systematic research, the authors contend that as drug users grow older, new pressures, new demands and new preoccupations will arise which must inevitably rub against drug-taking behaviour. Under these circumstances pressure to change may arise either from within the user or from shifting environmental exigencies. However, because this observation begs the rather more basic questions of *how* and *why* such pressures work, the practitioner is left with no other option than to wait around for the drug misuser to make a move toward change. This is a luxury which social workers cannot always afford, of course, especially if they work in one of the many agencies that tend the victims of the user's behaviour.

Adopting the kind of 'holistic' perspective advocated above, it is possible to arrive at an adaptation of Prochaska and DiClemente's (1983, 1984) and Kanfer and Grimm's (1980) 'stages of change' models, which guides a genuinely social work approach to addiction at every stage of change. This adapted model, which appears in

Figure 2.4, also provides the organising framework for the remainder of the book.

Under this model, the 'glue' (see Chapter 1) binding an individual to their substance of choice occurs at any or all of five system levels, though at different points in the change process different system levels will be more or less important. A weakness of Figure 2.4 is that

Figure 2.4   *Social work with addictions*

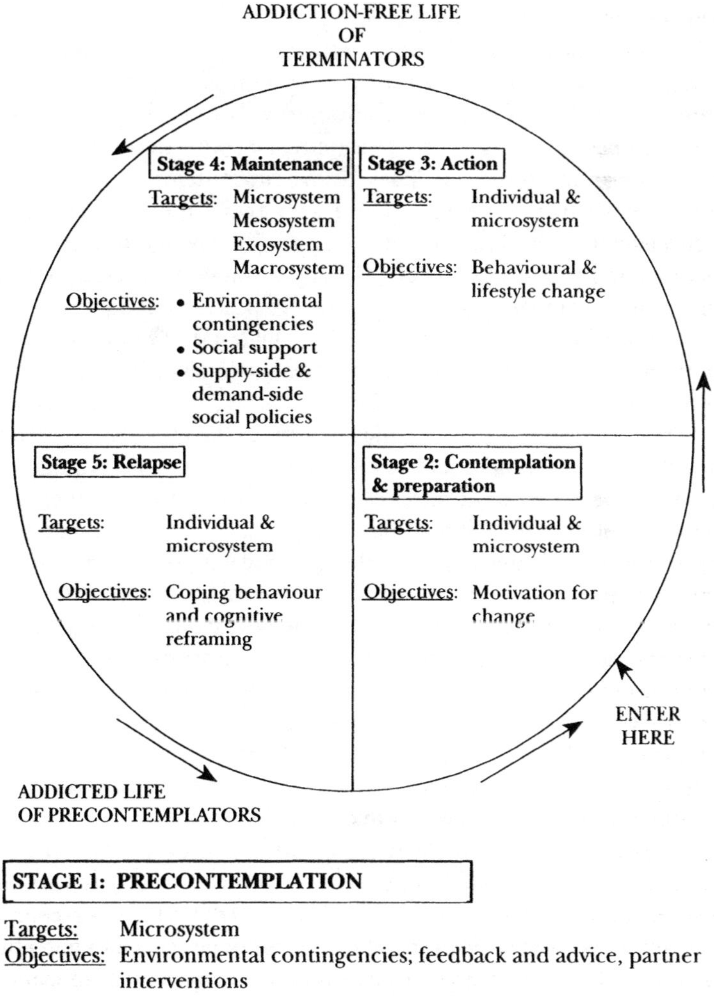

ADDICTION-FREE LIFE
OF
TERMINATORS

Stage 4: Maintenance

Targets: Microsystem
Mesosystem
Exosystem
Macrosystem

Objectives: • Environmental
contingencies
• Social support
• Supply-side &
demand-side
social policies

Stage 3: Action

Targets: Individual &
microsystem

Objectives: Behavioural &
lifestyle change

Stage 5: Relapse

Targets: Individual &
microsystem

Objectives: Coping behaviour
and cognitive
reframing

**Stage 2: Contemplation
& preparation**

Targets: Individual &
microsystem

Objectives: Motivation for
change

ENTER
HERE

ADDICTED LIFE
OF PRECONTEMPLATORS

STAGE 1: PRECONTEMPLATION

Targets: Microsystem
Objectives: Environmental contingencies; feedback and advice, partner
interventions

it presents the change process as cyclical and could therefore be seen to imply that with each relapse, the drug user has gained nothing from the efforts made and is all the way back to square one. As Prochaska *et al*. (1992) point out, this is unlikely to be the case and their spiralling arrangement of stages captures the idea of progress with each iteration of the change process better than Figure 2.4 does. On the other hand, provided the reader bears this qualification in mind, the circular arrangement of stages allows us to superimpose the levels of intervention dimension more neatly than Prochaska, DiClemente and Norcross's (1992) spiral.

From a social work viewpoint, intervention in the case of precontemplators would begin at the microsystem level with the aim of intervention at this stage being primarily to reduce the reinforcement value of drug-taking behaviour. This can be attempted by facilitating the flow of feedback to the precontemplator regarding the negative consequences of drugs in their life. It can also be approached by seeking to influence the behaviour of significant others and in some cases even by social workers themselves actively manipulating environmental contingencies. Precontemplation and these microsystem interventions will be elaborated in the following chapter. Once the user begins to express even the slightest ambivalence or desire to change, 'contemplation' has begun and the focus of attention must shift from the microsystem to the user. Thus Chapter 4 will deal with contemplation and show that the same principle of raising the salience of negative consequences which was at work during precontemplation should be reemployed during contemplation, only this time it is done through the eyes and with the cooperation of the user. As we shall see, the constructive interpersonal relationship between client and therapist that is advocated by Kanfer and Grimm (1980) in the pre-action stages of change is indispensable at the contemplation stage. During contemplation users are engaged at some level with a problem in decision-making (whether or not to change) and they can be assisted in this by a vigilant assessment of the pros and cons of their habit. For this reason, the psychology of decision-making will also be considered in Chapter 4.

Chapter 5 turns to the 'action' or 'treatment execution' stage of change. During this stage we continue to work intensively with the individual but we also begin to broaden our attention to take in microsystem interventions capable of reinforcing the user's tentative first steps towards change. Taking alcohol abuse as a platform for discussion, Chapter 5 outlines the steps involved in 'behavioural self-control training' (BSCT) and in order to maximise the practical utility of BSCT for non-drug-specialist workers, the technique will be presented in the form of a self-help manual.

Chapter 6 deals with the maintenance or 'treatment generalisation' stage of change. Since the best predictors of maintenance are almost all social (employment, stable relationships and so on), our work must incorporate multiple levels of change from the individual to the broader social environment. Not only must the quality of the user's immediate social context be considered, but social workers, more than any other of the helping professionals, must be prepared to press for social policies which minimise the risk of relapse. For this reason, the effectiveness of various drug prevention policy options will be considered in Chapter 6. Finally, Chapter 7 will review the approach presented and consider methods for evaluating the work done. Much of the material in the chapters ahead relates to alcohol. This is because alcohol is the best researched and most over-used substance in the Western world. Despite this concentration on alcohol, however, the principles involved in working with addictive behaviours remain the same, whatever the substance involved.

3

Precontemplation

In Chapter 2 the point was made that the most neglected stage of change is precontemplation. In part this gap is explained by Prochaska and DiClemente's own finding (1983) that precontemplators employ fewer of the ten change processes (see Chapter 2) than at any other stage in their relationship with drugs. Little if any time is spent in self-reevaluation, there is less openness with significant others, precontemplators have fewer emotional reactions to the negative aspects of their habit and they do little to shift their attention or environment in the direction of change. Such resistance to change obviously provides the drug counsellor with very little to work with.

Another likely reason for the dearth of literature on precontemplators is that most drug research is conducted by treatment providers, and precontemplators, by definition, fall outside their purview. But while specialist treatment agencies may be able to sever all contact with precontemplators (indeed, they rarely have any choice *but* to), the same cannot be said of social workers outside specialist drug agencies. As discussed in Chapter 2, social workers often encounter drug abuse in the context of some other, often more pressing social problem such as domestic violence, homelessness or poverty. In these circumstances, many of the individuals concerned will either deny that a drug problem exists or reject any suggestion that their behaviour should change. To date, the only researcher to have paid much attention to the early stages of change is Bill Miller (1983, 1991, 1998; Miller *et al.*, 1988; Miller and Rollnick, 1991). As we shall see in the next chapter, Miller's innovative work on 'motivational interviewing' does incorporate strategies for increasing the attractiveness of treatment and some of his ideas can be applied to precontemplators. On the other hand, most of Miller's strategies rely on there being at least some degree of ambivalence within the drug user which can be exploited by the counsellor.

For this reason, motivational interviewing belongs more to the contemplation than the precontemplation stage of change.

In one of the very few attempts to provide systematic guidelines for working with precontemplators, Tober (1991) adopted what she referred to as a 'damage limitation' stance. Tober rejects the proposition that heavy drinkers must be made to suffer in order to 'motivate' them to change. This argument, she claims, is based on two fallacious assumptions: (a) 'that greater suffering...will always lead to behaviour change', and (b) 'that behaviour change will result only from increased suffering' (p. 27). In Tober's view, greater suffering is just as likely to lead to more drinking as it is to a determination to change. Her own preference is to minimise the harm that is done by drinking while waiting for maturational or environmental factors to drive the client into treatment. Tober goes on to propose damage limitation interventions such as periods of enforced abstinence, nutritional precautions, changes of beverage type, greater access to primary health care, and supervised accommodation. For third parties like partners and children, she advocates examining their coping behaviours and introducing them to semi-formal support networks.

Tober is right to reject punitiveness as a motivational device. Not only does the crude psychology on which it is based lack supporting evidence, it ignores the research which shows that drug abusers are just as likely to change their behaviour for *positive* as for negative reasons (for example, Vaillant and Milofsky, 1982). Moreover, workers who seek to maximise suffering cast themselves in the role of persecutor, from which position it is almost impossible to exert a constructive influence on the client. On the other hand, if we accept Tober's approach in its entirety we are left without any semblance of a strategy for change. Tober seeks only to minimise harm, not to advance the client towards later stages of the change process. In addition, while it may be quite appropriate to provide drug abusers with all the regular services offered by the agency, it is highly inappropriate to seek to protect clients from the consequences of their decisions. To do so would be a contradiction of the fundamental premise on which all forms of drug treatment must be based – that addicts are responsible for their own behaviour.

We have now arrived at the fundamental dilemma confronting all who work with precontemplators: how can we provide services to these clients which ameliorate their problems without rewarding the very behaviour that is causing all the trouble? In trying to resolve this dilemma, we will assume that the drug user is unwilling to engage in counselling or that it would be pointless to try. Under these circumstances, our best, if not our only, hope of promoting change is to focus on the user's microsystem (see Chapter 2) and all the interventions described below are targeted there.

Feedback and advice

Prochaska and DiClemente (1984, 1988) have suggested that maturational and environmental influences are responsible for moving precontemplators forward. As we have seen, Tober (1991) is one author who has interpreted this suggestion as implying that the worker should simply wait for these forces to take effect. Consistent with the principles espoused in the previous section, however, we arrive at a rather different conclusion. Put simply, part of the worker's role must be to take every reasonable opportunity to reinforce whatever pressures are operative. What this proposition amounts to is a recommendation to facilitate the flow of objective feedback to the precontemplator concerning the physical and social consequences of drug consumption. Two indispensable characteristics of this feedback must be emphasised. First, it needs to be individualised feedback. Research has shown consistently that generalisations about the detrimental effects of drug consumption have little or no effect on drug-taking behaviour; only personal feedback about how drugs are affecting the individual is capable of promoting change (cf. W. R. Miller, 1989). A second characteristic of feedback is that it must be provided in an empathic and non-judgemental manner. Whereas compliance and behaviour change are known to be promoted by counsellor empathy (for example, Chafetz, 1961; Rogers *et al.*, 1978; Valle, 1981), the opposite is true of unaccepting or hostile counsellor behaviour (for example, Milmoe *et al.*, 1967; Lieberman *et al.*, 1973).

Where possible, the feedback provided by the worker should be based on standardised and objective tests, rather than being a mere expression of opinion. There are now numerous assessment procedures available (cf. Jacobson, 1989) and social workers in secondary settings could encourage their clients to undergo one of them. One example of a comprehensive alcohol screening procedure is the Drinker's Check-up (DCU) developed by Miller and his colleagues (Miller *et al.*, 1988). The DCU consists of a test battery designed to alert problem drinkers to any harmful effects that alcohol is having on them. The DCU normally requires a two-hour assessment followed by a separate feedback visit. During the assessment, the drinker is subjected to:

1. 'The Brief Drinker Profile' (Miller and Marlatt, 1987), which is a semi-structured interview schedule covering topics such as usual drinking pattern, life and family problems, physical symptoms and level of dependence.
2. Blood tests sensitive to the effects of alcohol on internal organs.
3. A collection of neuropsychological tests indicative of alcohol's effects on the brain.
4. Interviews with 'collaterals' who can confirm the client's self-reported consumption levels.
5. A standardised, self-report of drinking patterns known as the 'Alcohol Use Inventory' (Horn *et al.*, 1987).

Within one week of these tests the drinker returns for the results, including where they stand relative to the general population. As previously emphasised, the drinker is never admonished; results are presented in a friendly and objective fashion, with time allowed for clients to react and share their concerns.

Miller *et al.* (1988) have used the DCU as a free public screening procedure in which terms like 'alcoholic' and 'problem drinker' were deliberately avoided in favour of less threatening descriptors, and an emphasis on measuring fitness levels rather than disease. In this study, the researchers advertised a free 'check-up for drinkers who would like to find out whether their drinking is causing them any harm' (ibid., p. 255). Of the 42 drinkers who volunteered, over half displayed symptoms of neuropsychological impairment, and the alcohol intake of the group as a whole was well above recommended levels. Despite this, only eight had ever sought help for their drinking. Six weeks following the DCU, there was a 27 per cent reduction in consumption by the group overall. Moreover, this improvement was still evident at the eighteen-month follow-up. It must be conceded that for problem drinkers at the precontemplation stage, it is highly likely that an offer of assessment related specifically and solely to drinking would be rejected. Thus, Miller *et al.*'s invitation may need to be modified to refer to 'lifestyle' assessment rather than promoting the procedure as an assessment of alcohol-related harm specifically.

Indeed, there is obvious value in expanding the scope of health screening to include a range of other lifestyle problems as well. The most important point about the DCU for our present purpose, however, concerns its apparent capacity to prompt previously inactive drinkers to take action about their consumption. Whereas only eight of the 42 individuals involved in the study had ever sought treatment for their drinking prior to the DCU, twenty of them were in treatment by the eighteen-month follow-up point. In the absence of a satisfactory no-treatment control condition, it is not possible to attribute this increase in treatment participation to the DCU, but results are encouraging and clearly supportive of the proposition that workers can afford to be proactive in providing information about the need for change.

As well as its effects on health, drug abuse is certain to undermine and ultimately impoverish the user's broader social environment. Thus, users should be provided with feedback about the deleterious social consequences of their drug use wherever possible. One promising, but as yet under-researched, technique for achieving this objective has been described by Johnson (1973, 1986) and Treadway (1989). The procedure, known ominously as 'The Intervention', is a carefully orchestrated and rehearsed meeting in which family members and others within the drinker's immediate social network confront the drinker with what alcohol is doing to them and to the drinker personally. Following an assessment and one or more education sessions, family and friends are taught to write personal testimonials about how their lives have been diminished by the drinker's compulsive use of alcohol. These statements are intended to be as much a proclamation of the individual's love for the drinker as an expression of the writer's profound desire that the drinker seek help. The statements are then vetted by the group who check for blaming or judgemental accusations before the drinker is invited to an 'intervention meeting' in which these testimonials are read out one by one in a prearranged sequence with the most powerful statements being kept till last. Treadway acknowledges that 'The Intervention' is a high-risk strategy, which should only be attempted as a last resort. It is an emotional ambush which is just as likely to generate resentment as a change of heart within the user; but, as the author himself puts it, 'When the alcoholic is denying the problem, the intervention approach is often the only alternative to giving up. It's the last move' (Treadway, 1989, p. 57). A recent study by Miller *et al.* (1999) suggests that most families will not go through with an Intervention but for those who do, some degree of success can be expected.

While social workers might be quite comfortable with providing feedback, the emphasis in social work training on non-directiveness may make some practitioners feel uncomfortable with the notion that their clients should be offered advice. But to take just one example of the influence that expert advice can have, Russell *et al.* (1979) enlisted the help of 28 general practitioners in five group practices in London. Over a period of four weeks, these doctors asked all patients attending their clinics the question, 'Are you a cigarette smoker?' A total of 2138 patients answered the question in the affirmative, and these people were semi-randomly assigned (based on day of attendance) to one of four groups. Group One was a no-treatment control group in which patients simply had their names taken for follow-up purposes. Group Two completed questionnaires about their smoking habits and attitudes towards giving up, but otherwise received no advice or assistance of any kind. Group Three completed these same questionnaires, and they were given brief but firm advice by the general practitioner to stop smoking. Finally, Group Four completed questionnaires, were given advice to stop smoking, and were provided with take-home leaflets on how to stop. Results of the study suggested that this simple 'advice' intervention was sufficient to encourage substantial numbers of patients to quit smoking. Changes in motivation and intention to stop were immediately evident after advice was given to Groups Three and Four, and patients in Group Four (advice plus leaflet) displayed a significantly higher rate of trying to quit than controls (Groups One and Two) by the one-month follow-up. Most importantly, the two treatment groups showed much higher quit rates than controls at the twelve-month follow-up point. Compared with quit rates of only 0.3 per cent in Group One and 1.6 per cent in Group Two, quit rates at the twelve-month follow-up were 3.3 and 5.1 per cent in Groups Three and Four respectively. Extrapolated to the entire UK population attending general practitioners' surgeries in a year, Russell *et al.*'s (1979) results have quite staggering implications. In the authors' own words:

> The results suggest that any GP who adopts this simple routine
> could expect about 25 long-term successes yearly. If all GPs in the
> UK participated the yield would exceed half a million ex-smokers

a year. This target could not be matched by increasing the present 50 or so special withdrawal clinics to 10,000. (Ibid., p. 231)

A logically similar procedure has been described by Kristenson (1983) who identified from a health screening those individuals who had an elevated liver enzyme. He then gave half this group feedback about their liver enzyme results and told them that they should moderate their drinking. Five years later, this group displayed lower rates of alcohol-related sickness and absence from work than the other half who received no such feedback or advice. Indeed, Edwards *et al.*'s study (1977) implies that this kind of advice may even be as effective as an intensive treatment regimen. In this study, 100 alcohol-dependent males were randomly assigned to two forms of treatment. In the 'Advice Only' group, the drinker and his partner were told in a sympathetic and constructive fashion that responsibility for drinking lay in the drinker's own hands. Except for a prior screening assessment, this was all the treatment provided. A second group of drinkers also underwent an initial assessment before being assigned to an 'Intensive Treatment' condition in which the drinker and his partner were offered a variety of interventions including Alcoholics Anonymous, drug therapy, psychotherapy, marital therapy and inpatient detoxification if necessary. Despite the enormous discrepancy in time and resources invested in the two groups, both displayed similar reductions in consumption twelve months later.

We will return to the issue of brief versus intensive treatment in Chapter 5, but for the present it is enough to note that the 'advice' had been sufficient for some of the drinkers to modify their behaviour. What makes this result even more remarkable is that it was achieved by a group which, although voluntary in the formal sense, contained many individuals who had been placed under coercive pressure to attend. This finding would seem to imply that expert advice to modify one's addictive lifestyle can be effective with some drug abusers, even when those individuals have exhibited no prior determination to change. Just who should offer advice is an issue that has received insufficient research attention but it is interesting and potentially important to note that in all the studies reviewed, the adviser was a medical practitioner or an individual likely to be regarded by the lay person as an authority in the area. For non-specialist social workers this may pose something of a problem: their advice could be rejected, not because it is wrong, but because the advisers are not perceived as being expert enough. Where possible, therefore, it may be preferable for workers in non-specialist agencies to arrange for a medically or drug-trained individual to provide advice about addiction.

As well as who provides it, another aspect of advice that must be carefully considered is the manner in which it is proffered. Based more on their clinical experience than empirical research, Prochaska and DiClemente (1984) have proposed that the movement from precontemplation to contemplation is facilitated by counsellors who help clients experience the developmental and environmental pressures acting on them as positive rather than merely coercive in nature. Coerciveness on the counsellor's part is said to set up defensiveness in the precontemplator and impedes rather than promotes change. Prochaska and DiClemente (1984, 1988) make the point that precontemplators must first identify with the counsellor before they are open to being influenced by the counsellor, and this is a point which has received extensive empirical support (cf. Egan, 1989). It is significant that in all the successful feedback and advice studies reviewed earlier, authors were careful to emphasise the importance of conveying a sense of being *for* the clients, of respecting their clients as people. There was no sense in which information and advice were used as a cudgel to bludgeon the client into treatment.

Environmental contingencies

The 'environmental contingencies' approach to drug treatment is derived from Skinner's celebrated work (1953, 1966) on instrumental or operant conditioning. The basic principle on which all operant procedures rest is that behaviour is shaped by its environmental consequences and that therefore any given behaviour can be modified by altering the consequences that accrue to it. The worker's task is conceptually, if not operationally, simple: it is a matter of assessing the usual consequences of drug abuse and ensuring that the abuse is not inadvertently rewarded. On the contrary, the secret is to find ways of rewarding the incompatible behaviour of moderation or abstinence. This 'environmental contingencies' approach is clearly consistent with our stated principle of ensuring that users are not sheltered from the negative consequences of their actions. Moreover, under the environmental contingencies approach it is not essential (though clearly preferable) for clients to participate in developing the regimen. Thus, because client cooperation is not an immutable prerequisite of the strategy, environmental interventions provide another avenue for working with precontemplators.

Numerous studies into the effects of manipulating drug-related contingencies have appeared in the literature. For example, in one of a series of interconnected studies, Cohen *et al*. (1972) made the provision of an enriched or an impoverished inpatient environment contingent upon drinkers achieving a moderate level of consumption. The male clients were permitted to drink up to 10 fl.oz of alcohol per day for five consecutive weeks but in the 'contingent' condition, the clients were provided with an enriched environment if they drank less than 5 fl.oz per day. The enriched environment consisted of access to a private telephone and recreation room, participation in group therapy sessions, a varied menu, access to visitors and nursing staff, and various other material privileges. If any client exceeded the 5 fl.oz limit, he was placed in an impoverished environment by himself, provided only with puréed food, and access to any alcohol was removed on the day following the over-indulgence. The environmental contingencies operated during the first, third and fifth weeks of the study. In the second and fourth weeks, clients were exposed to an impoverished environment no matter how much they drank (that is, *non*-contingently). On comparing conditions of non-contingent impoverishment (weeks 2 and 4) with conditions of contingent enrichment/impoverishment (weeks 1, 3 and 5), the researchers found that all their clients drank less under 'contingent' conditions.

In a related experiment, Cohen *et al*. (1971) demonstrated that contingent reinforcement also produced declines in drinking relative to non-contingent enrichment. Bigelow *et al*. (1974) also allowed male alcoholics to drink up to a certain level each day while in hospital, but the immediate consequence of taking a drink was to spend a period of fifteen minutes in social isolation (or 'time-out'). This time was spent in a small booth and the only activities allowed were drinking and smoking. The result of this manipulation was roughly to halve the level of drinking in seven of the ten clients who participated.

While such experiments serve to illustrate the principle of 'environment contingencies', it must be conceded that they lack ecological validity when applied to the circumstances under which most non-drug-specialist social workers operate. Whereas Cohen, Bigelow and their colleagues worked within large treatment hospitals under strictly controlled conditions, most community-based social workers could not hope (or probably even want) to match this level of environmental control. A study by Miller *et al.* (1974), however, implies that an environmental contingencies approach can be successfully implemented even within the broader, urban community. In this experiment, the researchers set out to examine the effects of monetary reinforcement on a 'skid row alcoholic'. During the baseline (or A phase) of this single-subject experiment, the client was breathalysed eight times according to a random schedule of unannounced visits from a Research Assistant. In the next (B) phase of the study, the client was awarded $3.00 tokens whenever a negative blood alcohol reading was obtained. In the third (C) phase, $3.00 tokens were issued irrespective of blood alcohol levels (non-contingent reinforcement). And in the final (B) phase, contingent reinforcement was reinstated. Results of the study revealed that this simple contingent reinforcement intervention produced quite dramatic declines in consumption relative to baseline, and significant declines relative to conditions of non-contingent reinforcement.

Social workers who administer social services and material relief are obviously in a very strong position to provide some component(s) of their service contingently upon appropriate client behaviour. Naturally, any decision to invoke this power must not entail a denial of the client's legitimate access to the agency, and for this reason it may be that contracts will relate to services or resources over and above those normally provided by the agency. Moreover, the terms of the contract must specify realistic, achievable goals which take account of the need to 'shape' behaviour through the principle of 'successive approximations' (see Chapter 5) rather than set unattainable goals in the short term. Notwithstanding these qualifications, there is likely to be some aspect of the precontemplator's social environment that is open to a contingency contracting approach by the worker.

Partner interventions

For clients in a reasonably stable relationship, the principle of environmental contingencies can be extended to include 'partner contracting' interventions which specify the interpersonal consequences of drug abuse. These interventions invariably entail an element of *quid pro quo* and there is now solid evidence of their effectiveness, though not necessarily with precontemplators (cf. O'Farrell and Cowles, 1989). This literature and the principles involved in partner contracting will be discussed in greater detail in Chapter 6. For the present it is sufficient to note that partner contracting involves a structured procedure in which couples formally agree to exchange reinforcers. For example, Hunt and Azrin's (1973) system of counselling for couples where one of the partners is alcohol-dependent aims: (a) to provide reinforcement for the drinker to be a functioning partner; (b) to provide reinforcement for the partner for maintaining the relationship; and (c) to make alcohol abuse incompatible with the improved relationship. Twelve specific problem areas are discussed, including money management, family relations, sex problems, children, social life, attention, neurotic tendencies, immaturity, grooming, ideological difficulties, general incompatibility and dominance. Together the couple constructs a list of specific activities that each would agree to perform in order to make the other person happy. This list typically includes preparing meals, listening to the partner with undivided attention, picking up the children from school, redistributing the finances, engaging in certain sexual activities, visiting relatives and spending a night out together. In all cases, sobriety is a necessary precondition for reinforcers to be exchanged.

Where even the minimal level of cooperation required of precontemplators in 'partner contracting' cannot be relied on, workers may be able to focus their efforts on the drug user's partner alone. It is now well-known that the partner's coping behaviour can have a significant influence on the addict's relationship with drugs (Orford *et al.*, 1975; Djukanovic *et al.*, 1976; McCrady, 1988). This is *not* to suggest that one person can ever be held accountable for the drug-taking behaviour of another, but to make the more positive point that partners are not necessarily powerless when confronted with alcohol and drug addiction. For example, McCrady (1988) has suggested that nagging may actually cue drinking behaviour in heavy drinkers. Examples of nagging include repeatedly telling the drinker to cut down, issuing warnings about the dreadful things that will happen if drinking does not stop, or bringing up past hurts or problems in an aggressive or accusatory manner. Orford *et al.* (1975) have also eschewed what they refer to as 'controlling behaviours'. Examples of this kind of coping response include going to the pub to bring the drinker home, hiding or throwing alcohol away, taking total control of money, or attempting to place drinkers in a situation where they will cause themselves severe social embarrassment if they drink too much. Once again, the effect of this behaviour can be to cue further drinking. Indeed, Djukanovic *et al.* (1976) reported that 74 per cent of their sample of men seeking treatment claimed that their wives had stopped nagging or trying to control their drinking before they went into treatment.

While nagging and controlling behaviour may be counter-productive, we have made the point more than once that drug use must not be reinforced by seeking to pacify or shelter the user. Steinglass *et al.* (cited in McCrady, 1988), for example, reported that one or both members of a couple where one of the partners drinks excessively may change their behaviour immediately after drinking in such a way that more or better communication occurs between them. Similarly, Billings *et al.* (1979) have shown that in marital relationships where the amount of verbal interaction is usually low, drinking can result in a significant increase in the amount of verbal output – an outcome likely to confer on alcohol abuse substantial interpersonal advantages. In summary, then, the partner must perform a delicate balancing act. On the one hand, punitive or controlling behaviour can cue further drug-taking, but, on the other hand, overly supportive or conciliatory behaviour can reinforce it.

Some practical advice for the partners of precontemplators can be derived from Sisson and Azrin's (1986) 'reinforcement training programme'. Sisson and Azrin developed this technique in response to repeated requests for help from women who were suffering because of alcohol abuse by a family member who was unwilling to undergo treatment. Their programme aims to teach the non-alcohol-dependent family member: (a) how to avoid or minimise physical abuse to herself; (b) how to encourage sobriety; (c) how to coax the drinker into treatment; and, eventually, (d) how to assist in treatment. The total programme is a rather complex procedure comprising a number of distinguishable components, all of which have their roots in learning theory. After completing a checklist designed to draw attention to the ways in which her family member's drinking is diminishing her life, the client is invited to consider the ways in which she stands to gain from the programme. The aim of this part of the programme is obviously to promote the motivation necessary to remain in counselling over the weeks, or even months, ahead. Next, clients are taught how to use positive reinforcers when the alcohol abuser is not actually drinking. A list of possible reinforcers is drawn up by client and counsellor for deployment during periods of sobriety. At these times, the woman is also instructed in positive communication. She informs the drinker, for example, that she is providing certain reinforcers because he is not drinking. She expresses positive feelings for him, and asks that he remain sober. Clients are also instructed to schedule activities which they know the drinker will enjoy but at which it will be difficult if not impossible to engage in heavy drinking. Examples might include taking their children on a picnic or participating in certain organised activities.

As well as methods for preventing alcohol abuse, partners are taught how to behave when heavy drinking does occur. Where possible, the women is encouraged to be present at the time of drinking to encourage eating and consumption of non-alcoholic beverages. She is also instructed to make the drinker aware of how much he is actually drinking and to remind him how much she prefers him when he is sober. If despite these interventions her partner does become intoxicated, the woman is instructed to ignore him and remove all reinforcers. The drinker is held fully accountable for all his actions and the fewest possible concessions are made for his state. Late or extra meals are not provided; if he passes out on the floor or lands in jail, he is left there; if he becomes incontinent or vomits, he is not cleaned up. Only in life-threatening situations is the woman permitted to intervene. As far as possible, the drinker himself is left to correct the situation when he can. On the assumption that the problem drinker is most motivated to stop drinking when the negative consequences have been severe, the partner is also taught to exploit such opportunities by suggesting counselling when the drinker recovers. Finally, the 'reinforcement training programme' also attempts to train the woman in ways of enhancing and protecting her own life, independently of the drinker. She is guided in pursuing interests outside the home and away from the drinker. Where applicable, she learns to construct the sequence of events that leads to violence against her, and thereby to identify cues to protective behaviours. Rather than argue or inflame a volatile situation, the woman simply leaves the house. If violence does occur, however, she must agree to call the police and press charges.

In a controlled trial of the programme, Sisson and Azrin (1986) compared their reinforcement training procedure against a more traditional programme involving supportive counselling and a referral to Al-Anon. The authors found a significant advantage in favour of reinforcement training. All but one of the drinkers related to clients in the reinforcement training programme came into treatment, compared with none of the drinkers related to clients of the 'traditional' programme. Moreover, even before coming into treatment, drinkers with relatives in the reinforcement programme had already reduced their alcohol consumption significantly. While these results were most encouraging, the study suffered certain methodological limitations. Specifically, comparisons between the 'reinforcement' and 'traditional' were complicated by the fact that 'reinforcement' clients received considerably more intervention than 'traditional' clients did. Additionally, the total number of clients involved in the study was very small, making the external validity of the findings highly questionable.

A more recent study of the reinforcement training (now known as 'community reinforcement and family training' or CRAFT) (Miller *et al.*, 1999) produced more definitive results. In that study, CRAFT was compared with both Al-Anon and the confrontative Intervention technique developed by Vernon Johnson (Johnson, 1973, 1986). Unlike CRAFT, Al-Anon is not designed to influence the drinker, but rather to provide support to family members. In fact, Al-Anon teaches its members to detach themselves from the drinker's behaviour and not try to influence the drinker to change. The sole purpose of Al-Anon is to promote the well-being of family members and the underlying philosophy is entirely consistent with the Alcoholics Anonymous position that the drinker will only decide to change when they hit 'rock bottom'. As previously indicated, the so-called 'Intervention' is an aggressive procedure in which close family members and close friends are assembled for an ambush meeting with the drinker in which the drinker's loved ones take turns in confronting the drinker with the adverse effects drinking is having on them. In their controlled trial comparing CRAFT with Al-Anon and The Intervention, Miller *et al.*, (1999) found that CRAFT was significantly better than Al-Anon and The Intervention in bringing resistant clients into treatment but that all three unilateral approaches were associated with improvements in the psychological functioning of family members.

In our own work with the female partners and family members of precontemplators (cf. Barber and Crisp, 1995b; Barber *et al.*, 1995;

Barber and Gilbertson, 1996, 1997, 1998), we have developed a unilateral procedure known as the 'Pressures to Change Approach' (PTC). PTC has been applied in individual counselling sessions (Barber and Crisp, 1995b; Barber *et al.* 1995; Barber and Gilbertson, 1996, 1997, 1998) and in a groupwork setting (Barber and Crisp, 1995b), and has also been summarised in the form of a self-help manual (Barber and Gilbertson, 1998). In all of these forms, randomised controlled trials have shown PTC to be successful in reducing consumption, at least in the short term, and in coaxing previously resistant drinkers into therapy. Just as importantly, PTC has also been shown to improve the morale and coping skills of the drinker's partner (Barber and Gilbertson, 1996). Depending on format, PTC requires between one (self-help format) and six (group format) sessions and involves training the non-drinking partner in the use of environmental contingencies which are arranged in order of increasing pressure to change. What follows is a shortened version of the PTC manual used in Barber and Gilbertson's (1998) study. The manual is intended for the partners of heavy drinkers and it sets out in simple language the five levels of pressure involved in our procedure. The manual can be used as an adjunct to individual or group counselling or provided to clients as a self-help booklet if the client is unable or unwilling to engage in therapy. If you plan to use PTC as a counselling or groupwork procedure, you can use the manual as your own guidebook for structuring a series of sessions.

The 'Pressures to Change' manual

Partners and other members of a drinker's family suffer in many ways: disruptions to daily life arise from arguments over drinking, money shortages, the unreliability and unpredictability of the drinker's behaviour, and so on. Family members may experience feelings of anger, frustration, embarrassment and powerlessness. The situation is even more complicated when such feelings are tinged with love, loyalty and responsibility, or just the desire to keep the family together. It is a common belief that nothing can be done to change this situation until the drinker acknowledges that they have a problem and seeks help voluntarily. But while it is certainly true that only the drinker is responsible for drinking, research has shown that partners can sometimes influence the drinker's decision to cut down or seek help. The basic message of our programme is this:

YOU ARE NOT RESPONSIBLE FOR YOUR PARTNER'S DRINKING, BUT THIS DOES NOT MEAN YOU ARE POWERLESS TO DO ANYTHING ABOUT IT.

This booklet explains what you can do. The programme outlined here has three basic objectives:

- First, it aims to provide you with a greater measure of control over your life and relationship with your partner. It is a common complaint among the families of heavy drinkers that their lives are dominated by drinking. Whether you have a good day or a bad day, whether you go out or stay home, whether people visit you or stay away: such things often seem to be out of your control. For this reason, our first and most fundamental objective is to help you set limits and improve the quality of your own life.
- Second, the programme aims to reduce your partner's alcohol consumption. By decreasing the advantages of heavy drinking and increasing the advantages of remaining sober, we hope to provide your partner with the necessary incentive to change.
- Third, the programme aims to bring your partner into treatment. This objective is not as important as the other two because your partner may be able to solve the problem alone. Nevertheless, if your partner does approach a treatment agency, you and (more importantly) your partner will have proof of their desire to change. For this reason we will encourage your partner to contact an alcohol treatment agency, whether or not they want to go into counselling. Although we will refer to 'partners' of heavy drinkers throughout the programme, the strategies can be used by anyone who has a close relationship and frequent contact with the drinker: a parent, a child, a brother or sister, a close friend. The programme applies five different levels of pressure, and it is suggested that you spend about one week on each level before going on to the next one. As you add more levels, the pressure to change increases. The five levels of pressure are:

LEVEL I PRESSURE – INFORMATION AND PREPARATION
LEVEL II PRESSURE – INCOMPATIBLE ACTIVITIES

LEVEL III PRESSURE – RESPONDING
LEVEL IV PRESSURE – CONTRACTING
LEVEL V PRESSURE – INVOLVING OTHERS

CAUTION
Physical violence is sometimes associated with heavy drinking. If your partner is or has been violent towards you, you must at all times give priority to your safety and that of your family. If you feel there is any possibility that harm will result if you follow any of the steps suggested in this booklet, seek advice from a domestic violence agency before you start. It may be that this programme is not for you.

Now, let's begin.

LEVEL I PRESSURE: INFORMATION AND PREPARATION

Although drinking is widely accepted, even encouraged, in our society, alcohol is a strong drug. With regular use, the body becomes accustomed to receiving its usual dose. As with other drugs, regular, heavy consumption of alcohol means that the drinker must increase the dosage to obtain the same effect. The more you drink, the more you need to drink.

Having become accustomed to receiving its regular dose of alcohol, the body will complain if its supply of the drug drops below a certain level. This is called withdrawal and the higher the usual dose, the stronger the symptoms are likely to be. In mild cases, the drinker may experience craving, agitation, headaches or nausea. In severe cases, withdrawal may be experienced as 'the shakes' or hallucinations. Because these unpleasant symptoms are relieved by a dose of alcohol, having another drink provides the quickest solution. We begin Level I by considering how dependent your partner has become on alcohol. This will give us a better idea of the challenge confronting your partner if they decide to cut down or give up.

How dependent is my partner on alcohol?

Your answers to the following questions will give you some idea of the extent to which your partner depends on alcohol. This is a questionnaire in common use by drug and alcohol specialists. Instructions for scoring your answers are given after the questionnaire. The following questions concern your partner's drinking. Please read each of the questions and then circle the answer that you believe to be most likely.

1	Does he/she feel he/she is a normal drinker?	Yes	No
2	Do you or other near relatives ever worry or complain about his/her drinking?	Yes	No
3	Does he/she ever feel guilty about his/her drinking?	Yes	No
4	Do friends or relatives think he/she is a normal drinker?	Yes	No
5	Is he/she able to stop drinking when he/she wants to?	Yes	No
6	Has he/she ever attended a meeting of Alcoholics Anonymous?	Yes	No
7	Has drinking ever created problems between you and your wife, husband, a parent or other near relative?	Yes	No
8	Has he/she ever got into trouble at work because of drinking?	Yes	No
9	Has he/she ever neglected his/her obligations, his/her family, or his/her work for two or more days in a row because he/she was drinking?	Yes	No
10	Has he/she ever gone to anyone for help about his/her drinking?	Yes	No
11	Has he/she ever been in a hospital because of drinking?	Yes	No
12	Has he/she ever been arrested for drunken driving, driving while intoxicated, driving under the influence of alcoholic beverages?	Yes	No
13	Has he/she ever been arrested, even for a few hours, because of other drunken behaviour?	Yes	No

For questions 1, 4 and 5, score 1 for a 'no' response. For all other questions score 1 for a 'yes' response. The total should be somewhere between 0 and 13. A total of 3 or higher is normally taken to indicate some level of dependence on alcohol. In this programme we assume a degree of dependence on alcohol, so if your partner scored 3 or higher, read on.

How do people change?

Research has shown us that people who manage to solve an addiction problem typically go through the stages depicted in Figure 3.1 You can see from the diagram that the commitment to change involves progressing through a number of stages. The stages we are primarily concerned with in this programme are called the 'precontemplation' and 'contemplation' stages.

Precontemplation
The precontemplator is someone who gives little or no thought to their drinking. Any problems are ignored or blamed on other people or circumstances. The typical precontemplator says things like: 'I know lots of people who drink more than I do', or 'I don't have

Figure 3.1   *The revolving-door model of the stages of change*

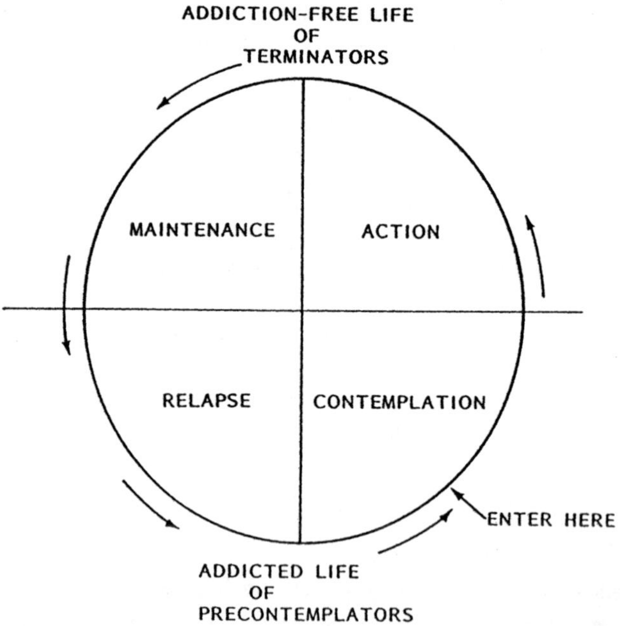

ADDICTION–FREE LIFE
OF
TERMINATORS

MAINTENANCE   ACTION

RELAPSE   CONTEMPLATION

ENTER HERE

ADDICTED LIFE
OF
PRECONTEMPLATORS

Reprinted from Prochaska, J. O. and DiClemente, C. C. (1988) 'Toward a comprehensive Model of Change', in W. R. Miller and N. Heather (eds), *Treating Addictive Behaviours: Processes of Change*, the Plenum Publishing Corporation.

a problem, you do. Why don't you get some counselling.' The pre-contemplator is outside the circle of change. The precontemplator doesn't have the slightest intention of changing.

Contemplation
During the next stage, contemplation, the drinker begins to think about cutting down. They are not yet ready to do anything. In fact, the contemplator usually doesn't want change if it can be avoided. They are just starting to weigh up the pros and cons. 'Maybe I do drink a bit too much sometimes . . . but I'm no alcoholic!', or 'Maybe I should cut down a bit . . . perhaps when things settle down at work', or 'Maybe I do drink a bit . . . but some of my friends drink more than I do', or '1 think I will cut down a bit, but not just now'. This is the contemplator: moving back and forth between the need to change and their love of drinking. A contemplator may go on like this for days, months, or even years before either giving up on change or taking some definite step towards change. That step may be to throw the bottle away, or call a treatment agency, or just promise to cut down or stop. When this occurs, the drinker enters the action stage.

Action
In the action stage, the heavy drinker reduces their drinking or abstains from alcohol altogether. This can occur with or without help from someone else.

Maintenance
The initial decision to change is the easy part, of course. Now the drinker is confronted by a new problem, maintenance, or the hard work of keeping the change going. In many cases, the maintenance stage is followed by the relapse stage.

Relapse
Relapse normally follows one or two occasions where the drinker slips up and drinks more than they wanted to. The old drinking pattern reemerges and the person goes back to being a precontemplator. They slide out of the change circle until circumstances change and contemplation begins again.

Perhaps the most important point about the circle of change is that this is the typical pattern, even for those who eventually solve an addiction problem. Research has shown that people with an addiction to alcohol go around the circle a number of times before the drinking problem is solved. So, if this is the normal pattern for people who solve the problem, you can see that relapse does not necessarily mean failure. The important thing is for the drinker to learn something about the circumstances that lead up to drinking. Knowing what happened when the first slip-up occurred makes it possible to change those circumstances in future or find other ways of coping with them.

Many of the partners who have been through our programme observe some short-term change in their partner's drinking. It is expected that, in keeping with the typical pattern, most of these drinkers will lapse or relapse after a while. If this happens with your partner, you may decide that you are not prepared to live with yet another failed attempt and you choose to end the relationship. But if you do decide to stay, remember that relapse is the usual pattern. The circle of change will come around again, particularly if you keep using the strategies we cover in this booklet. Do not give up on the strategies outlined even if you feel you have tried most of them before. Persistence and consistency are the keys to success in this programme.

Why do people change?

From Figure 3.1 you can see that our task is to encourage a precontemplator to become a contemplator or, better still, an 'actor'. We are trying to entice someone outside the change circle inside the circle. So, how does someone move from being a precontemplator to being a contemplator? Well, we know quite a lot about what does not work. Nagging, for example, doesn't work. Hiding the bottles doesn't work. Arguing, shouting and fighting also don't work. All these actions do is upset you and provide the drinker with an excuse for drinking: 'If you didn't nag so much, I wouldn't drink so much' or 'If you'd only leave me alone, I wouldn't have to go the pub'. You've probably heard this kind of thing before. As we have already said, you don't make your partner drink, but that doesn't necessarily stop them blaming you whenever possible.

Because we know that nagging and arguing don't work, it is most important that you do not confuse pressure with fighting or arguing. Try to avoid getting into shouting matches over your partner's drinking. All this does is upset you. We know it is easier said than done, but it is very important that you try to remain calm throughout the programme.

Now that we've looked at what not to do, let's turn our attention to what you can do. Basically, people change for one of two reasons: either their lives change in some important way, or they change because of pressure from the environment. Examples of the first reason include: turning 40 or 50, the birth or death of a child, the formation or breakdown of a relationship. In other words, life goes on, and with every new stage there is the chance and the challenge to change old patterns of behaviour. The other way people change is through pressure. This refers to the often slow build-up of negative consequences associated with an old behaviour. There may be no single incident that forces the change; it may merely be the realisation that one's life is not the way one wants it to be. Since we can't control the events and stages of your partner's life, our programme looks to the second reason for change. Our objective is to put just enough pressure on your partner to entice them inside the circle of change.

SUMMARY AND THINGS TO DO DURING THE COMING WEEK

1. Heavy drinkers are likely to do something about their drinking when the disadvantages of drinking outweigh the advantages.
2. During the next few weeks, you will be making all the disadvantages of drinking very clear to your partner.
3. Reduction in drinking is often followed by a return to old habits. Don't be too disappointed if this happens. It is part of the change process. Remember that nagging, anger and other direct attempts to control your partner's drinking do not work. Try to remain calm and focus on the strategies covered in this booklet.
4. Either fill in the questionnaire in the next section or read the next section and take note of your partner's drinking so that you can complete the questionnaire at the end of the week.

LEVEL II PRESSURE: INCOMPATIBLE ACTIVITIES

You might not think so, but drinking is doing your partner good. Sure, alcohol causes you both some pretty serious problems, but this just goes to show that your partner is getting something so valuable from drinking that it outweighs all of the problems involved. For this reason, it is important to be clear about what your partner is getting out of drinking. Alcohol may help your partner relax or celebrate or deal with feelings of sadness. Other people drink simply to get rid of the withdrawal symptoms they feel when they haven't had a drink for a while.

For the next exercise, write down in the space provided the times, situations and people involved in your partner's drinking. The example below shows what Carol wrote about Tony's drinking.

Tony drinks heavily:		
When?	**Where?**	**With whom?**
Friday nights	Pub	Frank and Graham
Saturday afernoons	Pub	Frank and Graham
After a win at the races	Pub	By himself

This example shows that Tony normally drinks too much in the company of others, although he will drink alone if he has something to celebrate. There are a number of other important things we now know about Tony's drinking. For one thing, he doesn't drink heavily every day. For another thing, he tends to drink when he is celebrating or relaxing; not when he is stressed or sad. Finally, Carol's list demonstrates the importance of two particular drinking friends. From all of this we are beginning to get a picture of Tony's high-risk times and the benefits he obtains from drinking.

Now make your own list. In compiling it, make sure you think of a typical drinking week. Do not pick the best or worst example.

My partner's typical drinking week looks like this:		
When?	**Where?**	**With whom?**

Now, what does your partner's drinking pattern tell us about the benefits they are getting from alcohol? Does it help your partner to relax? Does it help your partner to feel confident in social settings? In the space provided, write down what you think your partner gains from alcohol.

What my partner gains from drinking is:

1. _____
2. _____
3. _____
4. _____

This information about the people, places, times and benefits associated with your partner's drinking forms the basis for Level II pressure: INCOMPATIBLE ACTIVITIES. Incompatible activities are things your partner can do that interfere with their drinking but which provide some of the benefits of alcohol. For example, few people drink while they are engaged in vigorous activity, yet exercise can be another way of relaxing for people who drink when they are tense. For people who drink heavily when they are depressed, going to a concert or play can sometimes help to relieve sadness without the need or opportunity to drink.

ILLUSTRATION

Mrs Shepherd's times of highest risk were on weekends when her daughter, Theresa, was out. On Saturdays and Sundays, Mrs Shepherd started drinking at lunchtime and continued into the evening until she finally passed out in her chair.

Theresa knew that her mother now had limited mobility because of failing health and that Mrs. Shepherd was no longer able to work in the garden on weekends. Theresa tried to think of an interesting incompatible activity which would occupy her mother throughout Saturday and Sunday afternoons. Theresa suggested they have part of the pergola enclosed to form a hothouse. Mrs. Shepherd would then have a small, manageable area in which to work on weekends. Because Mrs Shepherd had always enjoyed gardening it was, for her, incompatible with both boredom and drinking.

Mrs Shepherd shifted most of her drinking to the evening mealtimes, limiting the time available for drinking. Although she still drank too much on weekends, she did reduce her boredom and her alcohol intake. It was the start of a new, less dependent relationship with alcohol.

Using the information you have from the last two exercises, try to work out a suitable incompatible activity that could be used occasionally to reduce your partner's opportunity to drink.

If you are unable to think of an activity which provides the benefits your partner obtains from drinking, any activity your partner will agree to try at times when they are very likely to drink too much will serve the purpose. Even if your partner takes part in the incompatible activity but starts drinking once it is over, the time available for drinking has been reduced and at least part of the 'high-risk time' has been negotiated without alcohol.

SUCCESSFUL INCOMPATIBLE ACTIVITIES WILL BEGIN TO DEMON-STRATE TO YOUR PARTNER THAT THEY CAN SURVIVE WITHOUT RESORTING TO ALCOHOL.

SUMMARY: THINGS TO DO DURING THE COMING WEEK

1. Using the forms and questionnaires you have completed, try to work out your partner's high-risk times and situations. When are they most likely to drink too much?
2. Try scheduling an incompatible activity for one or more of these times.

LEVEL III PRESSURE: RESPONDING

In this section we look at how to respond to your partner when they are drunk or sober. To begin, please complete the following drink diary. Think about your partner's drinking over the last week. For each day of the week, record whether or not they had too much to drink; then record the circumstances surrounding the drinking, much as you did in Level II. Now, and most importantly, record what you did in response to your partner's drinking on that day.

DRINK DIARY			
Day	**Intoxicated?**	**Situation**	**My response**

As you look at your answers to this questionnaire, compare the way you reacted when your partner drank too much with when they were sober. Even if your partner was drunk every day of the week, there would have been some time in the day when they were sober. Think about your reactions during the times of the day when they were drunk or sober. Now, the question we want to ask is: WAS THERE MUCH DIFFERENCE IN THE WAY YOU REACTED TO YOUR PART-NER'S DRUNK TIMES AND SOBER TIMES? You may have felt differently on the two occasions, but did you respond to your partner any differently. Did life go on pretty much as normal irrespective of the amount they had drunk?

In our work with partners we have repeatedly found that many people do not distinguish between drunk times and sober times. Because they have learnt to get on with life despite the drinker, they behave more or less the same way regardless of how much their partner drinks. Of course it is a good thing to live your own life and not be constantly worrying about your partner's problems, but their drinking does matter to you and your behaviour should convey this. Do you always prepare a nice meal, irrespective of how much your partner drinks? Are you always cheerful? Do you never initiate conversation about topics your partner enjoys, regardless of whether they are drunk or sober? Perhaps you and your partner don't talk much any more on good days or bad ones.

Some people are unintentionally friendlier when their partner has had too much to drink. For example, some drinkers will only talk about personal matters when they have been drinking and if you were freely available at these times, your partner would have a strong incentive to keep drinking: it makes them feel understood and close to you. All of these patterns demonstrate the importance of Level III pressure: RESPONDING. While you cannot control your partner's decision to drink, you can help to provide some incentive for your partner to choose in favour of staying sober. In this section we try to show you how.

Getting started

Make a list of all the benefits your partner gets from living with you. Your partner is staying with you, so there must be something they get out of it. The best lists are those that contain very tangible things like meals, sex, watching television together, and so on. There is nothing wrong with listing 'love' or 'happiness', provided you know precisely what these things mean in practice. For example, how do you show love? How do you make your partner happy?

The things my partner values in our relationship are:

_____

_____

_____

_____

_____

_____

Don't be discouraged if you had trouble finding things to write. It may have been a long time since your partner paid you a compliment, or you might feel that your relationship has deteriorated because of your partner's drinking. If you are really stuck, perhaps you could ask your partner at a time when they are sober and willing to talk to you.

With this information you are ready to work out your responding strategies. As unromantic as it sounds, the basic idea is to use the things your partner gets out of the relationship to provide incentives not to drink. TO THE EXTENT POSSIBLE, REMOVE WHATEVER YOUR PARTNER GETS OUT OF THE RELATIONSHIP WHEN THEY ARE DRUNK AND PROVIDE THESE THINGS CHEERFULLY WHEN YOUR PARTNER IS SOBER.

Think of your responses as a light switch: when the switch is on, your partner can see clearly, when the switch is off, your partner is in the dark. The difference in the world around your partner should be like night and day, depending on whether they are drunk or sober. If your partner is sober, the light is on. If they drink too much, the light goes off. If this happens reliably and predictably, two important consequences will follow. First, your partner will receive accurate feedback from the environment that they have had too much to drink. And since so many heavy drinkers are poor judges of when they have had too much, this is important information. Second, your partner will be faced with a real choice every time they drink: drink too much and everything I value in the relationship is removed; remain sober and what I want is readily available.

What to do when your partner is drunk

As you remove everything you can from the above list, accompany your actions with a calm but clear statement about what you are doing. Something like, 'You've had more to drink than I will accept, I'm leaving the room' should do the trick. Once you have made your statement, break off all contact with your partner until they sober up again. Do not prepare meals. Do not keep meals warm until your partner gets home. Do not enter into any conversation. Do not sit and watch television with your partner. If your partner collapses on the floor or gets sick, leave them to sort it out when sober.

Try to avoid negotiating or explaining your actions any more than you already have. Through it all, remember: NO ARGUMENTS AND NO RECRIMINATIONS. Say what you have to say firmly but calmly.

What to do when your partner is sober

To use our light switch idea again, how will your partner know that you prefer them sober if the lights don't come on again when they are no longer intoxicated? Show your partner you are pleased when they are sober. Be ready to do the opposite of what you did when your partner was drunk.

When your partner is sober, make a statement like, 'The way you are now is just what I want. This is the person I want to be with.' Having made your statement, give whatever you can from the list of things your partner values. Now is the time to prepare that special meal, go on that outing, or just sit and talk. Perhaps you could ask your partner if there is anything they would like you to do together. Whatever it is you are willing to do, make it clear that you are happy to do it because your partner is sober.

If all heavy drinkers ever hear is that they drink too much, they face the prospect of being seen by themselves and others as nothing but a drunk, a no-hoper. The only way to save themselves from this painful predicament is to deny that they have a problem with alcohol. By responding positively when your partner is sober, you are saying, 'There may be times when you drink too much, but there are other times when you are sober and good to be with.' This message helps your partner in two ways. First, it helps your partner distinguish between acceptable and unacceptable behaviour. Second, it shows your partner that they are not just a drunk; that while you may want your partner to do something about their drinking, you recognise that your partner has good qualities as well.

ILLUSTRATION

David often came home late for dinner after drinking with his friends in the pub. Irene would keep his meal warm in the oven and work around the kitchen while he ate dinner. She would then do the dishes and go to the living room where she would watch television for a while before going to bed. Irene didn't much care for television but would sit there for an hour or so because David wanted her to, and because it was just about the only time they spent together any more.

After going through the Level III exercise, Irene realised that the evening ritual of putting out the meal, talking while her husband ate and sitting with him in front of the television was quite important to David. Although the interaction between them was minimal, it was company for David and he did occasionally talk about work and other things that were on his mind.

Irene stopped keeping David's meal warm. She told him dinner would be served at 6.30 p.m. and if he was not home by then, dinner would be left on the table. Irene would tidy up after herself and go to her room to read. If David came in, Irene would tell him that she did not want to be around him when he had had too much to drink but that she would like to spend time with him when he was sober.

If David did come home sober, Irene would tell him how much it meant to her and would cheerfully engage in the little ritual that David seemed to enjoy so much.

What to do when a crisis occurs

Every once in a while most heavy drinkers will do something they regret while drunk. They may cause themselves embarrassment, get picked up for drink-driving or hurt someone they love. These are crisis times and they present you with a valuable opportunity. At these times, your partner will be very suggestible, so it is worth raising the subject of drinking and suggesting that your partner seek help. As always, the way the matter is raised will have a large bearing on how your partner reacts. Something like, 'I know you feel very badly about what happened, and I know it was related to your drinking. Why not call the counselling service and talk about your drinking (or cut down your drinking)?' should be about right. If your partner responds by getting angry or telling you to stop nagging, simply say that you were not intending to nag and drop the subject. Do not let the situation develop into an argument. Another crisis is sure to come around and you can make the same gentle suggestion when it does.

SUMMARY: THINGS TO DO DURING THE COMING WEEK

1. Fill in the Drink Diary and examine the ways in which you have been responding to intoxication and sobriety.
2. Compile a list of what your partner values in the relationship and be ready to remove these things when they have drunk too much, and provide these things when your partner is sober.
3. Remember that praising your partner when they are sober is just as important as withdrawing when your partner is intoxicated. You can't expect someone to behave appropriately if you only ever show them what is inappropriate. Be prepared to switch the light on as well as off.
4. Crises are times when your partner is most likely to decide to change or seek help. Exploit crises every time they come around.
5. Continue to arrange incompatible activities whenever possible.
6. Stay at Level III, RESPONDING, for at least one week before moving on.
7. Be consistent. Once you have worked out your strategy, stick to it. Your partner must know exactly what to expect when drunk or sober.
8. Try to resist the temptation to shout or argue if things don't work out straight away. Chances are this will only make you upset and your partner may use the argument as an excuse to drink too much.

LEVEL IV PRESSURE: CONTRACTING

By now your partner should know there are consistent and predictable changes at home according to how much they drink. However, up to now you have not sought a commitment from your partner to cut down by a specific amount or at specific times. Thus, the next level of pressure, CONTRACTING, involves asking your partner to make a contract with you about precisely how much alcohol they will consume on a given day or days. This strategy increases the pressure because it pins your partner down to definite drinking targets.

The best drinking contracts are those that begin by looking only a short way ahead, rather than forcing your partner to make promises about the rest of their life. You could begin Level IV by making a contract to limit drinking at a function such as a wedding or party, or you could make a contract for the next normal week. Whatever the details of the contract, try to follow these general principles:

(a) The contract should target a 'high-risk time' (see Level II). A high-risk time is a time when your partner is highly likely to drink too much. It could be on a Friday night or at a party or at some other time or place with which you are familiar.
(b) The contract should set a specific limit, for example, four glasses of beer or three glasses of wine.
(c) The drinking limit should be difficult but not impossible to achieve. If your partner is used to drinking a great deal at high-risk times, consider contracting to reduce consumption substantially rather than insisting there be no drinking at all.
(d) A contract involves two parties, not just one. If your partner agrees to do something as difficult as cutting down or abstaining on a high-risk day, offer to do something in exchange.

Once a contract has been made, there are only two possible outcomes. Either the contract will be honoured or it won't. If your partner honours the contract, they will have overcome a high-risk situation and started the process of change. Now you are in a position to negotiate a new contract for the week or fortnight or month ahead. However, if your partner breaks the contract, the situation can still be salvaged. Failure to honour the contract is a small crisis for your partner and we discussed how to deal with crises in Level III. Would your partner now consider talking to a counsellor about the drinking? Look up the number of a 24-hour drug and alcohol help line and give it to your partner. If your partner resists or expresses anger, pursue it no further. Keep responding as described in Level III and wait for an opportunity to negotiate a new contract.

Listed below are some possible steps to help you negotiate a drinking contract.

Contracts relating to a special occasion

• Step 1: Explain to your partner that although you would like to attend the function, you are concerned about how much they will drink. Do not labour the point and, as always, avoid arguing.

- Step 2: Acknowledge that your partner may find it difficult to limit the amount they drink, particularly if surrounded by others who are drinking heavily.
- Step 3: Offer to do something for your partner in return for cutting down so that your partner feels the contract is part of a cooperative relationship rather than being merely a command.
- Step 4: Come to a precise agreement, setting out how much your partner will drink and what (if anything) you will do in return.
- Step 5: IF YOUR PARTNER ADHERES TO THE AGREEMENT, you have an opportunity to respond as described in the previous Level III. Tell your partner how much their effort meant to you and offer to do the things you know your partner values in your relationship. IF YOUR PARTNER BREAKS THE AGREEMENT, raise the matter next morning. Point out that you believed your partner wanted to keep to the agreement. Ask your partner to call a 24-hour drug and alcohol help line and arrange an appointment.

Contracts relating to day-to-day drinking

- Step 1: Choose a time when your partner is sober and explain that you would like to come to an agreement about the maximum amount they will drink each day. Point out that you get on better together when your partner controls their drinking. Keep your approach matter-of-fact.
- Step 2: Set a realistic limit for each day of the next week. If your partner does not drink each day, limit the discussion to drinking days, and particularly to 'high-risk' days (see Level I). If your partner is accustomed to drinking, say, ten standard drinks on a high-risk day, make an agreement that they drink seven or eight on those days in the week ahead. Any movement towards change is to be encouraged at this point. Besides, the chances of success can be higher with a gradual reduction. Once your partner has adjusted to a lower level, further reductions can be easier to achieve.
- Step 3: Acknowledge that you have asked your partner to do a very difficult thing and offer to do something in exchange. This will show that you want to help and are willing make sacrifices too if need be.

- Step 4: Come to a definite agreement which clearly sets out your part of the contract as well as the maximum number and type of drinks your partner will have on any given day. For example, you might agree to go to the cinema with your partner on Saturday night, if they agree to drink no more than seven standard drinks on Friday night.
- Step 5: IF YOUR PARTNER ADHERES TO THE AGREEMENT, respond as described in Step 5 above and negotiate another contract for the week, fortnight or month ahead. IF YOUR PARTNER BREAKS THE AGREEMENT, respond as described in Step 5 above.

SUMMARY: THINGS TO DO DURING THE COMING WEEK

1. Find the number of your nearest 24-hour drug and alcohol counselling service and write it on a piece of paper.
2. Follow the steps outlined in this level to make a contract with your partner about their drinking.
3. Take advantage of any crises that occur by suggesting your partner ring for advice, and give your partner the number you have written down.
4. Continue to schedule incompatible activities when you can.
5. Respond positively when your partner is sober.
6. Withdraw whatever your partner values in the relationship when they are intoxicated.
7. Keep track of what is happening by filling out a drink diary (see Level III) each day.

LEVEL V PRESSURE: INVOLVING OTHERS

By now you have been applying the programme consistently for several weeks. Through your actions, your partner has been made aware of the negative consequences of a high blood alcohol content and the positive consequences of staying sober. Your partner's world now changes reliably with fluctuations in their alcohol consumption: sobriety means a pleasant home life, intoxication means the removal of everything your partner enjoys in the relationship.

If your partner still hasn't made a move towards cutting down or seeking help, it is time to progress to Level V, INVOLVING OTHERS. This strategy involves the same techniques you have been using up to now, but increasing the pressure by having one or more other people adopt the same tactics. It is no longer just you applying the pressure; now there are others as well. At Level V, there are two approaches you can use. One or both may suit your situation.

Strategy 1 – applying Levels I to IV

Anyone else you select to become involved in this strategy should satisfy all of the following criteria.

1. The person must have the love and respect of your partner. Never enlist someone your partner doesn't like or trust. That would do more harm than good.
2. The person must care deeply about your partner. It is not enough for the person to love and care for you, they should feel that way towards your partner.
3. The person or persons you choose must be capable of understanding and applying the strategies outlined in this booklet. For example, it is asking too much of young children to involve them in Level V pressure.
4. The person or persons you choose must have ample opportunity to interact with your partner. It is no use involving someone who sees your partner only rarely.

If you can identify one or more people who satisfy all of these criteria, go through this booklet with them and discuss the different levels. Explain what you have been doing and assist the other person or persons to adapt the same principles to their relationship with your partner. Of particular importance is Level III pressure. Discuss what these others can do when your partner is drunk or sober. For example, you might agree that any time you all have dinner together, the others will leave if your partner drinks too much. Also help the others to respond to any crises that might arise when they are with your partner.

Perhaps they could come around the next day and ask your partner to ring a drug and alcohol counselling service, just as we described in Level III.

If after some weeks this strategy also fails, you might consider moving to Strategy 2.

Strategy 2 – personal statements

It is important that the person who helps you with this strategy also satisfies the criteria listed for Strategy 1 with the exception that a good friend or a relative who occasionally visits from another part of the country could be ideal for Strategy 2.

Under the second strategy, one of your partner's friends or relatives writes a personal statement about your partner's drinking and the effect it is having on their relationship.

The personal statement consists of three sections:

1. A simple and sincere expression of love for your partner, and the importance of the relationship with your partner.
2. A description, with examples, of the ways in which alcohol is diminishing the relationship.
3. A gentle but clear request for your partner to do something about their drinking.

As such material is highly emotive, we recommend writing it down in a letter. Even if you judge it better for the person to speak directly to your partner, it is helpful if what is said has been written out to ensure that all three points are adequately covered.

ILLUSTRATION

Here is an example of a letter written by a woman to her father:

'Dad, I love you and I miss the way you used to be. I always looked up to you and I could never have gone to university and cared for the kids when they were younger without your love and support. I want to tell you how worried I am about your drinking. I'm worried that the way you drink is ruining your life and our relationship.

You've been complaining that you don't see much of your grandchildren. I've been making excuses for why we don't visit very often. The real reason is your drinking. When you're drinking you get very aggressive and I don't want the kids to see you that way. It's because of your drinking that I stopped

---

inviting you to lunch. You used to arrive drunk and everyone was on edge and embarrassed the whole time.

There's more I could say because these things have been going on for a long time. But all I really want to tell you is that I love you and really hope that you get help for your drinking. I'm sorry if saying all this is hurtful to you but I want you to get better. Please get some help.'

CONCLUSION

You have now reached the end of our programme and we hope the strategies described in these pages have helped you feel a greater sense of control over your life. We have tried to encourage you to set limits on what you are prepared to tolerate and we hope you are now acting firmly and consistently in accordance with those limits. We also hope your responses have your partner under constant pressure to change. If you have followed the steps outlined in this booklet, you have done all you can. The rest is up to your partner.

Summary

Working with precontemplators must surely be one of the most difficult challenges in the field of addictions. As we have seen, not only do precontemplators resist or deny the need for change, but most addiction researchers have responded by ignoring the precontemplation stage altogether. However, precontemplators cause most of the social harm brought about by drugs, and it is often social workers who are called on to assist. The procedures outlined in this chapter are designed to bring pressure on precontemplators to reconsider their resistance to change. Our objective has been to sow a seed of doubt in the user's mind about their drug-using behaviour. This degree of ambivalence may well be insufficient to carry the user through or even into treatment. Accordingly, we must be ready to accentuate early and tentative expressions of concern by the drug user about their lifestyle. The issues and tactics involved in achieving this will be discussed in the following chapter which deals with the next stage of change: contemplation.

4

From Contemplation to Preparation

Either because of the strategies outlined in the previous chapter or because of developmental and other changes in the drug user's life, many or most precontemplators will eventually consider the possibility of changing. Newly acquired or internalised information about the negative consequences of drug use impels them that way. By definition, however, these 'contemplators' are not yet ready to act on their emergent awareness. Rather, their response is likely to be one of deep ambivalence about the matter. On the one hand, social and maybe medical problems will be only too obvious to them, but on the other, they will want to resist any implication that they are not in control of their drug use. Besides, contemplators usually enjoy their drinking or drug use and they will be reluctant to lose this source of pleasure. W. R. Miller (1989, p. 70) has described the contemplation stage as akin to an internal 'seesaw which rocks back and forth between motivation to change on the one side and to stay the same on the other'. However, whereas the precontemplator may have been unwilling even to discuss the possibility of change, the contemplator is at least prepared to go that far. Accordingly, the focus of our analysis and our intervention must now shift from the user's microsystem to the user themself (see Chapter 3). While individual counselling may have been inappropriate during precontemplation, it now becomes imperative as the user struggles with the dilemma confronting them.

As discussed in Chapter 2, Prochaska and DiClemente (1982, 1983, 1988) propose that contemplators are most open to consciousness-raising interventions such as observation, confrontation and interpretation. As they become increasingly conscious of their drug problems, contemplators begin to reevaluate their ideals and their behaviour. This is a period of intense soul-searching and herein lies the first and most fundamental implication for practice during this stage: because verbal and cognitive processes are paramount at this time, the worker's task is to promote discussion and reflection, not behaviour change. Much of the literature on drug treatment, particularly from within the behavioural tradition, has focused too narrowly on the action stage and the mechanics of behaviour therapy to the neglect of what we might call the precommitment stages of change. Yet careful contemplation about the need for treatment in the first place is at least as important as the choice of treatment approach. Properly handled, the contemplation stage creates a firm foundation for intervention, motivates the client for change, develops goals and incentives, and promotes acceptance of responsibility for change.

In this chapter we shall consider the precommitment tasks of the contemplation stage and cover some of the verbal and cognitive interventions capable of facilitating the transition from precommitment to preparation and action.

Helping the contemplator decide

In attempting to explain how individuals solve their addiction problems, Orford (1985) has invoked the language and logic of decision-making psychology. According to this view, drug abusers are confronted with behavioural options which gradually shift in their subjective valence until the user must choose whether or not to abandon one option and pursue another. In the author's own words:

> the motivation for change derives from an accumulation of 'losses', 'costs', or harm resulting from behaviour ... these have accumulated to the point at which they exceed the 'gains', benefits, or pleasurable outcomes of appetitive behaviour to such a degree that the conflict between the desire to continue with the appetitive behaviour on the one hand, and other needs (to be a bread-winner, to be a family person, to enjoy life, to have a clear conscience, to have friends, to have self-respect, etc.) on the other hand, cannot be resolved by the defence mechanisms which have served up to that time. (Ibid., p. 272)

Orford coined the term 'choice point' to capture the crisis confronting the contemplator, and his view that theirs is a problem in decision-making sits quite comfortably with the term 'contemplation' used by Prochaska and DiClemente (1982, 1983, 1988) to identify the stage.

Over the years there have been numerous attempts to conceive of addictive behaviour in decision-making terms (see, for example, Astin, 1962; Heilizer, 1964; Horn, 1972; Armor *et al.*, 1978), but perhaps the most comprehensive and articulate of these is the model developed by Irving Janis and his colleagues (Janis and Mann, 1968, 1977; Janis and Rodin, 1979). Janis and Mann (1977) describe their approach as a 'conflict theory model' which grows out of the repeated finding that human beings are reluctant decision-makers who are prone to gross errors of judgement because of their desire to minimise the distress involved in facing important decisions. The relationship between decision-making and stress proposed by Janis and Mann can be summarised in five basic propositions.

First and most obvious is the idea that the degree of stress generated by the choice at hand is a positive function of the subject-ive importance of all possible outcomes. To put this another way, a decision is only stressful when the decision-maker realises there is much to gain and much to lose. Second, the prospect of change will be more stressful when the individual is highly committed to their present course of action. Third, when each alternative poses serious risks, the individual may lose all hope of solving the problem and adopt a kind of freeze response referred to by Janis and Mann as 'defensive avoidance'. Defensive avoidance is a counter-productive coping strategy in which the individual is given to 'selective inatten-tion, selective forgetting, distortion of the meaning of warning messages, and construction of wishful rationalizations that minimize negative consequences' (1977, p. 50). Fourth, the degree of stress is inversely related to the amount of time available to arrive at a decision. In other words, if an important decision must be made quickly, the individual has an emergency on their hands. Finally, rational problem-solving will occur only when there is both a basic level of stress (to provide motivation) and a reasonable expectation of resolving the dilemma. In summary, then, the best, most rational decisions require the three core conditions of *stress, hope,* and *time*: a moderate amount of stress, hope of finding an acceptable solution, and time to consider all the options. Only when these preconditions are satisfied does 'vigilant' decision-making become possible. Vigilant decisions are defined operationally by the authors as those in which the individual:

1. thoroughly canvasses a wide range of alternative courses of action;
2. surveys the full range of objectives to be fulfilled and the values implicated by the choice;
3. carefully weighs whatever he [*sic*] knows about the costs and risks of negative consequences, as well as the positive consequences, that could flow from each alternative;
4. intensively searches for new information relevant to further evaluation of the alternatives;
5. correctly assimilates and takes account of any new information or expert judgement to which he is exposed, even when the information or judgement does not support the course of action he initially prefers;
6. reexamines the positive and negative consequences of all known alternatives, including those originally regarded as unacceptable, before making a final choice;
7. makes detailed provisions for implementing or executing the chosen course of action, with special attention to contingency plans that might be required if various known risks were to materialize. (Ibid., p. 11)

Taken together, these seven criteria provide client and worker with something of a yardstick for establishing when contemplation is complete and the client is ready to move to the action stage of change.

Under the model (Figure 4.1), contemplation would begin when a change in the antecedent conditions presages imminent loss or threat. The user will respond with the first question, 'Are the risks serious if I don't change?' If after considering whatever additional information is salient at the time (antecedent condition), the probability that the threat will materialise is judged to be minimal or the magnitude of the danger is low enough to be tolerated, the contemplator will answer 'no' to this question (mediating process) and return to the drug usage of the precontemplator. This return to baseline is known as unconflicted adherence and in this state there is simply insufficient stress to motivate change. If, on the other hand, the answer to the first question is 'yes' or 'maybe', stress will result and the contemplator will begin searching for some means of escape from the threat. The question at this point becomes, 'Are the risks

***Figure* 4.1** *Janis and Mann's conflict theory of decision-making*

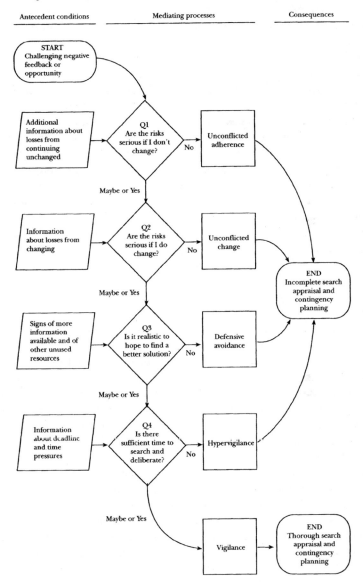

Reprinted from *Decision Making: A Psychological Analysis of Conflict, Choice, and Commitment* by Irving L. Janis and Leon Mann. © 1977 by The Free Press.

serious if I do change?' Information about the losses likely to result from changing one's drug use is processed (antecedent condition), and if the contemplator is satisfied that there will be no serious consequences (mediating process), stress will subside and they will embark on change with confidence and composure: a response referred to as unconflicted change. If the contemplator considers that change is going to exact a heavy price, the answer to the second question will be 'yes' or 'maybe', stress will persist and may even increase, and the drug user will search for more information, more options and better solutions. Eventually, the third question, 'Is it realistic to hope to find a better solution?' must be faced, and if the answer is 'no' the contemplator will revert to drug use and seek to protect themself from stress through defensive avoidance of any subsequent warning signs. However, if the contemplator possesses hope of finding a better solution than the current situation, they will move to the final question, 'Is there sufficient time to search and deliberate?' If the contemplator answers 'no' to this question, they will become hypervigilant, or panicked, and in such a state contemplators will foreclose on their options by gravitating towards the most obvious and simple-minded solutions. Needless to say, such decisions are rarely optimal. Assuming the contemplator has sufficient time to weigh all the options, however, vigilant decision-making becomes the probable response.

It is important to realise that the five coping patterns of unconflicted adherence, unconflicted change, defensive avoidance, hypervigilance and vigilance are all within the behavioural repertoire of every decision-maker. Janis and Mann's (1977) model seeks to predict which response is likely to prevail by linking each of them with the conditions relating to conflict, hope and time that mediate the five responses. The implications of Janis and Mann's model for work with contemplators are straightforward: the counsellor must aim to moderate the amount of stress involved in the decision, while providing the necessary hope and time for the contemplator to exercise decisional vigilance. Although the second and third of these core conditions are clear enough, providing sufficient threat to motivate change but not so much as to produce hypervigilance can be difficult to achieve in practice. Fortunately, Miller's (1983, 1998; Miller and Rollnick, 1991) work on 'motivational interviewing' provides a rich source of guidance in this regard and we will discuss his procedure in the next section.

Once the core conditions have been satisfied, Janis and Mann (1977) suggest the use of a 'decisional balance sheet' to promote vigilance. The balance sheet is based on research showing that the types of expected consequence of each alternative course of action can be classified into four main categories: (a) utilitarian gains and losses for self; (b) utilitarian gains and losses for significant others; (c) self-approval or self-disapproval; and (d) approval or disapproval from significant others (see Janis, 1959; Janis and Mann, 1968). 'Utilitarian gains and losses for self' refers to the expected instrumental effects of the decision on the decision-maker's utilitarian objectives. Gains resulting from change could include such things as a happier home life or better job security, for example. Utilitarian losses, on the other hand, might include sacrificing some old friendships or losing a source of relaxation. The category 'utilitarian gains and losses for significant others' extends similar considerations to those with whom the decision-maker is identified or affiliated. 'Self-approval or self-disapproval' refers to the effect(s) of any given decision on the individual's internalised moral standards. More specifically, some decisions are likely to bring shame and some will bring pride in doing what is morally right according to the decision-maker's own standards. The need for drug counsellors to show more interest in the contemplator's values and moral standards is an issue which has been taken up by Orford (1985), who points out that some of the most powerful incentives to change frequently have little to do with utilitarian considerations but are related to what the user thinks is proper behaviour. Finally, the 'approval or disapproval by significant others' of each alternative under consideration is another source of potential gains and losses, so this category too must be carefully assessed before opting for one course of action over another.

Janis and Mann (1977) propose a six-step counselling procedure which operationalises their decisional balance sheet idea and this procedure can be readily incorporated into a broader intervention plan for contemplators. The first step is an open-ended interview in which the counsellor asks the client general questions about the most salient alternatives and their expected consequences. In the early stages of contemplation, the user may be able to think of only two options: to stop immediately and altogether or to continue using in the same way and at the same level as now. Whatever alternatives the contemplator has thought of, he or she is asked to rank them in order and focus on the top two. The contemplator is then asked to

***Figure* 4.2**   *The decisional balance sheet alternative*

Alternative # _____

	Positive Anticipations +	Negative Anticipations –
1. Tangible gains + and losses – for SELF		
2. Tangible gains + and losses – for OTHER		
3. Self-approval + or self-disapproval –		
4. Social approval + or disapproval –		

Reprinted from *Decision Making: A Psychological Analysis of Conflict, Choice, and Commitment* by Irving L. Janis and Leon Mann. © 1977 by The Free Press.

think of all the possible arguments for and against the two highest alternatives. The second step of the procedure is to introduce the balance sheet grid as seen in Figure 4.2.

The aim of the balance sheet is to promote reflection by the client on all the non-salient consequences of the alternatives under consideration. The contemplator is introduced to the four outcome dimensions discussed above and helped to fill in the grid using information obtained from the first step in the counselling procedure. In step three, the client is encouraged to search for any other pros and cons that they may not have thought of before. At this stage, it is quite legitimate for the counsellor to draw the client's attention to factors which the counsellor may be aware of, provided that the client is the judge of how important these factors are. Having now completed balance sheets for each alternative, the client is helped to identify the most important consequences in step four. (The authors recommend assigning a score out of seven for each entry.) In step five, balance sheets are filled in for any new alternatives the client may have thought of since the procedure began. For example, as a result of steps one to four or simply because other options have presented themselves in between counselling sessions, the contemplator and/or the counsellor may suggest entering a treatment programme rather than trying to give up alone; or moderating consumption rather than giving up altogether; or giving up over time rather than all at once. New possibilities such as these are analysed in the same way as the earlier options. Finally, in step six, the client again ranks the various options but is encouraged to keep an open mind for a little longer, to permit any unforeseen consequences to present themselves.

There is ample evidence to show that failure to undertake the kind of painstaking appraisal of consequences outlined above leads to post-decisional regret and eventual relapse. For example, smokers who take insufficient account of withdrawal effects when deciding to give up are very likely to relapse when the severity and perseverance of the symptoms become apparent. Indeed, it is probable that a lack of decisional vigilance is one of the chief reasons for Prochaska and DiClemente's (1988) finding that most of those who solve an addiction problem require more than one cycle through the stages of change. Behind each relapse there is usually some unanticipated or insufficiently weighted consequence of change which needs to be understood in future decision-making.

Promoting motivation for change

In the previous section we looked at the vital role of stress, hope and time during the contemplation stage of change. We saw that a moderate degree of stress is essential if contemplators are to have the necessary motivation to engage in vigilant decision-making. In this section we will look more closely at techniques for moderating stress or, more positively put, for promoting motivation for change. The preeminent thinker in this field is Bill Miller, whose work on 'motivational interviewing' (Miller, 1983, 1998; Miller *et al.*, 1988; Miller and Rollnick, 1991) was hailed as the most important advance in the treatment of addiction 'in more than a decade' when it first appeared

(Heather, 1992). Interestingly, though, much of what Miller actually does will sound familiar to social workers who are schooled in most of the non-directive counselling techniques he advocates.

Motivational interviewing is built on a fundamental objection to the traditional, disease-oriented model of motivation. According to the traditional approach, motivation is a characteristic of the user. Individuals are said to possess a certain level of motivation for change which is carried about with them like any other relatively stable personality trait. It follows that drug abusers who resist treatment must be deficient in this trait. This proposition is normally followed by the added suggestion that in order for motivationally deficient users to 'become motivated' it is necessary for them to 'hit rock bottom', that is, for the user's life to deteriorate to the point where 'denial' becomes manifestly absurd, even to the user. Only then will resistance break down and the user face up to the desperate need for change. The notion of 'denial' looms large in the traditional explanation of treatment failure. Denial, in the sense of rejecting the label 'alcoholic', is seen as an adjustment strategy or defence mechanism which largely accounts for the drinker's plight. A latent consequence of this idea is that the user can be held fully responsible for resistance to or failure in treatment. The therapist, on the other hand, is totally exonerated!

Miller and his colleagues (Miller, 1989; Yahne and Miller, 1999) dispute the traditional approach to motivation on a number of grounds. First, there is simply no evidence to support the notion that the 'alcoholic' has an inherently deficient personality. In particular, all the research into the alcoholic personality points to the conclusion that alcohol abusers are indistinguishable from the general population in terms of denial and other defence mechanisms (Chess *et al.*, 1971; Donovan *et al.*, 1977; Skinner and Allen, 1983). Second, as we saw in the previous chapter, it is far from being a universal rule that the motivation to change requires the user to 'hit rock bottom'. Many individuals change for positive reasons, not because their lives have become intolerable (for example, Vaillant and Milofsky, 1982). Third, it is well established that factors external to the user can promote or inhibit change. Finally, therapist characteristics are known to play a major role in treatment outcome (Greenwald and Bartmeier, 1963; Raynes and Patch, 1971; Rosenberg *et al.*, 1976), so it cannot be that deficiencies within the user are solely responsible for treatment failure.

In contrast to the traditional model of motivation, Miller's (1983) own approach begins with the proposition that 'denial is not inherent in the alcoholic individual, but rather is the product of the way in which counselors have chosen to interact with problem drinkers' (p. 150). After all, counsellor and client are engaged in social inter-action and each can be expected to influence the other in a dynamic pattern of exchange. For instance, Miller regards it as axiomatic that the effect of confronting a contemplator with the need for change will be to elicit resistance in that client. This prediction follows from the repeated finding that direct argumentation is an ineffective way of producing attitude change because it prompts the receiver to consider all the potential counter-arguments. Thus, therapists who endeavour to browbeat contemplators towards change may end up having exactly the opposite effect. Miller (1983) himself advocates that the counsellor try to draw the arguments for and against drug use from the client and thereby assist the client to convince themself of the need for change.

If, as Miller asserts, motivation is not a personality trait, then we might well ask, 'What exactly is it?' According to Miller, motivation is a behavioural probability or, in his own words, it is 'the probability that a person will enter into, continue, and adhere to a *specific change strategy*' (Miller, 1991, p. 19, my emphasis). Two aspects of this definition warrant careful attention. First, motivation relates to a behavioural tendency rather than the imputed possession (or non-possession) of an attitude or trait. Second, motivation is situation-specific. Thus, a person may be 'motivated' to engage in one form of treatment but not another, or to work with one therapist but not another. Moreover, the ultimate behavioural tendency (motivation) in any given situation will be the outcome of all the pressures towards accepting change minus all the pressure towards resisting change. One way of capturing this approach is to think of motivation as a state rather than a trait.

In sharp contrast to the traditional model, Miller's motivational interviewing approach deliberately de-emphasises labelling. Clients are not cajoled into acceptance of labels such as 'alcoholic' or 'drug addict'. What really matters is that client and counsellor establish what problems the user is having in relation to drug use, and what needs to be done about them. Moreover, motivational interviewing places responsibility on the client to decide how much of a problem there is and whether or not to change. It is not for the counsellor to confront clients with 'the truth' as the counsellor sees it. Because the goal of counselling is to increase clients' intrinsic motivation for change and belief in themselves, the strategies of motivational interviewing are more supportive than argumentative. As in client-centred counselling (Rogers, 1951; Carkhuff and Anthony, 1979; Ivey, 1983; Egan, 1989), resistance in clients is not met with confrontation but with empathy and reflection, both as a means of displaying respect for the client and of creating the kind of positive atmosphere which is conducive to change. Consistent with Miller's emphasis on self-directedness is the injunction to promote internal attributions for drinking and for drug-taking, as well as for any successes in changing behaviour. In other words, motivational interviewing, unlike the disease-oriented approach, views the decision to drink or not to drink as a free choice. The individual is not helpless; there need be no 'loss of control' unless the user so chooses. These fundamental differences between the motivational interviewing approach and the confrontational, traditional approach have been summarised in Table 4.1.

Table **4.1**   *Differences between the traditional approach and the motivational interviewing approach*

Traditional approach	Motivational interviewing
Heavy emphasis on acceptance of self as having a problem; acceptance of diagnosis seen as essential for change	De-emphasis on labels acceptance of 'alcoholism' or other labels seen as unnecessary for change
Emphasis on personality pathology, which reduces personal choice, judgement and control	Emphasis on personal choice and responsibility for deciding future behaviour
Therapist presents perceived evidence of problems in an attempt to convince the client to accept the diagnosis	Therapist conducts objective evaluation, but focuses on eliciting the client's own concerns
Resistance seen as denial, a characteristic trait requiring confrontation	Resistance is seen as an interpersonal behaviour influenced by the therapist's behaviour
Resistance is met with argumentation and correction	Resistance is met with reflection
Goals of treatment and strategies for change are prescribed for the client by the therapist; client is seen as 'in denial' and incapable of making sound decisions	Treatment goals and change strategies are negotiated between client and therapist based on data and acceptability; client's involvement in and acceptance of goals are seen as vital

Reprinted from Miller, W. R. and Rollnick, S. (eds) (1991) *Motivational Interviewing: Preparing People to Change Addictive Behavior*, p. 53, Guilford Press.

In a review of the empirical literature, Miller (1985) identified a number of interventions and preconditions which are known to be associated with the successful promotion of motivation. Taken together, these interventions comprise a kind of toolbox for motivational interviewing. The first intervention that is known to work is ADVICE, but as this technique was fully discussed in the previous chapter, there is no need to dwell on it here. A second motivational intervention is to identify and where possible remove BARRIERS to change. Such barriers often relate to quite practical concerns such as the lack of alternative child care, or not wanting to be seen attending a drug treatment centre. The more that obstacles such as these are removed, the more likely it is that a client will enter treatment. Third is the notion of CHOICE, and there is ample evidence to suggest that treatment is more effective (Kissin *et al.*, 1971; Thornton *et al.*, 1977; Sanchez-Craig, 1990) and client attrition is lower (Costello, 1975; Parker *et al.*, 1979; Sanchez-Craig and Lei, 1986) when clients are given choices within and between treatments. Accordingly, the counsellor must seize every opportunity to provide alternatives throughout the process, rather than adhering rigidly to a standard treatment formula for all clients. Because the contemplation stage is a time of weighing up the pros and cons of continued drug use, the most fundamental counselling strategy is to decrease the DESIRABILITY of drinking or drug usage.

In Miller's terms, the tactic is to tip the 'internal seesaw' towards change by subtly adding weight to that side of the fulcrum. Once again, this objective is not normally achieved by direct argumentation but by drawing attention to the client's values and emotional reactions. In this process it is important that the user be encouraged to present all the desirable aspects of alcohol or drug use. Not only does this minimise post-decisional regret (see above), but the counsellor is alerted to the factors which need to be undermined or counterbalanced. EXTERNAL CONTINGENCIES and FEEDBACK are also part of the motivational interviewing toolbox, and these, too, were quite comprehensively discussed in Chapter 3. GOAL SETTING is the seventh building block of Miller's procedure and it refers to the motivational power of comparing one's present state to one's important life goals. Feedback will only be useful to the extent that it provides information about the discrepancy between goals and progress towards those goals. For this reason, assisting clients to clarify their basic goals in life, as well as their specific goals with respect to alcohol or drug use, provides the foundation on which most other motivational strategies can be constructed. Finally, counsellors need to adopt a HELPING ATTITUDE if the interaction between them and their clients is to be productive. This quality will probably be more familiar to social workers as 'empathy' which can be defined as the capacity to convey a sense of being for the client through active listening and accurate reflection of the client's statements and feelings. Drug counsellors who adopt this empathic approach have been shown to produce favourable long-term results with problem drinkers (Edwards *et al.*, 1977b; Kristenson, 1983), as do therapists who convey optimism about the client's chances of success (Leake and King, 1977).

Three central themes run through the eight characteristics of motivational interviewing listed above. The first of these is the need for affirmation which produces the positive relationship necessary for the counsellor to have influence with the client. The second has been referred to by Miller and his colleagues (Miller, 1983, 1998; Yahne and Miller, 1999) as awareness, by which they mean the recognition of discrepancies between the 'real' and the 'ideal', between one's values or goals and one's present behaviour. More than anything else, it is discrepancy which provides the stress said by Janis and Mann (1977) to be necessary for vigilant decision-making to occur. Finally, the provision of alternatives is important because it demonstrates clearly that the problem is both solvable and within the client's competence to do something about it. Thus, the end result of providing alternatives is likely to be the promotion of client self-efficacy, and the importance of this objective would be clear from our earlier discussion of Janis and Mann's decision-making model. Without a sense of self-efficacy, the contemplator will be unable to answer 'yes' to the question, 'Is it realistic to hope to find a better solution?', and a negative expectation will almost certainly result in abandoning change altogether.

The eight characteristics of motivational interviewing can be combined with the three central themes as seen in Figure 4.3.

Figure 4.3 indicates that affirmation acts as a moderator variable which determines the extent of any effects on discrepancy and self-efficacy exerted by the eight strategies discussed earlier. In turn, discrepancy and self-efficacy determine the ultimate level of motivation for change.

Figure 4.3   *A diagrammatic representation of the motivational interviewing approach*

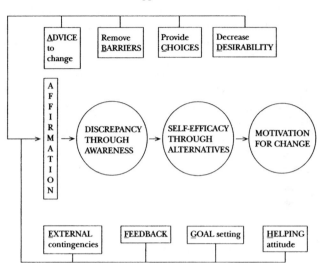

Putting all these principles together, it is possible to derive the following five-step counselling procedure which can be used as a brief intervention by non-specialist workers. The five steps are:

1. Broaching the subject
2. Exploring client concerns.
3. Providing objective feedback and information
4. Summarising Steps 2 and 3
5. Negotiating alternatives.

Step 1: Broaching the subject

Undoubtedly, the way in which the subject of drug use is raised with an early-stage contemplator can be a vital determinant of whether or not the client will be prepared to engage in vigilant decision-making. Especially at this early stage, it is imperative to avoid labelling and confrontation. Both Miller (1983) and Rollnick *et al.* (1992) empha-sise the importance of open-ended questioning regarding the client's own concerns. An almost exclusively empathic, reflective stance should be taken by the counsellors at this stage; although Miller (1983) points out that reflection should be deliberately yet subtly selective. Client statements about the need for change can be reinforced simply by giving these statements greater attention or by the counsellor displaying positive non-verbal responses such as smiles, head-nods and an open, interested body posture. The primary aim of this step should be to provide the 'affirmation' component of the model, but the counsellor should also take every opportunity to begin generating the 'discrepancy' which impels the contemplator towards change. In Janis and Mann's (1977) terms, the counsellor would listen attentively for the four basic decision-making questions and use the tactics described to steer the contemplator towards affirmative answers.

Step 2: Exploring client concerns

As the client opens up and begins to volunteer their concerns, the real work of motivational interviewing begins. The objective of accentuating the discrepancy between the client's goals and their current state should now come to the fore. Table 4.2 summarises the flow of discussion that I have found useful during this step.

Table 4.2   *Topics for discussion during Step 2 of a motivational interview*

Topic	Objective	Possible starter questions
Substance use in general	To begin discussion of behaviour and feelings	'Tell me about your drinking'
A typical day	To obtain a detailed profile of consumption	'Describe for me a typical drinking day'
Past and present consumption	To draw attention to increased consumption and tolerance	'How has your drinking changed over time?'
Positive functions of substance	To begin delineating high-risk situations and to acknowledge the benefits of drug use	'When do you really look for a drink?' or 'What would you lose if you gave up drinking?'
Concerns about drug use	To promote discrepancy directly	'What concerns do you have about your drinking?'

The counsellor seeks to draw the client towards change by moving from a general discussion of drug-taking behaviour to a more detailed and specific analysis of the pros and cons of continued usage levels. The client is prompted to think about how much they use now and, by comparing this with past levels, helped to recognise the sometimes dramatic increase in tolerance (see Chapter 1) that has developed. In Step 2, the client also begins to consider the situations which trigger over-use (see also Chapter 5) as a means of introducing the benefits of drug use. The pros of drug consumption should then be discussed explicitly before moving to the personal concerns and costs of continuing to use.

Step 3: Providing objective feedback and information

Miller (1983) recommends interrupting the interviewing process at about this point to conduct or provide relevant, personalised information and feedback. Guidelines for the provision of feedback were referred to in Chapter 3 so the reader will be familiar with the requirements for optimising its effectiveness. In general terms, however, the purpose of this step is to provide the user with information about how much (if any) is safe for them to consume, where the user currently stands with regard to safe usage levels, what effects of drug use on the client are already apparent, and anything else the client may wish or need to know. For example, contemplators typically want reassurance that they are not 'sick', so it is appropriate at this point to discuss the nature of addiction (see Chapter 1) and dispel any unhelpful stereotypes that may be harboured by the contempla-tor. In this context, the counsellor should take the opportunity to emphasise the client's control over and responsibility for their own behaviour.

Step 4: Summarising Steps 2 and 3

Having covered all this ground, the counsellor should draw the dis-cussion together into a summary statement. Particularly in view of the very open-ended discussion that ensued during Step 2, there is an obvious need for a clear, concise summary which provides some incentive to continue. It must be emphasised, however, that the statement is primarily a summary of the client's responses and comments, it is not merely an opportunity for the counsellor to offer opinions or propose solutions. The client should be asked to respond to the counsellor's summary and consider what needs to be done now. In listening to the client's reply, the counsellor listens for any sign that the client is moving towards 'preparation' or a decision to change. If the opportunity arises, it can be a very powerful tactic at this point to advance some gentle arguments in favour of the decision not to change because this is likely to prompt arguments for change by the client. In this way clients can be encouraged to talk themselves into changing. Alternatively, Janis and Mann's (1977) 'balance sheet' exercise can be used to help clients systematically rehearse the arguments for and against change.

By the end of this fourth step, counsellor and client should have negotiated the first two of Janis and Mann's (1977) decision-making questions, namely, 'Are the risks serious if I don't change?', and 'Are the risks serious if I do change?' Assuming the client does have serious problems in relation to drug use, the answer to both questions should by now have been answered in the affirmative. In Miller's (1983) terms, this means that the counsellor has been successful in generating discrepancy between the client's real and ideal state. The fundamental precondition of motivation for change has been established.

Step 5: Negotiating alternatives

While discrepancy may be a necessary component of motivation, it is not sufficient. The client must have a realistic expectation of solving the problem. In order to achieve this, the motivational interviewing technique requires that time be spent by client and counsellor considering all the options for change. From Janis and Mann's (1977) viewpoint, this step deals with the third and fourth of their decision-making questions: 'Is it realistic to hope to find a better solution?', and 'Is there sufficient time to search and deliberate?' Affirmative answers to these questions ensure that the final precondition of motivation for change is provided, namely, self-efficacy or the belief that one has the capacity to solve the problem. For this reason, client and counsellor now think broadly about all the treatment options. For example, should the client aim for abstinence or moderation?

Should the client enter treatment at all? If so, what kind of treatment? What about self-help methods? And so on. For each of the alternatives, a decisional balance sheet (Janis and Mann, 1977) can again be completed. A motivational interview need not end with an agreement by the client to do anything. It may simply be an opportunity for the client to reflect on the concerns and considerations which were avoided during the earlier precontemplation stage. While there is always the danger that a client may get stuck at the contemplation stage, ultimately it is up to the client to make the next move. Besides, the chances of the client prevaricating indefinitely will be considerably reduced if the fifth step in the procedure is completed successfully.

In recent years, motivational interviewing has been subjected to numerous controlled trials in a very wide range of clinical settings, and the weight of evidence has so far been very favourable. For example, motivational interviewing has been shown to improve treatment compliance in psychiatrically ill alcohol and drug users (Martino *et al.*, 2000; Swanson *et al.*, 1999), to improve treatment outcomes among illicit drug users on probation (Harper and Hardy, 2000), to reduce smoking dependence among hospitalised adolescents (Colby *et al.*, 1998), and to promote reductions in consumption among pregnant drinkers (Handmaker *et al.*, 1999). Assuming that the client does make a resolution to change through the application of motivational techniques, a new set of strategies needs to follow. These strategies are directed to helping the client gain control of their *behaviour* and they are appropriate for people who have arrived at the action stage of change. Thus, it is to the action stage and behavioural self-control procedures that we must now turn.

5

Action Strategies

While the counselling received at the contemplation stage may convince users of the need for change, many will need further help to gain control of their behaviour. This task requires a different set of procedures from those outlined in the previous chapter but the primary focus of the intervention will remain the user. This chapter looks at a simple set of strategies for use at the action stage of change. Not only are the interventions conceptually simple but there is considerable evidence that if they are going to work, they will do so quickly and efficiently. In fact, we shall see that carefully designed self-help materials may be all that is required to bring about change in some drug misusers. This is not to say that addictive behaviours are easily resolved or that change will always last. The point is merely that the best treatment methods are not necessarily the most complex or protracted.

Fundamental principles in the behavioural treatment of addictions

As discussed in Chapter 1, the behavioural model of addiction is predicated on the notion that addictive behaviour is learned behaviour, and therefore that the modification of drinking and drug-taking is partly a problem in learning. Many researchers in the behavioural tradition have used a kind of shotgun approach, in which numerous psychological treatments ranging from simple blood alcohol discrimination training to marriage guidance counselling are fired at clients in the hope that one or all of them will assist the client in learning to drink appropriately, or not at all (for example, Vogler *et al.*, 1977). Such approaches have been referred to as 'multimodal' and one review of the literature (Miller and Hester, 1986) has identified up to twenty separate treatment components that have been advocated in various combinations by behaviourally oriented clinicians. Although multimodal approaches often claim considerable success, they are highly labour-intensive, sometimes requiring up to one year of therapy with a trained therapist.

In this chapter we will consider a simpler, more focused behavioural procedure. At the heart of the approach is what is known as the 'functional analysis' of both antecedent events and expected consequences of drug-taking behaviour. There is now a great deal of evidence to show that addictive or excessive behaviours are influenced by a variety of antecedent events. These events (or cues) can be subjective states such as negative emotions or external events such as certain sights, sounds or smells, but whatever they are, they constitute danger signals to the user who is trying to give up that they are at risk of using a drug. Fortunately, the range of situations which cause drug abusers to relapse has been found to be quite limited. Cummings. *et al.*, (1986) identified only eight kinds of 'high-risk situation' which together accounted for all the relapses that occurred in their sample of 327 heroin users, alcohol abusers, binge eaters, smokers and gamblers. Five of the situations were intrapersonal in nature (that is emanating from within the user) and three were interpersonal determinants. Table 5.1 presents Cummings *et al.*'s (1986) summary of these high-risk situations.

***Table* 5.1**   *High-risk situations (percentages)*

	Drinking	Smoking	Heroin use	Gambling	Overeating
Intrapersonal	**61**	**50**	**49**	**79**	**46**
Negative emotions	38	37	19	47	33
Negative physical states	3	2	14	–	–
Positive emotions	–	6	10	–	3
Testing personal control	9	–	2	16	–
Urges and temptations	11	5	4	16	10
Interpersonal	**39**	**50**	**51**	**21**	**52**
Interpersonal conflict	18	15	13	16	14
Social pressure	18	32	34	5	10
Positive emotions	3	3	4	–	28

Reprinted from Cummings, C., Gordon, J. R. and Marlatt, G. A. (1986) 'Relapse: prevention and prediction', in W. R. Miller (ed.), *The Addictive Behaviors*, p. 303, Pergamon Press, New York.

Under intrapersonal determinants the authors distinguish between five kinds of pressure. First are 'negative emotional states' such as feelings of depression which occur in reaction to negative events of a non-interpersonal nature. 'Negative physical states' refers to any kind of somatic discomfort, whether or not the discomfort is related to previous drug overuse. Under 'positive (intrapersonal) emotional states', the authors lumped all feelings of happiness or celebration which do not occur in or derive from social contact. 'Testing personal control' relates to occasions when individuals are tempted to try their drug to prove to themselves that they are truly 'cured' and can therefore now handle the drug in moderation. As the label implies, 'urges and temptations' relates to withdrawal effects and the temptation to use in order to deal with craving for the drug itself. Under the heading of interpersonal determinants, Marlatt and Gordon (1980) include 'interpersonal conflict', 'social pressure' and 'positive (interpersonal) emotions'. Interpersonal conflict refers to all disagreements, arguments and other negative confrontations with other people. Social pressure includes all occasions of direct interpersonal coercion as well as indirect pressure, such as being surrounded by people in the act of drinking or using. Finally, positive interpersonal emotional states relates to situations in which individuals turn to drugs to enhance positive social occasions.

As shown in Table 5.1, Marlatt and Gordon (1980) found that 74 per cent of alcohol relapses were preceded either by negative emotional states like depression (38 per cent), interpersonal conflict (18 per cent) or social pressure (18 per cent). Heroin users, on the other hand, were most troubled by social pressure (see also Barber *et al.*, 1991), negative emotional states, negative physical states and interpersonal conflict. Interestingly, only a small minority of drug users (6 percent overall) claimed that craving for the substance, in and of itself, was responsible for their relapse, even though Marlatt and Gordon's sample was drawn from a clinical population of severely dependent persons (see also Cummings *et al.*, 1980). It would seem to follow that craving is normally secondary to some other cue or cues.

Such findings serve to clarify how drug abuse can be considered functional: the user turns to drugs in order to cope with the situation at hand. Put simply, the user does not so much have a drug problem as a drug solution and much of the art of drug treatment lies in delineating the positive consequences of alcohol or drug abuse and finding ways of substituting more adaptive behaviours to achieve these ends. For example, the drinker who turns to alcohol to ameliorate stress may need to practise relaxation exercises (behavioural strategy), as well as go through certain prearranged mental routines such as calling to mind things like the reasons for wanting to cut down, the drinking limits that have been set for the day, and one or two simple self-statements (cognitive strategy).

As well as coping skills, behavioural interventions normally make use of a number of other principles derived from work in the psychology of learning. For example, it is well-known that keeping a record of progress (self-monitoring) increases awareness of habitual actions and this feedback can have a significant influence on motivation. Also, it is known that the self-regulation of human behaviour depends to a large degree on the individual's goals, but that setting goals which are difficult or unattainable can lead to a feeling of being overwhelmed or frustrated. For this reason, it is better to set short-term goals rather than try to achieve too much too soon. By focusing attention on the next day or the next week instead of the rest of one's life, we can help break the cycle of helplessness that addicts often feel caught up in. The final principle is self-reward. This refers to the simple if somewhat contrived tactic of making an agreement with oneself that adherence to the treatment goal for the next day or the next week will lead to certain rewards such as outings or purchases. The use of self-reward has been shown consistently to produce better results than self-monitoring on its own (Mahoney, 1974). This is not merely because people like to go out or because they like to buy things; the major function of self-reward is to act as a signal to the user that the goal for the week (or the day) has been achieved. In other words, self-reward provides tangible feedback that the client's self-management programme is working.

A ten-step intervention plan for the modification of drinking and drug-taking behaviour

Putting all the foregoing principles together, it is possible to derive a number of key components of any cognitive-behavioural intervention strategy. In this section and the next we will illustrate how such a strategy would work by applying it to the most common drug – alcohol. It is worth reiterating, however, that although alcohol is the subject of discussion, the same general approach can be extended to any drug of dependence (see Chapter 2).

After outlining the structure of the intervention in this section, the next section will be presented in the form of a programmed instruction manual based on our ten-step plan. This approach has two advantages. First, it moves discussion from a set of abstract principles to quite tangible prescriptions for practice. Second, the programmed instruction format allows the text to be transcribed or paraphrased for clients and made available in the form of a self-help manual; and the benefits of self-help materials like these will become clear towards the end of the chapter when we look at the literature on brief intervention methods. Moreover, each step in our programmed instruction manual constitutes a straightforward summary of the techniques contained within the strategy and the references that appear throughout can be used by the reader to delve further into the various procedures.

Before presenting the programmed instruction manual, however, it is necessary to consider a diagrammatic overview (Figure 5.1) of the intervention plan on which it is based. The first step in our model consists in deciding whether to aim for moderation or abstinence. Naturally, this decision should be made by the client after taking account of all the considerations (including legal and financial) that are involved (see Chapter 4). For example, there is considerable consensus in the literature that a moderation goal is not for everyone. Of particular importance is the repeated warning that individuals with high levels of alcohol dependence should be encouraged towards abstinence because their ability to sustain controlled drinking has never been reliably established (see Pendery *et al.*, 1982; Heather and Robertson, 1983; Foy *et al.*, 1984; Miller and Hester, 1986, 1988; Heather and Tebbutt, 1990). Apart from high levels of dependence, abstinence should always be recommended to clients with alcohol-related organic damage of any kind, including brain damage. Pregnancy and the concurrent use of certain kinds of medication may also necessitate abstinence, irrespective of level of dependence. Nevertheless, it is not for the worker to browbeat clients at this first stage of the intervention, if only because there is firm evidence that clients who are allowed to participate in the choice of crucial elements of their treatment programme do better than those whose treatment is forced upon them (Miller and

Figure **5.1** *The ten-step intervention plan*

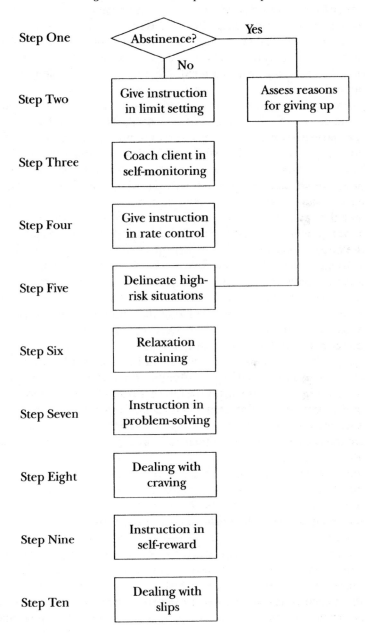

Step One — Abstinence? — Yes

No

Step Two — Give instruction in limit setting — Assess reasons for giving up

Step Three — Coach client in self-monitoring

Step Four — Give instruction in rate control

Step Five — Delineate high-risk situations

Step Six — Relaxation training

Step Seven — Instruction in problem-solving

Step Eight — Dealing with craving

Step Nine — Instruction in self-reward

Step Ten — Dealing with slips

Hester, 1988). If a client insists on continuing to drink despite advice to the contrary, they should not be dismissed as 'unmotivated' as is so often the practice. For one thing, it may be possible to attenuate the damage of extreme drinking through controlled drinking therapy, and for another, clients can be helped to come to the realisation through treatment that abstinence is the only viable option.

Having taken the fundamental decision about the goal of treatment, Step Two for those who choose an abstinence goal is to review their reasons for giving up so as to maximise the motivation for change. Following this step, abstainers proceed directly to Step Five of the model. For individuals who choose controlled drinking, on the other hand, Step Two involves setting realistic limits based on accurate normative information about how much is safe. At Step Three, controlled drinkers are coached in monitoring their drinking behaviour and at Step Four they are given instruction in controlling their rate of intake. Irrespective of the treatment goal, all clients proceed to Step Five where the functional analysis of drinking behaviour that was referred to in the previous section is conducted. Depending on what high-risk situations are identified, drinkers are provided with training in coping skills designed to address the problem(s). At Step Six, clients are exposed to relaxation training under the assumption that they will be more capable of calling on coping skills if they are able to control their anxiety when confronted by a high-risk situation. At Step Seven, clients are coached in problem-solving before moving on to methods for dealing with craving at Step Eight. Under our model, clients are instructed to use self-rewards at Step Nine, and in the final step they are helped to make contingency plans in the event that a lapse occurs.

A programmed instruction manual for clients

Having developed the basic structure of our intervention plan, we can now illustrate the approach through a programmed instruction manual based on Figure 5.1. The manual begins at Step Two of the model (that is, after the treatment goal has been set) and is addressed directly to clients.

Step Two (abstinence goal): Why give up?

Whether you like to admit it or not, giving up alcohol will have costs as well as benefits for you. You are going to feel discomfort and frustration; you might even lose some friends or find yourself with nothing to do from time to time. So take some time to think back over your reasons for wanting to give it up as well as your reasons for wanting to keep drinking. For example, you might be drawn towards giving up because of your health or because of what alcohol is doing to your home life; but, on the other hand, you might feel drawn to drink because your friends drink, or because drinking helps you relax. You are only ready to give it up when you are convinced that the pain of not drinking is going to be less than the pain you will suffer if you keep drinking.

It can be helpful to write down the reasons why you have chosen to give it up. There will be some difficult days ahead and referring to your list from time to time may help you to deal with the urge to drink again. (Go directly to Step Five.)

Step Two (moderation goal): Set a realistic limit

In order to cut down, the first thing you need to know is how much alcohol is too much.

Different kinds of drinks contain different amounts of alcohol but because of the different-sized glasses used, the following glasses all contain about 8 to 10 grams (half an ounce) of alcohol. They are called units of alcohol and are what is normally served in a pub:

1. A small or 120 ml (4 fl.oz) glass of wine;
2. 60 ml (2 fl.oz) glass of fortified wine such as sherry or port;
3. A half-pint (285 ml/10 fl.oz) glass of beer;
4. One nip or 30 ml (1 fl.oz) of spirits such as brandy or whisky.

It is a good idea to work out how many units of alcohol there are in a bottle. For example, a bottle of regular strength beer contains about four units of alcohol, and a bottle of wine contains about seven units of alcohol.

To be a safe drinker, an average-size man should drink no more than four units of alcohol in a day and an average-size woman should drink no more than two units of alcohol a day. However, it is important to point out that the effect of alcohol on the body is actually determined by the amount of alcohol in the bloodstream at any one time. Since it takes time for your body to burn up the alcohol in your bloodstream you must space out your drinking, otherwise your blood alcohol concentration just builds up and up. Even the recommended level of four drinks for men and two for women can be unsafe if you drink them too quickly. As a rough guide, you should aim to drink your recommended drinking levels over two or more hours.

Figure **5.2** *The personal agreement sheet*

I agree that I will have no more than
..............drinks a day in the next normal
week. This means that I will not have more
than..............drinks each week.
Signed..............
Dated..............

Now that you know how much alcohol is too much, you need to set yourself realistic drinking limits in the weeks ahead. If you are drinking a lot more than the recommended level, cut down gradually. It is very hard to change habits overnight, so why not aim to drink a little less each week until you do reach safe levels. You could fill in the 'personal agreement sheet' (Figure 5.2) which is a kind of contract with yourself to start cutting down.

Use the 'personal agreement sheet' to set a realistic limit for the next normal week. For example, if you normally drink around ten drinks each day, aim to drink eight. Although this amount is still unsafe, it is a good start for someone who is used to ten drinks a day, and when that reduction has been achieved, the recommended level will begin to look easier.

Step Three (moderation goal): Always know how much you are drinking

Now that you have set yourself a limit, you are ready for one of the most important steps of all: getting into the habit of always counting your drinks.

In order to control your drinking, it is crucial that you always know precisely how much you are drinking. Some people find it helpful to keep a drink diary. To use the diary method you need to carry a daily record card with you at all times. Every time you have any alcohol, write on your card what kind of drink it was and how much the glass contained. Try to record units of alcohol; so if you filled a beer glass full of wine, that would be about one and three-quarter units of alcohol. One thing to remember is that it can be very difficult to know how many drinks you have had if you keep topping up your glass. My advice is that you fill and finish one glass at a time. Stop people from topping up your glass if you possibly can.

As well as the kind and amount of drink you have, record the date and time you had it. And very importantly, keep track of the drinking situation. You may have noticed that you drink more in some situations than in others. For example, some people drink more when they are in a crowd while others drink more when they are alone. Some people drink more when they are in the pub with friends while others drink more when they are entertaining their friends at home. The situation around you can be a more powerful influence on your drinking than you might think, so it is important that you learn to recognise which situations lead you to drink more than is safe. Are there certain people you tend to drink too much with? Are there certain places where you tend to drink too much? Are there times and days when you drink more than at other times? Are certain activities associated with too much drinking (for example, watching television or playing cards)? Do you drink more when you have certain feelings (for example, feeling unhappy or excited)? If the answer to any of these questions is 'yes', then you must learn to avoid these circumstances or change the way you respond to them. You will learn more about this in Step Six.

To sum up this step, then, make sure you are aware of the type and amount of drink you have as well as the time, date and situation in which you have it.

Step Four (moderation goal): Things to do while drinking

The next step in your plan should involve things to do during drinking sessions. Consider how you might slow down your intake; for example, heavy drinkers very often gulp their drinks causing them to drink much faster than light drinkers. The next few times you drink, count the number of mouthfuls it takes you to consume a glass. Once you have a good idea of how many mouthfuls you normally get out of a glass, aim to increase the number. Simply increasing the number of sips to a glass can be a very effective (and almost painless!) way of slowing you down.

You can also try setting a time limit for each drink. Give yourself, say, 20 to 30 minutes for a drink and do not allow yourself another one until the time has elapsed. If you finish your drink before time, have a soft drink 'spacer' to fill in the time. And when you drink, put the glass down and take your hand off it between sips. It really cannot run away, but if you hold on to it, chances are you will drink from it more frequently. Another thing to try is activity. People are more inclined to drink when that is the only thing they are doing. If you are in a situation where you can do something active (like playing darts or dancing), then that can help slow you down too.

To sum up Step Four, then, try to:

1. Take smaller and slower mouthfuls.
2. Set a time limit for each drink.
3. Have a spacer drink between alcoholic drinks.
4. Put the glass down and take your hand off it between each mouthful.
5. Do something active during the drinking session.

Step Five: Know your high-risk situations

Everyone who drinks uses alcohol to attain some desired goal, such as feeling relaxed or refreshed. Problems arise, however, when alcohol becomes your only means of achieving such goals. For example, if a few drinks is the only way you have of relaxing at the end of the day, then alcohol becomes very important to you: you need it in order to relax. For this reason it is helpful to spend sometime reflecting on the reasons why you use alcohol at all. Once you know what alcohol does for you, you can explore other ways of achieving the same things without the need for it.

One helpful way of clarifying what alcohol does for you is to think about the situations you are going to find hard to handle without it. Are there certain people you will be tempted to drink too much with?

Are there certain places where you will be at risk? Are there times and days when you drink more than at other times? Are certain activities associated with too much drinking? Do you drink more when you have certain feelings? These are your high-risk situations and you must find ways to deal with them. Obviously the best way is to avoid them altogether but you may not always be able to do that, so in the next few steps we will look at some simple strategies for surviving high-risk situations without getting drunk.

Table 5.2 presents a list of common reasons people have for drinking. Go through the list and check the reasons that apply to you. Check as many or as few as you like. Add some reasons of your own if none of the ones listed adequately covers your reason(s). Once you have done this, go to the appropriate section indicated on the right-hand side of the page.

Section 5.1: When you feel down

There is no avoiding unhappy times. They are a part of life. But you have indicated that you turn to alcohol when you feel down or depressed so you must find a better way of dealing with unhappiness. Probably the best and simplest place to start is by telling someone about your unhappiness. You might try a family member or close friend, or maybe a counsellor or telephone counselling service.

Table 5.2 *High-risk checklist*

Reason	Section
I drink when I feel down or depressed	5.1
I drink because it gives me confidence	5.2
I drink to celebrate	5.3
I drink because it helps me relax	5.3
I drink when I have arguments or conflicts with others	5.3
I drink because of social pressure from others	5.2
I drink because it makes me feel at ease with other people	5.2
I sometimes drink to test my willpower by showing that I can stop when I want	5.3
I drink to help me stop worrying about things	5.1
I drink if I feel physically sick or my stomach is tied in knots	5.3

Another thing to try is activity. When you feel depressed, you can lose interest in the things you usually like doing. But this also works in reverse. If you do not do the things you like to do, you become depressed. So, when you are down, try to force yourself to do the things you usually like doing. You might go to the cinema or for a walk in a park or listen to your favourite music. Becoming active when you are depressed can take effort but chances are that if you persist, your feelings of despair will begin to go away.

Very often, though, it is our own thoughts that make us feel down. You see, at the root of most bad feelings are attitudes or beliefs which you may be only half aware of but which nevertheless determine the way you feel. Much of the difficulty in dealing with unhappiness is that we do not realise that emotions are really decisions we make. In other words, nothing makes us feel bad, we decide to be upset, and upsetting decisions are based on irrational beliefs that pop into our minds as soon as something bad happens. Very often we are not aware of the belief because the feeling itself is too strong, but it really is what you think about the situation that makes you feel the way you do.

So how do you change your beliefs when you get upset about something? There are five basic steps:

1. *Identify the primary feeling:* What was the emotion that made you uncomfortable? Was it anger or embarrassment or depression or what?
2. *Rehearse what actually happened:* Do not carry on about how awful it was. Just relive the events that led up to the emotional reaction. For example, 'I asked her out but she turned me down'. No opinions, just fact.
3. *Identify the thoughts that upset you:* In other words, try to figure out the things you said to yourself about the situation. For example, you might have said things like: 'Oh no! She doesn't like me!' or 'How embarrassing. I've been made to look like an idiot'. I am sure you know the kind of thing I mean. Now, can you pick the irrational belief behind these thoughts? In this case, for example, our jilted lover seems to think that it is a disaster if a relative stranger or acquaintance does not like him.
4. *Dispute the idea that is hurting you:* Ask yourself, is this a rational idea? In the example I have just given, the answer has to be no! Things have to go wrong sometimes – it is just a fact of life. Is that really so disastrous? Dispute ideas like that when they upset you.

You do not have to put up with them. If you keep telling yourself that things are awful, they get worse and worse.

5. *Set out to change your irrational beliefs*: When you have spotted the idea that is making it tough for you, practise saying more rational things to yourself. For example, 'OK, so maybe she isn't crazy about me. It really isn't the end of the world. That's life. I'll try someone else.' Got the idea! It really is all a matter of how you look at things and that is something you do have control of. (See Ellis *et al.*, 1988.)

Section 5.2: Assertiveness

One reason why you drink seems to be that it gives you confidence. An important fact to remember is that confidence is a skill, just like driving a car or working a machine. People learn confidence, they are not born with it. This means that you can practise the skill of confidence and thereby learn to be more confident.

But where do you start this learning? First, think of a person you know who shows confidence, just to get a feel for the idea. What does the person do that makes you think they are confident? When you have a clear idea of how a confident person behaves, try to imagine doing similar things yourself.

Picture yourself in a high-risk situation and imagine how you could behave so that you will not need to drink. Go through the whole process mentally at first. It is a good idea to rehearse the scene with someone you trust so that you are clear on what to do. Now when you are next with other people and you feel pressured to drink, try to act in this confident fashion. In other words, act as if you are confident. Say whatever you have to say in a confident way, no matter how you feel. Sure, you may feel uncomfortable at first but with some practice you will soon find that behaving as if you are confident will actually make you feel more confident.

'Come off it!' you will say. 'Life is not that simple! I can't change the way I feel just like that!' Well, let me repeat: I am not saying you can change the way you feel immediately, only that you can change the way you act! And once you get used to acting differently, you'll eventually start to feel differently.

One more thing. It is not just the things you say that make you a confident person – it is also the way you look. There are two basic rules. First, make eye contact. When you are talking to people, look at them! One way of telling whether a confident person is confident or not is by noticing whether they are prepared to look you in the eye. If you have trouble looking straight into someone's eyes, look at the bridge of their nose – chances are they will not know the difference. Do not stare, of course. Look away occasionally but be prepared to make eye contact more often and for longer than you look away. Why not watch how that confident person you know does it. Second, watch your body posture. If you are sitting, lean towards the other person slightly so that it is clear you are not backing away. If you are standing, face the other person and do not fold your arms in front of you, otherwise you look as though you are protecting yourself. At all times try to appear comfortable! Once again, watch how that confident person you know does it. (See Chaney *et al.*, 1978; Chaney, 1989.)

Section 5.3: Other risky situations

I want you to imagine yourself in one of the 'high-risk situations' you have identified. Assuming that it is impossible for you to avoid the situation in the first place, what do you think you can do to help you survive the situation without resorting to alcohol to pull you through? Go through the whole process mentally at first. It is a good idea to rehearse the scene with someone you trust so that you are clear on what to do when and if the situation recurs. If you have trouble working out what to do, defer this exercise until we have covered problem-solving in Step Seven. You can use this problem-solving method to help you work out a strategy for coping with high-risk situations.

In this step you learnt to identify your 'high-risk situations'. When you confront situations like these, you are going to need two important skills to come through them. The first is the skill of controlling your emotions because if you can avoid getting too upset you will find that the urge to drink will not be as strong and you will be better placed to work out how to survive the situation. We will cover this skill next in Step Six. The other skill you will need is that of problem-solving because you are in danger of turning to alcohol if you cannot think of a more effective way of coping with the situation. We will cover problem-solving in Step Seven.

Step Six: Learning to relax

There is a very simple way of relaxing which does not involve alcohol. All it requires is practice. To use this method it is best to lie flat on your back with your arms by your side. Close your eyes and relax like that for a few seconds. Then, as you lie there, clench your right fist as tightly as you can. Clench it tighter and tighter and feel the tension that builds up first in your hand and forearm and then throughout your whole body. Hold the fist for about five seconds and then relax it. Attend carefully to the difference in the way you feel when your right hand is relaxed. Let the feeling of relaxation get deeper and say the word 'relax' quietly to yourself as you breathe out. After you have relaxed like that for a few seconds, repeat the exercise with your left fist, making sure you attend to the dramatic difference between the way you feel when your fist is clenched and when it is relaxed. Now repeat this same process of tensing and relaxing all these other parts of your body as well:

The biceps in your right arm, by clenching your right fist and trying to touch your fist on to your right shoulder. Hold it for five seconds. And relax. Repeat.

The biceps in your left arm.

The triceps in your right arm by extending your right arm by your side and trying to push your hand through the floor beneath you.

The triceps in your left arm.

The toes in your right foot by curling your toes back as far as they will go.

The toes in your left foot.

The calf muscle in your right leg by bending your whole right foot back as far as it will go.

The calf muscle in your left leg.

Tighten the muscles in your right thigh and relax.

Now the muscles in your left thigh.

Then move to the muscles in your stomach by first of all pulling your stomach in. Make it quite hollow. Hold it. And relax. Repeat.

Then take in a huge breath. Hold it for as long as you can. Feel the tension build up. And now slowly exhale and feel the difference.

Next, clench your teeth tightly together. Hold the tension. Study it. And relax. Repeat.

Next, raise your eyebrows as far as you can (keep your eyes closed). Study the tension. And relax. Repeat.

Now frown.

Each time you release the tensions in a part of your body, say the word 'relax' quietly to yourself. While you are saying 'relax' to yourself, it can be helpful to imagine yourself in a very relaxing situation; perhaps lying on a beach or asleep in bed. When you have been through all parts of your body, just lie or sit there as long as you like. You should set aside at least 5–15 minutes each day and faithfully go through this exercise; over time it will help you to become a much calmer person. (See Benson, 1975.)

Step Seven: Solving problems without alcohol

In everyday life, people are constantly being confronted with situations that require them to take some action. Coming across problems and attempting to solve them are normal, unavoidable parts of life. I want to give you a general method for solving problems as they arise. If what is said just seems like common sense, that is because common sense is all it is.

The first step in being a good problem-solver or conflict-solver involves being realistic. The way people look at their lives can have a big effect on how they react to any problems which arise. In order to make the most effective decisions about problems and arguments, you must accept that problems will happen. Trying to pretend otherwise just makes problem-solving that much harder. Also, stay calm and give yourself a chance to solve the problem. When a serious problem arises, people often react by doing the first thing that comes into their head. When faced with a problem, do not rush in. Give yourself a chance to find the best (which is not necessarily the first) solution you can.

Given that you manage to stay calm and face up to the problem, what do you do then? Before being able to work out the answer to any problem, you need to be very clear about precisely what the problem is. If you have trouble doing this just by thinking about it, try explaining the problem to someone else. Often when you force yourself to put your thoughts into words, your ideas become clearer.

After you have clearly defined the problem, your next step should be to come up with as many possible answers as you can to increase the likelihood that one of the answers is the most effective possible. There really is only one rule to go by when coming up with possible solutions, and that rule is: there are no rules! Having no rules really means that you must not criticise your ideas until after you have had them all. It does not much matter how wild your ideas are, start by writing them all down. After you have drawn up your list of options, go through each one and try to imagine what would happen if you put each idea into action. Write down the reasons for and against each option. By the time you reach the end of your list, you should have one or a small number of possible actions which you think could solve the problem.

To sum up, then, successful problem-solving involves five steps:

1. Accept that problems will arise and stay calm.
2. State the problem as simply and clearly as you can.
3. Come up with as many solutions as you can.
4. Write down the pros and cons of each solution.
5. Now make your decision. Pick the option with the most pros and the fewest cons and go with it. (See D'Zurilla and Goldfried, 1971.)

Step Eight: Dealing with craving

When you cut down or give up drinking, you must expect to feel a strong urge to drink from time to time. Craving is a normal part of the body's readjustment to life without alcohol. However, once the readjustment is complete, craving will stop altogether. So the first step in dealing with craving is to realise that it is a perfectly normal reaction and does not mean anything terrible is going to happen to you. Do not imagine that the craving will just build up and up until it gets completely out of control. That just does not happen. Craving does not build up and up indefinitely. It reaches a peak and then it fades away. At first, the craving will come back again but the longer you stay off it, the less intense it will be and the less often it will occur; until eventually the craving will leave you forever. The important thing is how you respond to craving while the body is readjusting.

One thing to try is distancing yourself from the craving. The best way to explain what distancing means is to consider the difference between a person who feels craving and reacts by saying 'Oh no! I feel like a drink', and a person who reacts by saying: 'I feel tense, it must be a craving for alcohol that I'm feeling.' The first person identifies with the feeling and it takes over that person, whereas the second person thinks of craving as mere information. The second person does not allow craving to become part of their or her self-image.

Since it is usually easier to put a drink off than go without, another thing to try is delaying that next one. If you keep postponing it, you will not go out of control. The urge will pass, no matter how much you are used to drinking. So, when craving troubles you:

1.   Think of it as providing information that you need to stop and take control. Say to yourself, 'I feel craving. It is time to act.'
2.   Use your relaxation skills to avoid becoming too anxious about the craving.
3.   Go over in your mind the reasons why you have decided to change your drinking. Remember what alcohol has done to your life.
4.   Remember that the craving will go away if you are patient.
5.   Try to distract yourself with some other activity.

Step Nine: Reward your successes

If you are going to stick to your drinking plan, you need to be rewarded for your successes along the way. Like any difficult job, changing a habit requires considerable effort over a long period of time and we are all more willing to make that kind of effort if we receive encouragement. So reward yourself for each success you have at controlling your drinking. The types of rewards you choose are really up to you, but here are some suggestions.

First, there are material rewards such as going to a film or concert or sports event. Material rewards just refer to things that you personally find pleasurable. What I am suggesting is a kind of contract or agreement with yourself in which you agree to allow yourself some luxury in exchange for sticking to a drinking plan.

Because material rewards usually cost money, why not put the money aside that you would have spent on drink if you had not cut down and use this money to buy something at the end of a day or a week or a month. Some people find that opening a separate bank account helps them stick to their drinking plan. This way they can buy things which clearly come from their achievements. Indeed, simply checking the growing bank balance from time to time provides enough incentive to keep many people going. Whatever you choose to reward yourself with, though, make sure it is something over and above what you normally have. There is no point rewarding yourself with something you have all the time anyway!

Another thing to keep in mind is that rewards tend to work better if they are delivered fairly soon after your success, so at first you may like to find little rewards to use every day you are successful. However, as time goes by you should start to extend the amount of effort required to receive a reward.

For most of us, though, the feeling of pride that comes from a job well-done is a very powerful and spontaneous reward in its own right. This is a mental reward and you should capitalise on it by pausing to congratulate yourself whenever you manage to cut down your intake of alcohol. Some people even practise self-statements like, 'Today I showed that I can do the hard things in life'. Maybe you can make up your own self-statement and repeat it to yourself at the end of a day when you have kept to your drinking plan.

Apart from self-statements, there are two other sure ways of gaining mental rewards. The first is simply to keep a chart or record of progress. Make a graph of the amount you drink from day to day. Watching the graph decline can be a very rewarding experience!

The other tactic for gaining mental rewards is to tell a trusted friend or relative about your desire to beat your drinking problem. If your friend really cares about you, it is certain that they will praise and encourage you after every step you take towards achieving your goal.

So, to sum up:

1. Be prepared to reward your successes.
2. Rewards can be material or mental.
3. Mental rewards include self-statements, records of progress, and encouragement from friends.

Step Ten: Dealing with lapses

Finally, what if you do slip up on one occasion despite your best efforts and drink more than you should? If everything fails and you do give in to the temptation to drink, you must be prepared for a new challenge – picking yourself up and having another go. You cannot change a drinking habit overnight and you certainly cannot do it without a struggle.

There are two understandable but mistaken reactions you can have to a lapse. The first is to be too hard on yourself. It is certainly true that it is up to you whether or not you choose to drink, but it is also likely that there was something happening around you that contributed to your slip. For example, you may have been with some of your old drinking friends, or you may have had an argument with someone close to you. If that is the case, you should recognise that and, without trying to make excuses for yourself, realise that such events will not always occur. As a matter of fact, you may have just learnt about a high-risk situation that you need to avoid or learn to deal with in the future.

The other mistake people sometimes make when they slip up is to change the way they look at themselves. Whereas they see themselves as reformed drinkers while they are not drinking, they suddenly go back to thinking of themselves as alcoholics again as soon as they slip up once. When you start to think of yourself as an alcoholic again, you have had it!

Obviously no one wants you to slip up, but if you do, you must expect to feel pretty bad about yourself for a little while. But you must not let that feeling get out of hand. Here is what to do:

1. Settle down! Remember one lapse does not mean you're through unless you make that decision.
2. Go back over your reasons for making the break in the first place. (It can help if you have written those reasons down somewhere so that you can read over them.)
3. Think of the times you have been tempted but have not given in. You may have had one failure but you have probably had many successes. Derive courage from those times.
4. Think back over the events that led to the lapse. You are bound to find that the slip did not come out of the blue. Is there something you can learn from these events to help you in the future?

Brief intervention methods

It is probably fair to say that most people would assume that when it comes to drug addiction, more treatment is likely to be better treatment. But there is actually very little evidence to support this assumption. In the case of alcohol, for example, whether we are dealing with severely alcohol-dependent individuals or secondary-stage problem drinkers, when two treatments of differing intensity have been compared, the less intensive one has usually proved as effective as the more intensive one (Ritson, 1968; Edwards *et al.*, 1977b). And in two large-scale controlled trials conducted in the United States recently, brief interventions delivered by non-specialist health workers, were found to be effective in reducing drinking (Fleming *et al.*, 1997; Israel *et al.*, 1996), alcohol-related problems (Israel *et al.*, 1996) and the drinker's use of health care services (Fleming *et al.*, 1997).

In the case of self-control training like that outlined in this chapter, the procedure was initially designed to run over about ten sessions of educational counselling with a trained therapist. However, towards the end of the 1970s Miller and his colleagues (Miller, 1977, 1978; Miller and Taylor, 1980; Miller *et al.*, 1980; Miller *et al.*, 1981a) became interested in the possibility of condensing self-control procedures and even committing them to a self-help manual that could be given to problem drinkers to work through at their own pace. In one of their studies, for example, Miller *et al.* (1980) placed advertisements in the newspapers and called for referrals from doctors and welfare workers for problem drinkers to be involved in a controlled drinking research project. The researchers randomly assigned their clients to one of four treatment groups: (i) a Self-help Group which was interviewed only once before being given a self-help manual (Miller and Munoz, 1976); (ii) a Brief Self-control Training Group which received one session per week for six weeks with a trained therapist before being given the self-help manual; (iii) an Extended Self-control Training Group which received the same treatment as the second group plus a further twelve sessions of intensive (multi-modal) therapy; (iv) another Extended Self-control Training Group which was identical to the third group, except that members of this group were able to select the additional therapy they received. The result of the experiment was that all groups reduced their drinking by comparable amounts, even the group which received only one session.

Heather *et al.* (1986) also placed advertisements in the paper to attract people who felt they were drinking too much. Almost 800 people responded to the advertisement and half of these were sent a booklet which contained general information about drinking and drinking problems, while the other half were sent a self-control training manual written by the researchers. Six months after the material was sent, the people remaining in the study (less than half) were surveyed about their consumption habits. Results indicated that prior to receiving the booklets respondents were drinking just over 49 units of alcohol per week or 70 grams per day before receiving the manual. Six months later, the group sent the self-control manual was drinking 5.5 units of alcohol a day. Thus, both groups had improved considerably with very minimal help, but the group exposed to self-control training showed greater improvement than those who were given more general advice. Heather *et al.* (1987) reported that of those they were able to recontact, reductions in consumption had been maintained up to twelve months later. It should be acknowledged that the Heather *et al.* studies do suffer serious methodological problems, including the fact that the level of subject attrition meant that consumption figures were collected at all three points for only a minority of the participants who started out in the project. Another problem in the Heather *et al.* studies is the absence of a no-treatment group which disallows the conclusion that improvements can be confidently attributed to the manuals themselves. Nevertheless, Heather *et al.*'s results are certainly consistent with the proposition that self-control training can be conveyed cheaply and effectively in the form of self-help manuals.

The author (Barber, 1989, 1990, 1991b, 1993; Eltringham and Barber, 1990) has also tried to produce change quickly and without recourse to a therapist, but in our case behavioural self-control training was committed to interactive computer software. The computer has the advantage over self-help manuals of being able to react to user input and thereby individualise treatment in much the same way that a therapist would. In a controlled field experiment into the effectiveness of the computer programme (Eltringham and Barber, 1990), men attending a drink-drive programme were divided into three groups: (1) Group Therapy plus Counselling which involved a structured group programme running over a weekend, as well as one or two individual counselling sessions with a trained therapist; (2) Group Therapy only; and (3) Computer Therapy Only. Participants in the experiment were randomly assigned to the computer programme and the others were allowed to choose between the other two treatments. As with the self-help manual studies, the results of the trial revealed significant reductions in consumption in all groups, with no difference between treatment options.

Cue exposure and scheduled withdrawal

In addition to the behavioural self-control procedures outlined above, two additional techniques – cue exposure and scheduled withdrawal – are currently enjoying considerable interest in the addictions field. Both techniques are based on classical conditioning principles and seek to extinguish the power of internal and external cues to trigger the craving for drugs. The basic idea common to both techniques is that if we can break the association between certain stimuli and drug consumption, we should eventually eliminate the power of those stimuli to cue drug use altogether. The technical term for this process is *extinction* and there is considerable evidence that it works for many other conditioned responses.

Scheduled withdrawal involves the user gradually reducing their consumption according to a fixed schedule in which consumption occurs whether or not the user wants the drug at that time. The best way to explain this idea is by illustration. For example, in their carefully controlled trial, Cinciripini *et al.* (1994) first asked smokers how many cigarettes they normally smoked in a given week. The researchers then asked their clients to reduce that amount by one-third over the next week and, most importantly, to smoke their quota of cigarettes according to a precise fixed-interval schedule that spread consumption evenly across their waking hours. The number of cigarettes was reduced by another third in the next week and the fixed-interval schedule recalculated. Thus, smokers would be required to smoke at times when they would not normally smoke and to postpone smoking at times when they would normally look for a cigarette. In this way, the association between smoking on the one hand and customary cues on the other hand would eventually be broken. In Cinciripini *et al.*'s study, scheduled withdrawal was combined with behavioural self-control training and results of the study were most encouraging. However, research into the technique is still in its infancy and there is no reliable evidence that the approach works with other drugs of addiction.

Cue exposure therapy can be divided into two kinds – *imaginal* and *priming dose* cue exposure (Rankin *et al.*, 1983). As with scheduled withdrawal, the objective of cue exposure is to eliminate the power of classically conditioned cues to evoke drug use, but in cue exposure this is achieved by repeatedly exposing users to drug cues while being preventing from using. Imaginal cue exposure involves asking clients to imagine scenes they would normally associate with heavy drinking. While holding those scenes in their minds, clients are unable to drink and are sometimes taught to relax while picturing the scene. Priming dose cue exposure entails providing the user with a small amount of alcohol and then preventing further drinking. The rationale for doing this is that the most powerful cue to excessive drinking is the first few drinks. The first drinks are referred to as the 'priming dose', and the argument is that if the drinker can be taught to break the association between the first drink or two and further drinking, the priming dose will cease to cue drunkenness.

In an illustration of priming dose cue exposure, Heather *et al.* (1993) asked a heavy drinker to describe his high-risk situations in considerable detail. In subsequent therapy sessions, the client was taken into a simulated bar setting and provided with a drink of water to reduce any thirst he may have been experiencing at that moment. The client was then given a priming dose of two standard drinks over a twenty-minute period. Next, a third standard drink was placed in front of the client and he was told that although he would not be prevented from drinking it, the object of the exercise was to resist the urge. The therapist instructed the client to handle the glass and sniff its contents, without actually drinking any.

In order to focus their attention on the drink, cue exposure clients are also normally asked to report on their thoughts, their level of desire to continue drinking, and changes in their level of desire. The procedure lasts for around ten minutes before the client is given a few minutes' break and the trial is repeated once or twice per session. Controlled trials of this procedure have produced promising results when the object of therapy has been to eliminate drinking altogether (for example, Drummond and Glautier, 1994; Monti *et al.*, 1993). The procedure has also been used to try to teach moderately dependent drinkers how to control their drinking rather than abstain altogether. Results so far have been encouraging (for example, Sitharthan *et al.*, 1997), although there is some evidence that cue exposure may not be as successful in teaching controlled drinking as the behavioural self-control procedures outlined earlier in this chapter (for example, Heather *et al.*, 2000). Cue exposure has also been extended to the treatment of numerous other addictive behaviours, including opiate use (Franken *et al.*, 1999), smoking (Hepple and Robson, 1996), gambling (Symes and Nicki, 1997) and binge eating (Jansen, 1998), with most studies reporting quite good levels of success.

Gender- and ethnic-sensitive treatment

In this chapter we have looked at a simple cognitive-behavioural strategy for use at the action stage of change. It needs to be recognised, however, that because women are so greatly under-represented in addiction research and treatment, our existing methods have largely been developed by and for men. While the ratio of men to women in high-risk alcohol groups is only around 2:1 (Risk Prevalence Study, 1990), estimates of the ratio of men to women in treatment range between 3:1 and 10:1 (Sokolow *et al.*, 1980). There is a vicious cycle here. Participants in research are overwhelmingly male because treatment facilities are dominated by men; but treatment facilities are unlikely to attract women when they are based on procedures which have been validated only on men. What research has been done in relation to gender suggests that women and men may indeed differ in their treatment needs. For instance, the gender difference in treatment-seeking behaviour can be accounted for partly by the fact that women are more likely to have child-care responsibilites that interfere with programme attendance (Marsh and Miller, 1985). It follows, then, that drug treatment for women should make provision for child care (Finkelstein, 1994). Among other commonly reported findings are that female drug users are more likely than their male counterparts to suffer depression and/or anxiety (Culbertson, 1997; Griffin *et al.*, 1989), and to report higher rates of sexual abuse (Wallen, 1992). While these gender differences are not limited to drug users, they are nevertheless relevant to drug treatment. There is evidence, for example, that confrontation tactics are particularly damaging for women who are inclined to react with feelings of shame, guilt and stigmatisation arising from preexisting feelings of depression and low self-esteem (Reed, 1987; Murray, 1989). For this reason, Moras (1998) has suggested that a focus on self-esteem enhancement is likely to be a valuable adjunct to treatment of the kind described earlier in this chapter. It has also been suggested that women do better in women-only groups than in individual counselling, particularly when women also act as the therapists (Dahlgren and Wilander, 1989; Copeland *et al.*, 1992). It must be said, however, that the evidence for this suggestion remains largely anecdotal.

Regardless of the treatment methods used, Reed (1982) proposes that drug treatment services for women must be guided by certain core principles. First, and as previously indicated, treatment should address the fact that many drug-dependent women suffer from low self-esteem, depression and anxiety due to conflict between their lifestyle and female role stereotypes. Second, treatment methods should take into account and build on women's strengths, which are usually different from men's (for example, expressive and relationship skills). Third, women should be assisted to develop capacities and skills such as assertiveness which may be limited by women's gender-role socialisation. Fourth, treatment methods should be compatible with women's styles of thinking and expressing themselves. Fifth, women are likely to need non-drug support services such as child care and training in protective behaviours. Finally, chemically dependent women need interaction with other women in order to develop support networks, work together on common problems, and minimise self-blame. Consistent with Reed's principles, the National Institute on Drug Abuse (NIDA) (1999) advocates a comprehensive approach to treatment for women that both assesses for and provides access to a range of social services, including: food, clothing and shelter; transportation; job counselling and training; legal assistance; literacy training and educational opportunities; parenting training; family therapy; couples counselling; medical care; child care; social support; psychological assessment and mental health care; assertiveness training; and family planning services. NIDA considers that traditional drug treatment programmes may not be appropriate for women because these programmes are unaccustomed to providing such services. Research also indicates that, for women in particular, a continuing relationship with a treatment provider is an important factor throughout treatment (NIDA, 1999).

Because ethnic minorities are more inclined to occupy marginal positions in society, they tend to be over-represented in the case-loads of public welfare professionals like social workers. The research evidence is that counsellors who are culturally different from their clients have less potential to effect constructive change in their clients (Vontress, 1971; Sue, 1975); so to maximise our effectiveness, social workers must begin by recognising the ways in which culture is relevant to the problem. Irrespective of the presenting problem, Jones (1985) considers that cross-cultural therapists should attend to the following issues: (a) the client's reactions to racial oppression; (b) the influence on the client of the majority culture; (c) the influence of the traditional culture on the client; and (d) the endowment of individual and family experiences. In Jones's view, all these factors interact and all will have some bearing on the problem at hand. In the language of behavioural self-control training, the factors identified by Jones are relevant to our functional analysis of drug-taking behaviour. In order to appreciate the positive functions of drug use to the client, the therapist needs to understand the cultural and contextual factors which make the behaviour adaptive. De La Cancela (1985) adds that cross-cultural therapists need to be aware that because ethnic minorities are frequently low-income earners, they often face practical impediments to treatment such as transport problems or difficulty in negotiating time off work. De La Cancela also reminds the therapist that English is often the client's second language, so interventions which de-emphasise literacy and complex dialogue are more likely to be effective. Consistent with this claim, there is some evidence that the task-focused, cognitive-behavioural procedures outlined in this chapter are more suitable for ethnic minority groups than more insight-oriented counselling (ibid.).

By the end of the action stage described in this chapter, the client should have reduced or ceased drug use. However, the major challenge – maintaining the change – still lies ahead. Relapse rates are notoriously high in the addictions field and much of the pressure to relapse is social in nature. In the next chapter, we turn to the difficult task of relapse prevention and consider ways of helping clients deal with the pressures to give up on their decision to change. We will see that an exclusive focus on the individual user, which is appropriate when the user makes the initial move towards change during the action stage, is insufficient to maintain change.

6

Maintenance

The problem of relapse is undoubtedly the most important single challenge currently facing the field of addictions. As Westerberg (1998) points out, however, relapse is not an altogether straight-forward notion to define. If, for example, relapse is defined as *any* drug consumption following treatment for abstinence, then around 90 per cent of drug users will normally relapse within twelve months of treatment (Hubbard and Marsden, 1986; Orford and Edwards, 1977; Shiffman, 1987). But if relatively long periods of moderate drinking or abstinence punctuated by occasions of heavy use can qualify as success, then perhaps as many as half of those in drug treatment can expect to succeed (for example, Armor *et al.*, 1978; Project MATCH, 1997). This more liberal definition of success is not mere obfuscation by treatment providers either. For one thing, it is known that a proportion of those who revert to drug use after treatment will limit their consumption. Another group will return to pre-treatment consumption levels for a short period of time only. Finally, it is now widely recognised that relapse itself can be an intrinsic part of the change process (see Chapter 2). Nevertheless, most treatment providers recognise that relapse users do need to be prepared to meet the challenges involved in maintaining their commitment to change over the long haul.

In the past, relapse prevention tended to involve either elaborating or extending treatment. For example, some clinicians tried bringing their clients back for periodic 'booster' sessions in which the ground that was covered in treatment was rehearsed and reinforced (see, for example, Lichtenstein, 1982; Wilson, 1985); others tried 'multimodal' approaches like those referred to in the previous chapter, in which a wide range of treatments were administered in the hope of preparing clients for as many eventualities outside treatment as possible (see, for example, Sobell and Sobell, 1973; Hamburg, 1975; Caddy and Lovibond, 1976; Alden, 1978; Miller and Hester, 1986). Perhaps the most extreme of the methods based on extending treatment is Alcoholics Anonymous in which the individual is seen as eternally recovering, never recovered, and therefore treatment must continue for a lifetime. However, none of these approaches has succeeded in reducing relapse rates relative to much briefer and simpler treatment methods. As a result, the trend nowadays is towards conceiving of maintenance as a problem which is distinct from the initial treatment. Thus, a given treatment strategy may be effective in initiating behaviour change in a client, but may be ineffective in maintaining that change. This way of viewing things renders the notion of booster treatment redundant and encourages targeted, rather than multimodal, strategies aimed at relapse prevention specifically. Similarly, if maintenance is a discrete stage with a beginning and an end, the need for lifelong treatment has also been obviated.

In this chapter we will look at some of the more promising directions for intervention at the maintenance stage of change. In Chapter 2, the point was made that it is at this maintenance stage that social work's holistic perspective on human problems is both most needed and most neglected. As we shall see, this is because the quality of the user's social environment is a (perhaps *the*) crucial determinant of relapse, yet the relapse prevention literature is dominated by clinical psychology. In line with the social work model described in Chapter 2, relapse prevention will be discussed at multiple system levels. At the first and lowest level are psychological interventions aimed at enhancing the individual's coping skills. Beyond this are microsystem interventions which seek to manipulate elements of the client's immediate social network. And beyond this are meso- and exosystem measures which address the political and cultural forces that are known to influence relapse rates in the community as a whole.

Level I: Interventions at the level of the individual

The first and most obvious target for intervention during the maintenance stage is the individual user, and probably the most influential contemporary writers on the psychology of relapse are Marlatt and his colleagues (Marlatt and Gordon, 1980, 1985; Brownell *et al.*,

1986; Weingardt and Marlatt, 1998). The model of relapse prevention developed by Marlatt and Gordon begins with an analysis (presented in Figure 6.1) of the process leading up to relapse.

As Figure 6.1 illustrates, relapse is viewed as a set of responses linked by chain reaction to a high-risk situation. Confronted by a high-risk situation (see Chapter 5), the user begins by searching their behavioural repertoire for an appropriate coping response. If no alternative to using readily presents itself, the addict is predicted to become anxious and suffer a lowering of self-efficacy. Self-efficacy refers to confidence in one's ability to 'organize and execute courses of action required to attain designated types of performance' (Bandura, 1986, p. 391), and this quality is said to influence behaviour by determining the initiation and persistence of coping efforts. In other words, individuals who are firmly convinced of their capacity to deal with a high-risk situation will execute a coping response more readily, with greater intensity, and with greater perseverance in the event of a setback than will individuals with weaker efficacy beliefs. Coping behaviours and self-efficacy are therefore mutually reinforcing, and in the absence of a salient coping response, a high-risk situation will diminish self-efficacy which, in turn, will diminish the effectiveness and perseverance of whatever the individual does try.

***Figure* 6.1**   *Marlatt and Gordon's model of relapse*

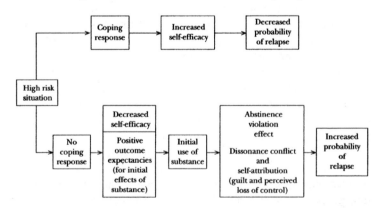

Reprinted from *Relapse Prevention* by G. Alan Marlatt and Judith R. Gordon (eds). © 1985 by the Guilford Press.

The role of self-efficacy is so important within the cognitive-behavioural tradition that Annis and Davis (1986, 1988, 1989) have asserted that any treatment procedure will be effective only to the extent that efficacy expectations are increased. Consistent with this proposition, several studies have found high self-efficacy to be associated with positive outcome in the treatment of smoking (Condiotte and Lichtenstein, 1981; DiClemente, 1981; Prochaska *et al.*, 1982; McIntyre *et al.*, 1983; Killen *et al.*, 1984; Supnick and Coletti, 1984), drinking (Chaney *et al.*, 1978), and eating disorders (Chambliss and Murray, 1979; Gormally *et al.*, 1980). By way of qualification, however, it is important to note that more recent research (Haaga and Stewart, 1992) has found that excessive self-efficacy (over-confidence) about one's capacity to recover from a lapse is actually associated with higher relapse rates.

Under the Marlatt and Gordon model, along with a decline in self-efficacy will normally go an increase in the individual's expect-ations about the positive benefits of alcohol or drug use. The indi-vidual will selectively recall the benefits of alcohol or drug use that they have experienced in the past. Ingesting the drug is seen as a (perhaps the only) means of dealing with the crisis at hand. When this occurs, the individual is drawn towards using from two direc-tions. On the one hand, they have not been able to find a construct-ive coping response, and on the other, there is the old familiar stand-by of drinking or drug-taking which promises an expedient solution. A crucial step towards relapse is taken if the person does give in to the temptation and uses. Marlatt and Gordon (1985) refer to such an occasion of use as a 'lapse' in order to distinguish it from the state of relapse in which the addict reverts to their former pattern of consumption. This distinction is central to the Marlatt and Gordon approach, and perhaps their most important contribution to the field. A lapse, they emphasise, is but a single occurrence and need not necessarily result in reinstatement of the addiction. The authors repudiate the AA axiom, 'One drink, one drunk', and assert that a lapse is just that, it is not necessarily a return to a previous state.

Whereas the term 'lapse' places emphasis on the process of backsliding or slipping up, relapse refers to a potential outcome or end point of that process. In support of this distinction, Brownell *et al.* (1986) point to research showing different determinants for lapses and relapses among smokers (Coppotelli and Orleans, 1985) and dieters (Dubbert and Wilson, 1984). The implication of the distinction between lapse and relapse is that it is the individual's response to an occasion of reuse that will determine whether or not a slip becomes a step towards relapse. Relapse is made more likely, however, by the so-called 'abstinence violation effect', which is the final step in Marlatt and Gordon's (1980, 1985) relapse model. The abstinence violation effect refers to the dual cognitive problems of (a) cognitive dissonance, and (b) an internal causal attribution. Cognitive dissonance operates when the former addict is confronted with the contradiction that they are supposedly reformed but have nevertheless just given in to the temptation to use again. These dissonant cognitions create an aversive psychological state and it is well-known that people will act to reduce dissonance of this kind (Festinger, 1964; Weiner, 1978).

Faced with a clash between self-image and behaviour, the individual is at risk of reducing cognitive dissonance by bringing their self-image into line with the behaviour. In other words, the former addict thinks: 'I have just used again. I really must be a junkie after all!' This altered self-image clearly makes further use more likely. The internal causal attribution component of the abstinence violation effect refers to the tendency towards excessive self-blame and self-recrimination that often follows a lapse. While the Marlatt and Gordon approach does not seek to relieve the individual of ultimate responsibility for lapsing, the authors point out that environmental pressures frequently play a role in the individual's decision to reuse, so failure by the individual to give these factors due credence is both unreasonable and discouraging. The dual psychological processes comprising the abstinence violation effect leave the individual extremely vulnerable to the temptation to keep using as a way of coping with the negative emotions they are experiencing.

Having delineated the stages in the relapse process, it becomes theoretically possible to construct interventions to prevent or mitigate the problems at each stage. The relapse prevention model developed by Marlatt and Gordon (1980, 1985) which seeks to accomplish this is presented in Figure 6.2.

As previously stated, the first and most fundamental intervention is for the addict to identify their own particular 'high-risk situations'. This can be approached by simple self-monitoring techniques like keeping a diary (see Chapter 5) and/or by having the client fantasise within the treatment session about potentially high-risk situations.

Figure 6.2 A model of relapse prevention

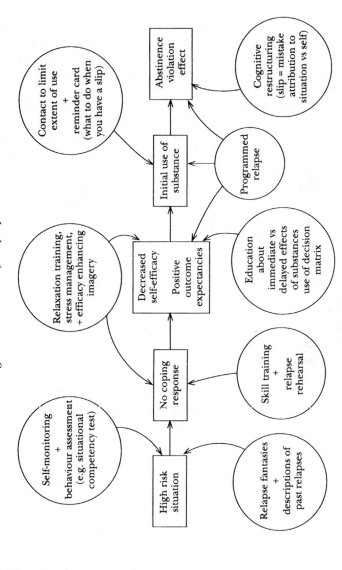

Reprinted from *Relapse Prevention* by G. Alan Marlatt and Judith R. Gordon (eds). © 1985 by the Guilford Press.

The basic objective is to teach the client to recognise the cues associated with entering a high-risk situation and to learn to use these cues as signals to engage in coping behaviour. As the notions of self-monitoring and high-risk situation were dealt with in Chapter 5, the reader is referred there for a fuller discussion of how to deal with this aspect of relapse prevention. Because it is not possible to train the individual to respond mechanically to every eventuality, Marlatt and Gordon also advocate a number of global strategies to support the more specific skills training the client has received. One important global skill is relaxation training which the individual can call on to deal with the emotional arousal that accompanies a situation of high risk. The rationale is that if the situation can be faced calmly, it is more likely that the person will be able to call on the coping skills they have been taught.

Similarly, a general method to facilitate problem-solving should help the person size up the situation, weigh options and act rationally no matter what they are confronted by. The general problem-solving procedure covered in Chapter 5 (D'Zurilla and Goldfried, 1971; Goldfried and Davison, 1976) is therefore also appropriate at this point. This problem-solving method is comprised of (a) initial problem definition and formulation; (b) generation of alternatives; (c) decision-making; and (d) action followed by monitoring verification of the outcome. Next, to deal with the possibility that positive outcome expectancies will attach to drug use in high-risk situations, the individual needs education which can take the simple form of reminding the person of all the effects alcohol or drugs have had on their life – not just the immediate pleasurable drug effect that can be expected. As previously noted, skills training is important not merely because of the new coping behaviours that are acquired, but because the acquisition of these skills should also engender an efficacy expectation. In addition to coping skills, however, Marlatt and Gordon's model addresses self-efficacy directly by having the person remind themself of past or anticipated successes in coping with high-risk situations ('efficacy-enhancing imagery').

Although not concerned with the modification of addictive behaviour specifically, Goldfried and Robins's (1982) analysis of self-efficacy theory nevertheless provides valuable guidance for the promotion of self-efficacy at the maintenance stage of change. Because by this time clients will have already made significant changes in their behaviour, Goldfried and Robins advise encouraging them to contrast the changes with their previous behaviour patterns. This should have the effect of helping clients see just how far they have actually come, and this, in turn, should obviate any tendency for clients to minimise their progress through the application of discouragingly high or inappropriate standards. A second tactic advocated by Goldfried and Robins is to help clients view changes from both an objective and a subjective vantage point. This is because most people have a built-in tendency to see the cause of novel success experiences as being due to external causes rather than to their own efforts (for example, Jones and Nisbett, 1971). By providing clients with an external, more objective perspective on the changes occurring in their lives, then, the therapist is trying to undermine this self-defeating attributional tendency. A third strategy is to encourage clients to retrieve past success experiences. Clients are instructed to self-monitor, even to the point of recording, their successful coping efforts and then to report on these experiences in counselling. Finally, Goldfried and Robins recommend trying to align the sequence of events involved in confronting threats: (i) expectancies for success in the situation; (ii) anticipatory feelings; (iii) behaviours; (iv) objective consequences; and (v) subsequent self-evaluations. According to the authors, because self-efficacy expectations often lag behind behaviour change, there are frequently inconsistencies among these phases of action. In seeking to realign the entire sequence so that each phase is more consistent with the others, the therapist seeks to discredit any negative expectancies, anticipatory feelings or self-evaluations that may still be associated with successful coping responses.

Annis and Davis's (1989) method for enhancing self-efficacy is to provide the client with 'homework' assignments involving exposure to progressively more challenging risk situations. In other words, clients deliberately expose themselves to risk in order to prove to themselves that they are capable of controlling the urge to drink or use. Based on their reading of self-efficacy theory, the authors propose six criteria for selecting homework tasks. First, the task must be sufficiently challenging to ensure that if the client deals with the situation, they will derive satisfaction and self-esteem from success. Second, the task must not be so challenging that the individual is highly likely to yield to the urge to use. A moderate degree of effort should be the objective. Third, the client must be encouraged to make an internal attribution for success rather than being put in a position where the outcome can be interpreted as due to some external aid like a spouse or therapist. Fourth, each homework task should form part of a broader plan so that the individual comes to see each homework assignment as bringing them closer to achieving a total victory over addiction. In other words, the tasks should become harder and more comprehensive in scope. Fifth, the successful completion of each task should be seen by the client as demonstrating greater control over what was previously compulsive behaviour. Finally, the homework tasks must be relevant to the idiosyncrasies of the client's drug problem. There is clearly no point in demonstrating to clients that they can successfully confront situations that are atypical of their own situation.

Should a lapse occur, however, the Marlatt and Gordon model proposes certain interventions for preventing a full-blown relapse. Essentially, the client is taught behavioural skills to moderate or terminate consumption and cognitive skills for dealing with the abstinence violation effect. At the level of behaviour, the client may be asked to sign a contract with the therapist stating that the lapse will end after the first occasion of use, should one occur. Additionally, the client may carry a reminder card around that sets out what must be done in the event of a lapse. Such behaviours might include phoning the therapist, engaging in vigorous physical exercise, calling on a friend, or employing the kind of rate control procedure described in Chapter 5. At a cognitive level, Marlatt and Gordon (1980, 1985) suggest that the client be prepared for the possibility of a lapse and for the remorse and self-recrimination associated with the abstinence violation effect. This issue must be handled with extreme care as it is clearly a fine line between preparing someone for the possibility of a lapse and giving permission to go out and use again. Nevertheless, clients should be educated about the difference between a lapse and relapse and encouraged to learn from slips rather than see themselves as starting all over again. In Marlatt and Gordon's own words:

> A slip is not all that unusual. It does not mean that you have failed or that you have lost control over your behaviour. You will probably feel guilty about what you have done, and will blame yourself for having slipped. This feeling is to be expected; it is part of what we call the Abstinence Violation Effect. There is no reason why you have to give in to this feeling and continue to drink

(or smoke). The feeling will pass in time. Look upon the slip as a learning experience. What were the elements of the high-risk situation which led to the slip? What coping response could you have used to get around the situation? Remember the old saying: One swallow doesn't make a summer? Well, one slip doesn't have to make a relapse, either. Just because you slipped once does not mean that you are a failure, that you have no willpower, or that you are a hopeless addict. Look upon the slip as a single, independent event, something which can be avoided in the future by the use of an appropriate coping response. (Marlatt and Gordon, 1980, pp. 447–8)

One of Marlatt and Gordon's more controversial proposals is the programmed relapse. As its name implies, this intervention involves actually scheduling a relapse in advance and, preferably, in the presence of the therapist. This technique is advocated for individuals whom the therapist fears are on the point of reusing. Because the therapist rather than the client sets the terms for the relapse, the hope is that the abstinence violation effect can be minimised. Moreover, by scheduling the event to occur in a neutral setting such as the therapist's office, the nexus between a high-risk situation and drug use should be broken. Finally, since Marlatt and Gordon's clinical experience is that the actual effects of the substance are normally disappointing from the client's viewpoint, the scheduled relapse gives the therapist an opportunity to disabuse the client of their positive outcome expectancies and plan more successful strategies for dealing with high-risk situations. Although this aspect of the Marlatt and Gordon model has some intuitive appeal, caution is warranted until further research is more convincing about whether the procedure is successful and, if so, for whom and under precisely what circumstances.

The obvious emphasis in the cognitive-behavioural approach to relapse prevention is on producing change within the user. With relatively few exceptions, the techniques advocated by Marlatt and Gordon (1985), Annis and Davis (1989) and others within this tradition are demonstrably reductionist; they are based on the assumption that individuals can overcome addictive behaviours with an act of will and a few social skills. This assumption should be rejected for two fundamental reasons. First, an exclusive or over-emphasis on individual change ignores the overwhelming research evidence that the quality of one's social network is a crucial determinant of whether or not relapse will occur (for example, Bromet *et al.*, 1977; Cronkite and Moos, 1980; Tuchfeld, 1981; Billings and Moos, 1983). Second, Marlatt's method fails to take seriously his own finding (Marlatt and Gordon, 1980) and ours (Barber *et al.*, 1991; Barber *et al.*, 1992) that much drug consumption (particularly heroin consumption) is a social behaviour driven by social forces. In our own follow-up work with heroin-addicted prisoners who had been through a Drug Unit programme (Crisp and Barber, 1992), we found that all those whose heroin habit was fully re-instated after treatment attributed their relapse to social pressures of one kind or another – unemployment, interpersonal conflict, social isolation, peer group pressure, and so on. And although change on the part of the user may be a necessary precondition to solving such problems, it cannot be sufficient. After all, the ex-user can be only one of the players in an interpersonal dispute or can take only one part in the negotiations about employment. Put simply, social problems require social – not merely psychological – solutions. Again, the point is not that psychological interventions are inappropriate, it is merely that they are insufficient and must be supported by interventions at systemic levels beyond the individual. Thus, it is to these more social interventions that much of the rest of this chapter is devoted.

Before leaving interventions focused on the individual, however, it is necessary at least to mention the potentially invaluable role of pharmacological agents in the prevention of relapse. In the case of heroin, for example, so-called 'methadone maintenance' therapy has been shown to be particularly effective, provided that the dosage is adequate. Methadone is an opioid antagonist that is taken orally and which produces cross-tolerance to all opioid drugs, of which heroin is the most common. Methadone is classified as an opioid antagonist because it attaches itself to opioid receptor cells in the brain and either pushes out or blocks other opioids from stimulating the receptor cells. Thus, a dose of methadone alters the brain so that its responsiveness to opioids is greatly reduced, and this, in turn, reduces the attractiveness of opioids by suppressing the pleasure associated with their use. For this reason, methadone has been referred to as a form of 'narcotic blockage'. Moreover, because methadone is long- and slow-acting, there is no need to administer the drug more than once daily for it to be effective. Numerous controlled studies have indicated that methadone can prevent heroin relapse and, with it, criminal behaviour and mortality among users provided that it is administered in high enough doses (> 60 mg) and that it is offered in combination with follow-up psychosocial services like those described in this chapter (McLellan *et al.*, 1993; Ward *et al.*, 1998; Strain *et al.*, 1999). This is not to say that the use of methadone is entirely without problems. In the first place, methadone itself induces dependence and produces an abstinence syndrome which is slower in onset and, although less severe at its height, actually lasts longer than heroin. For this reason, methadone requires phased removal if it is not to cause more problems than it solves. In the second place, it could be argued that it is curious, perhaps even perverse, to use one drug of dependence to treat another drug of dependence. This practice not only reinforces the idea in the user's mind that drugs are a ready solution to coping with problems, but it once again raises the question of why some addictive drugs should be legal and others illegal (see below and Chapter 1).

In addition to methadone, LAAM (levo-alpha-acetylemethadol) is another opioid antagonist that was recently approved by the American Food and Drug Authority for use in the treatment of heroin and other opioid dependence. LAAM is comparable to methadone in reducing opioid use (American Psychiatric Association, 1995) but is longer-acting and therefore need only be administered three times a week. A partial opioid antagonist known as buprenorphine has also been the subject of much clinical and research interest in recent years (Strain *et al.*, 1994). Buprenorphine is an analgesic and because it causes a significantly lower degree of sedation and respiratory depression than other opiates, it is a relatively safe drug to use; although it too produces withdrawal symptoms, even if they are milder than for methadone and LAAM. One opioid antagonist that is non addictive is naltrexone. Because controlled trials into naltrexone remain sparse, the use of naltrexone in the treatment of addictions is controversial, particularly when used as an adjunct to so-called 'rapid detoxification' (Mattick *et al.*, 1997). However, naltrexone's advocates claim that it is a highly effective relapse prevention treatment that has minimal side effects and has no potential for abuse or diversion for unprescribed use (Tai and Blaine, 1997).

In the case of alcohol, numerous medications have been tried over the years with very little success. One medication that is widely prescribed today is the antidipsotropic agent disulfiram (marketed as Antabuse) which produces extreme nausea, racing pulse and high blood pressure when taken in combination with alcohol. The experience of drinking after taking disulfiram is so aversive that the medication acts as a powerful deterrent to drinking. However, disulfiram is only as effective as the client's compliance with their daily dose. Primarily for this reason, controlled trials have produced very mixed results regarding the effectiveness of disulfiram (Porterfield, 1992; Goldstein, 1994) and many clinical researchers are unconvinced about its usefulness (for example, Horgen and Brownell, 1998). By contrast, the opioid antagonist naltrexone is growing in popularity in the prevention of alcohol relapse as it has been shown to reduce craving (Miller *et al.*, 1998). Unlike disulfiram, then, naltrexone works not by preventing a single drink but by reducing the priming effect of a drink through its capacity to suppress craving for the next one.

In the case of smoking, there is now very solid evidence in support of nicotine replacement agents in the prevention of relapse (Fiore *et al.*, 1994; Hajek, 1996). Two types of nicotine replacement are available: nicotine gum and nicotine patches placed on the skin. Both have been shown to be effective, and there is some evidence that combining the two forms is more effective than either of them alone (Fagerstrom *et al.*, 1993; Fagerstrom, 1994).

In contrast to heroin, nicotine and, to a lesser extent, alcohol, no medication has yet been shown to be effective for other drugs of addiction, including cocaine, marijuana, benzodiazepines or designer drugs. Moreover, it bears repeating that whatever pharmacological agents are used in the prevention of relapse, all of the research evidence suggests that pharmacotherapy alone is insufficient. The best outcomes are achieved through a combination of medication (where appropriate) and psychosocial intervention. We turn, then, to psychosocial interventions at system levels beyond the individual.

Level II: Interventions at the level of family, work and social support networks

As previously mentioned, it is now well-established that certain factors in the individual's personal environment play a crucial role in determining treatment outcome. Employment status, for example, is among the best predictors of relapse. Although only 30 to 40 per cent of drug users in the British treatment population are in regular employment (Raistrick and Davidson, 1985), these individuals represent the bulk of the 'stable' or non-using clients at any one point in time (for example, Stimson and Ogbourne, 1970). The causal direction of this association is debatable of course, but it is safe to assume that work and the maintenance of change are mutually reinforcing. In their longitudinal study of problem drinkers, Orford and Edwards (1977) reported that not simply employment but also occupational status at intake were also related to long-term treatment success: men from the four top occupational status categories (professional, administrative, supervisory, and other non-routine, non-manual occupations) were much less likely to relapse than men from lower-status occupations. This same association between occupational status and long-term maintenance has also been reported by Finney and Moos (1981), though one qualification introduced by these studies was the unremarkable finding that where high occupational status entailed high stress, the prognosis was less favourable. Further evidence of the importance of socio-economic factors comes from Robins and Ratcliff's (1979) finding that extreme poverty increases the risk of adult anti-social behaviour, including alcohol abuse and illegal drug use.

Of most importance in the Orford and Edwards (1977) study, however, was the social–emotional atmosphere of the ex-user's immediate environment. Drinkers from relatively cohesive domestic relationships were more than twice as likely to maintain treatment gains as drinkers from non-cohesive relationships. In this study, non-cohesiveness was characterised by a lack of affection, the use of few socially desirable adjectives or phrases by partners to describe each other, a lack of participation by the male in family tasks, and opinions about the future of the relationship which tended to be pessimistic (see also Bromet and Moos, 1977; Billings and Moos, 1982, 1983; Moos and Billings, 1983). This finding led Orford and Edwards (1977) to propose that 'A breakdown in the mutual rewardingness of marital or other family relationship is predictive of a relatively unfavourable outcome following treatment or consultation for any psychological disorder' (p. 74). It is important to note that the Orford and Edwards study included only married men, so their findings can hardly be seen as normative for the entire treatment population. Nevertheless, more recent research on this topic indicates that, if anything, cohesive and supportive relationships are even more important to long-term maintenance in women (Tucker, 1982; MacDonald, 1987). Furthermore, Cohen and Lichtenstein (1990) and Billings and Moos (1983) have produced results similar to Orford and Edwards (1977) with samples comprised of both men and women. As well as domestic relationships, the atmosphere at work is also known to play an important role: individuals who are involved in their jobs and enjoy cohesive relationships with co-workers and supervisors are less affected by negative life events and much less likely to revert to heavy drinking (Bromet and Moos, 1977, 1982).

With regard to smoking cessation, those successful at giving up also report more positive support from significant others than do relapsers or continued smokers (Coppotelli and Orleans, 1985; Mermelstein *et al.*, 1986), and measures of partner and co-worker support for giving up generally predict long-term quit rates among treated and untreated smokers alike (Lichtenstein *et al.*, 1986). According to Cohen *et al.* (1988) social support facilitates change in addictive behaviour via four 'macroprocesses': (i) by buffering stress; (ii) by influencing motivation to initiate or maintain behaviour change; (iii) by influencing the availability of smoking cues in the environment; and (iv) by applying social influence to abstain. The importance of buffering stress stems from the repeated finding (see above) that drug users turn to using in order to deal with negative affect. Hence, to the degree that social support elicits effective alternative stress coping strategies or results in potentially stressful events being appraised as benign, it should aid persons trying to stay off drugs. With regard to motivation, because change and the maintenance of change require self-control, Wilson and Brownell (1980) argue that 'continued self-regulatory behaviour requires social support; like any other behaviour, it will extinguish in the absence of the appropriate reinforcement' (p. 76). In other words, social support aids motivation by providing positive reinforcement for appropriate behaviour change. Cohen *et al.* (1988) make the added point that social support is likely to affect motivation less directly as well, by increasing self-esteem through the awareness that others care about and want the user to succeed. The significance of environmental cues in precipitating drug use has been referred to repeatedly throughout this book, so the association (or lack of it) between cues within one's social network and drug treatment outcome should now be obvious to the reader. Similarly, we know from the previous section that direct and indirect social pressures to use are powerful influences on relapse, so this too is an aspect of one's social support network which is likely to play a role in determining treatment outcome.

In a fascinating analysis of the effects of social support on smoking cessation known as 'The Oregon Process Studies' (Brown *et al.*, 1984; Mermelstein *et al.*, 1986), the researchers found not only that social support was indeed related to treatment outcome, but that the different kinds of support variables became important at different stages of the change process. Briefly, their results indicated that high levels of partner support for giving up (motivational support) and the perceived availability of general (stress-buffering) support were assets early in the change process (that is, during the initial decision to give up and at the three-month abstinence point). However, these support variables played no role at the long-term (twelve-month) follow-up point, by which time the presence of smokers in the subjects' social networks had become the key (environmental and social pressure) variables.

In view of such evidence, it is a popularly held view among drug researchers and practitioners alike that increasing social support from a potential quitter's spouse, friends and co-workers should make it easier to give up and stay off drugs of all kinds (for example, Colletti and Brownell, 1982; McCrady, 1988; Orleans *et al.*, 1991). Unfortunately, however, it does not follow merely because aspects of naturally occurring networks play a role in treatment outcome that artificially created social support will have the same effect. Indeed, the hard empirical evidence about such strategies is actually rather discouraging. Lichtenstein *et al.* (1986), for example, reviewed smoking cessation studies which have tried to increase specific support germane to changing smoking behaviour, either by: (a) training network members to be supportive; (b) training persons to influence their own networks; or (c) creating new networks. Their findings suggested that none of these strategies was consistently able to influence relapse rates. For example, neither training network members to be supportive nor involving partners in treatment appears to exert any significant effect on relapse (for example, McIntyre-Kingsolver *et al.*, 1986; Lichtenstein *et al.*, cited in Cohen *et al.*, 1988).

Admittedly, the evidence concerning spouse training is less clear-cut in relation to the treatment of obesity (for example, Brownell *et al.*, 1978; Murphy *et al.*, 1982), but research with alcohol abusers is so far largely consistent with the smoking studies (for example, McCrady, 1988). With regard to creating new social networks, an early study by Janis and his colleagues (Janis and Hoffman, 1970; Janis, 1983) on the influence of establishing a support network for those giving up did give some cause for optimism. In this study, the researchers found that individuals who had daily telephone contact with another quitter designated as a 'buddy' had a lower mean smoking rate at the end of treatment and at six-week, one-year and even ten-year follow-ups compared to control groups. However, similar projects by Hamilton and Bornstein (1976) and by Rodriguez and Lichtenstein (1977) could find no evidence that scheduled phone contact buddy systems improved maintenance rates; and buddy systems in work-site programmes similarly have so far not produced positive results (Marlott *et al.*, 1984). Finally, in our own work (Barber and Crisp, 1995) with alcohol abusers, recent graduates from various treatment programmes were introduced to community-based 'mentors' (heavy drinkers who had been abstinent for more than two years) whose role was to provide social support and non-alcohol-related recreational opportunities, but we found no difference in relapse rates between these individuals and controls.

So far, the only microsystem intervention to display consistently positive effects on relapse is the so-called 'community-reinforcement approach' (CRA) developed by Nathan Azrin and his colleagues (Hunt and Azrin, 1973; Azrin, 1976; Sisson and Azrin, 1989; Miller and Meyers, 1999). The fundamental objective of CRA is to rearrange the vocational, family and social reinforcers of alcohol abusers in such a way that time out from reinforcement will occur if they begin to drink. The technique involves a painstaking assessment and, if necessary, total reconstruction of the drinker's microsystem, including but going far beyond social support variables. In its final form CRA involves at least seven components:

1. A prescription for disulfiram (otherwise known as antabuse)
2. A programme for ensuring that the client continues to take disulfiram
3. 'Reciprocity' marriage counselling
4. A job club for unemployed clients
5. Resocialisation training
6. Recreational activities
7. An early warning system

In addition, certain versions of CRA also make provision for 'environmental enrichments' of various kinds which are likewise contingent on sobriety (Hunt and Azrin, 1973; Azrin, 1976).

CRA begins with an interview to which the drinker's partner (or significant other) is invited. The clients are asked why they wish to do something about the drinker's alcohol intake before the drinker is asked to complete questionnaires which interrogate the drinker further about the precise ways in which alcohol is impoverishing their life (see Sisson and Azrin, 1989). The intention here is to enhance the drinkers' motivation to participate by requiring them to reflect carefully on their current lifestyle. While the drinker completes these instruments, the counsellor continues to interview the other partner in another room about the problems caused by the drinker's behaviour and the efforts made by the 'non-drinking' partner to cope. The primary aim of this part of the intervention is to form an alliance with the drinker's partner. Next, the intake questionnaires are reviewed with both partners. The couple are then given an introduction to the role of disulfiram by the counsellor who stresses the importance of taking the medication regularly and as prescribed. Sometimes an agreement is struck whereby the drinker agrees to try disulfiram for a short trial period before it is reassessed by all three parties. In a typical CRA intervention, the first dose is normally taken in the presence of the partner and the counsellor, and the occasion is treated as cause for celebration and congratulations. At this session it is also advisable to review with both partners the situations in which the drinker is likely to be sorely tempted to drink and rehearse some of the possible responses. Azrin (1976) and Sisson and Azrin (1989) also recommend negotiating an early warning notification system to alert the counsellor if problems are developing.

As well as these 'antabuse assurance procedures', CRA also provides for a structured partner intervention known as 'reciprocity marriage counselling' (see Azrin *et al.*, 1973) which is designed to teach the partners how to communicate better with each other. To begin, the couple are administered the Marriage Adjustment Inventory (Manson and Lerner, 1962) which identifies twelve specific problem areas in the marriage: money management, family relations, sexual problems, children, social life, grooming, 'neurotic tendencies', attention, immaturity, value or ideological differences, general incompatibility, and dominance by one or other partner. Within each of these twelve domains, the partners identify problem areas and agree to exchange reinforcers which are contingent on the drinker remaining sober. In the words of Hunt and Azrin (1973, p. 94), 'This list typically include(s) preparing meals, listening to the partner with undivided attention, picking up the children from school, redistributing the finances, engaging in sexual activities of a particular type or at a minimal frequency, visiting relatives together and spending a night out together'. In the case of clients without a stable relationship, a similar procedure is followed with a significant other such as a parent or family member. Where the client is totally isolated, however, Azrin (1976) and Hunt and Azrin (1973) advocate trying to create a 'synthetic' family consisting of anyone who may have a natural or legitimate reason for maintaining regular contact with the client, for example, a minister, employer or relative. Synthetic family members are encouraged to invite the client for dinner and other outings contingent upon their sobriety. Hunt and Azrin (1973) and Sisson and Azrin (1989) make the point that reciprocity marriage counselling is far easier in theory than in practice, and the counsellor should be prepared to invest around five or more sessions in coaxing partners to negotiate and work through the many difficulties that arise between sessions.

As part of CRA, clients who are unemployed are also referred to a 'job club' (see Azrin and Besalel, 1980), the purpose of which is to help clients find work. Participants are coached in preparing résumés, finding a job lead, responding to job advertisements, presenting themselves in job interviews, and so on. Consistent with the behavioural tradition from which CRA emerged, the potentially complex task of securing employment is broken into discrete, manageable steps and clients are given highly specific instructions on how to behave at each point before being asked to role-play the various skills involved. The job club intervention can be conducted in a group setting with therapist and clients working together to identify potential jobs and guiding each other through the process of applying. At a time of severe economic recession such as we are experiencing throughout the industrialised world and beyond, it would be inadvisable to involve some (maybe even most) clients in the job club component of CRA, as repeated unsuccessful attempts to find work is known to have adverse psychological consequences (Barber, 1982) which would almost certainly impede the client's progress in treatment.

CRA also directs attention to the quality of the client's broader social life, that is, beyond home and work. The so-called 'resocialisation procedures' of CRA aim to arrange for the client to have a happy and satisfactory social life with persons who would encourage them to remain sober. Because Azrin and his colleagues were unsuccessful in their efforts to connect clients with suitable community-based 'resocialisation groups' such as church groups, Alcoholics Anonymous and others, the researchers established their own self-governing social club (Hunt and Azrin, 1973) which met at weekends for social and recreational activities with alcoholic and non-alcoholic guests. In addition, clients were assisted by the researchers to identify and participate in developing hobbies outside the social club which would further enhance their motivation to remain sober. Next, arrangements were made for each client to have a mentor or 'buddy' whose task it was to meet regularly with the client to provide advice and encouragement. As part of their regular meetings, the pair discussed ways of solving problems that were pressing and relevant to staying sober. The requirements for a 'buddy' were:

> He should be a former alcoholic, have been sober for at least a year, reside near the client, or have been a former client in this [CRA] program, be similar in age and social–economic status to the client, desire to help the client and be respected by the client, and agree to meet regularly with the client and to report regularly to the counsellor. (Azrin, 1976, p. 343)

Finally, in order to make the client's home a more attractive place, to facilitate communication with potential employers, and to increase access to friends and social occasions, CRA goes to the extent of helping clients obtain radio and/or television sets, take out subscriptions to local newspapers, obtain a driver's licence and have a telephone installed. If necessary, the initial costs of these environmental enrichments are met by the CRA programme. According to Hunt and Azrin (1973), a secondary benefit of arranging environmental enrichments is that the ongoing financial commitments they entail provide an additional incentive for their drinkers to remain abstinent or moderate.

Perhaps not surprisingly, the results of CRA have been quite impressive: drinkers who receive CRA have been shown to drink less, work more, spend more time with their families and out of institutions than do matched drinkers who do not receive CRA (Hunt and Azrin, 1973; Azrin, 1976). More importantly for our present purposes, these results are stable over a two-year period (Azrin, 1976), indicating that the procedure is an effective form of relapse prevention. However, an obvious disincentive to use the interventions outlined above is that the total package is extremely costly and labour-intensive to implement and, no doubt, impossible to replicate in every detail. The average client in Hunt and Azrin's (1973) original study required some 50 hours in therapy alone (that is, not including the time spent looking for work, participating in prearranged recreational pursuits, and so on), and even Azrin's (1976) revised method requires around 30 hours of therapy per client. Thus, in order for the CRA to become a workable adjunct (or perhaps alternative) to the psychological interventions outlined in the previous section, the procedure needs further refinement so that it becomes more affordable and transferable from agency to agency.

Level III: Intervention at the level of social policy and culture

At the level of the exosystems and macrosystems, we are concerned with the broadest social and cultural context within which drug-taking behaviour occurs. At this level it is possible to identify complex but potentially modifiable social and legal forces that are certain to influence relapse rates within the community generally. Thus, a genuinely comprehensive relapse prevention strategy must give attention to the promotion of public policies which create a climate that acts for rather than against the maintenance of treatment gains. In this section we will concern ourselves with prescription medicines only to the extent that trafficking in them is a criminal activity. The regulation of the medical and pharmaceutical industries themselves is obviously beyond the scope of this book.

In a quasi-economic sense, drug control policies can be divided into strategies for reducing the demand for drugs (demand-side policies) on the one hand, and strategies for reducing the supply of drugs (supply-side policies) on the other. These are not mutually exclusive categories, of course, but the distinction does help to clarify the primary intent of the different drug-related policy options we will consider. Figure 6.3 is a diagrammatic representation of some of the more important of the policy options that are relevant to relapse prevention.

As Figure 6.3 illustrates, the first and most fundamental policy decision concerns the legal status of the drug itself. This decision will have both demand-side and supply-side implications. Put bluntly, if reduction of drug addiction were the only goal of drug policy, the evidence does not support those who advocate the legalisation of currently illegal drugs such as heroin, even though current law enforcement efforts are far from perfect (Clayton, 1989). The problem is, of course, that addiction is only one consideration in the current drug policy debate. Policy-makers must weigh addiction rates against organised crime and (in the case of injectables) HIV infection rates, both of which could be lowered by legalising and regulating the use of illicit substances.

Turning first to illegal drugs, among the favoured, and certainly most expensive, supply-side controls are crop eradication and interception of drug traffic. Source-country crop eradication through chemical or physical means has been vigorously pursued by the United States Bureau of International Narcotics Matters (BINM) in South America and the Golden Triangle region comprised of Thailand, Burma and Laos. But despite huge investments of capital and personnel in this effort, even the President's Commission on Organized Crime (1986) concedes that the BINM has met with only very limited success. In the first place, some countries are reluctant participants and only half-heartedly administer the programme because illicit drug money is important to their political and economic survival. It has been estimated, for example, that somewhere in the order of 25 per cent of Colombia's gross domestic product is derived directly or indirectly from the illegal drug trade (*New Internationalist*, 1984).

In any case, the governments of source countries are unable to control the most powerful producers. In Burma, for instance, the insurgent Burmese Communist Party and the Shan United Army rely on drug trafficking to support their political campaigns, and both groups possess fortified jungle refineries which process opium to a crude level before shipping it to Bangkok for distribution and further refinement. Even when crop eradication is successful in one place, it normally only has the effect of increasing supply from another place, as was amply demonstrated when the BINM eradication of opium production in northern Mexico during the 1970s dramatically increased opium traffic from the Golden Triangle (President's Commission on Organized Crime, 1986).

As well as crop eradication, all Western countries, but especially the United States, have invested heavily in efforts to intercept and

Figure **6.3** *Policy options for the prevention of relapse*

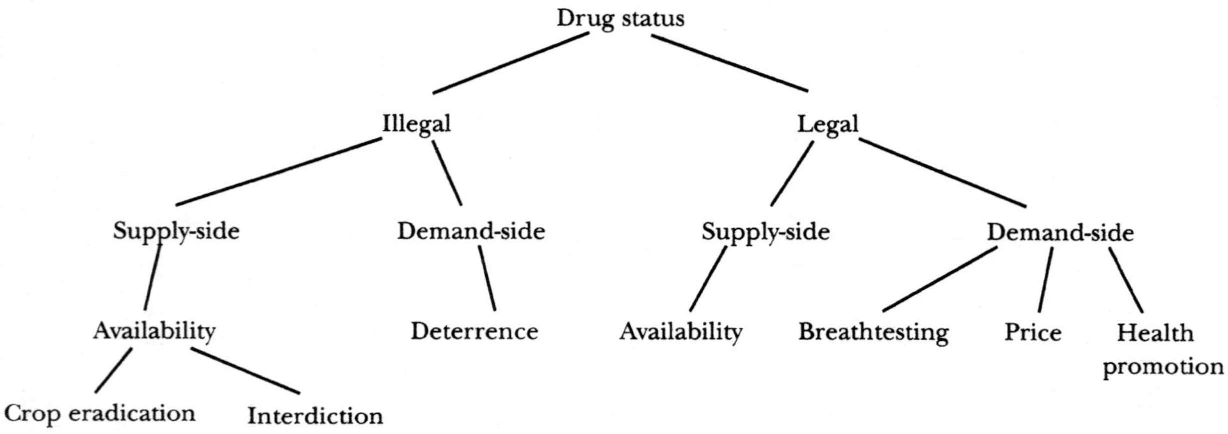

stop the flow of drug traffic by land and sea. In fact, the 'interdiction' programme, as it is known in the United States, consumes by far the bulk of the world's drug prevention funding (Fraser and Kohlert, 1988). While it is impossible to estimate the success of interception efforts with any real degree of accuracy, the strategy clearly cannot be equally effective for all substances. Bulky drugs like marijuana, for example, are much more easily detected than substances like heroin or cocaine; yet the United States Drug Enforcement Administration estimates that even in the case of marijuana, only 25–30 per cent of American shipments are intercepted (President's Commission on Organized Crime, 1986). At this rate the core of the supply network is left largely untouched. Indeed, Polich *et al.* (1984) have estimated that only between 4.3 and 11.2 per cent of the middlemen (let alone organisers) are arrested annually.

On the demand side, law enforcement and tough penalties for trafficking and possession are great favourites with the public (Grichting and Barber, 1986, 1988), but the problem with deterrence is that it is only as good as the numbers caught. As Fraser and Kohlert (1988, p. 109) put it: 'The research seems to suggest that increasing the severity of punishment, without increasing the likelihood of apprehension and the capacity to mete out sterner punishments, is insufficient to alter behaviour.' All this is not to suggest that it is pointless keeping drugs illegal. Not only is the supply of illegal drugs less than it would be if the trade were legalised or decriminalised, but the public perception of what is acceptable behaviour is greatly influenced by the law (Grichting and Barber, 1986, 1988), and there is no doubt that demand for illegal drugs increases with more liberal legalisation, as evidenced by the increase in marijuana use that occurred in the state of South Australia when possession of small amounts was decriminalised in the mid-1990s.

With regard to preventing alcohol and tobacco relapse, the supply-side and demand-side policy context is once again a crucial consideration. Susan Farrell's (1985) definitive review of the evidence for the World Health Organisation makes it clear that aside from raising the legal drinking age, consumption levels are affected by price, availability and, in the case of alcohol, the probability of detection and punishment for drink-driving. When the price of alcohol and tobacco relative to other commodities rises, per capita consumption declines (see also Addiction Research Foundation, 1981; Cook, 1981; Moore and Gerstein, 1981; Lewit and Coate, 1982).

Among other data, Farrell (1985) herself cites figures from the West Indies between 1966 and 1975 showing that the number of alcohol-related road accidents rose and fell predictably with rises and falls in the cost of alcohol relative to per capita income. And in the United States between 1960 and 1974, 63 per cent of the tax increases that occurred across 38 states during that time were followed by a reduction in cirrhosis of the liver mortality as well as declines in road fatalities. Of course, the degree to which consumption will fall in response to increases in price is certain to vary from one country to another and even within the one country over time, but fall it will.

Moreover, the reduction in drinking due to price rises is not confined to light drinkers. As in the United States, the evidence from around the world (see, for example, Seeley, 1960; Leu, 1975; Beaubrun, 1977; Kendell, 1983) is that even the rate of liver cirrhosis is affected by price, and cirrhosis is a condition which is only associated with very high levels of drinking. Indeed, while raising the price of alcoholic beverages may further impoverish some already poor families, Farrell (1985) asserts that because poorer families overall are more inclined to reduce their alcohol intake than pay more, price rises may actually increase the disposable income of low wage earners and the unemployed. Among the factors likely to moderate the effect of price on consumption are the magnitude of the price increase, the relative price of different alcoholic beverages, changes in disposable income, the extent to which alcoholic beverages are available from legal home production, and the interaction of price with other influences on the availability of alcohol, such as the number of liquor outlets.

The availability of alcohol and tobacco outlets has also been shown to exert a direct effect on consumption. For example, while the American experiment with prohibition in the 1920s is rightly, though some would say uncritically (Aaron and Musto, 1981), regarded as a mistake, it is a fact that all indicators of alcohol-related problems (except traffic accidents) reached their lowest levels ever during that time. More recently, strikes in the liquor industry in Finland in 1972, New Zealand in 1976 and in Norway in 1978 all brought about sharp declines in alcohol-related strife, including admissions to detoxification centres, drunk and disorderly arrests, domestic violence reports and hospital admission rates. In 1981 in Poland, alcohol rationing was accompanied by a 20 per cent reduction in per capita consumption and commensurate declines in liver cirrhosis, detoxifications and alcoholic psychoses. Once again, given the nature of the indicators from around the world, we can be very confident that declines due to restricting supply will not be limited merely to social drinkers.

On the demand side of alcohol control, one measure for which, under certain circumstances, there is now firm evidence is random breathtesting (Reed, 1981; Ross, 1982; Forcier *et al.*, 1986; MacKinnon and Woodward, 1986). Based on the cumulative experience of France, the Netherlands, Canada, New Zealand, the United Kingdom, Australia and the United States, Ross (1982) and Farrell (1985) conclude that the critical elements of any drink-drive policy are that: (a) driving with a blood alcohol concentration (BAC) higher than a specific level be a legal offence in itself, that is, irrespective of whether or not another traffic violation has occurred; (b) the BAC be established by objective chemical means; (c) the police be empowered to conduct BAC testing either in the event of a traffic violation or merely at random; and (d) the punishment for being over the legal limit or for test refusal be severe. It is also clear that breathtesting does not diminish alcohol consumption unless the public perceive there to be a high risk of detection (Reed, 1982). For this reason, Farrell (1985) favours highly publicised and visible 'blitzes' rather than indefinite or unobtrusive testing. In a similar vein, Jonah and Wilson (1983) advocate stopping drivers during main drinking hours, rather than throughout the week, and locating road stops where they will be highly visible to as many people as possible.

In addition to these supply- and demand-side options for combating drug use, most countries throughout the Western world and beyond also now incorporate harm minimisation strategies to a greater or lesser extent within their drug policies. The harm reduction philosophy starts with the assumption that abstinence is an unrealistic objective for many users, at least in the short term, and therefore promotes a number of strategies to reduce harmful use, to minimize use, and to reduce the social costs of using. Harm minimisation strategies typically include needle exchanges to reduce the incidence of blood-borne diseases, media campaigns advertising sensible ways of using drugs and, for opiate abusers, drug substitution programmes such as methadone maintenance (see above). In the case of legal drugs, controlled drinking programmes like those reviewed in Chapter 5 also qualify as harm minimisation techniques because they take it for granted that some heavy drinkers will reject the idea of abstinence.

There are formidable methodological obstacles involved in proving that harm minimisation works (see, for example, Lennings, 2000), but among the most unambiguous research findings so far belong to the heroin prescription trials that are currently underway in Canada and a number of European countries. In one of these trials, for example (van den Brink *et al.*, 2002), the Netherlands' Central Committee on the Treatment of Heroin Addicts (CCBH) administered regulated doses of heroin to a total of 549 users between 1998 and 2001. The average participant in the study was 39 years old with a 16 year addiction. The heroin was dispensed at a clinic three times a day either for smoking or injecting under medical supervision. Participants in one group were prescribed heroin and methadone for six or twelve months, while a control group received only methadone. The effect of discontinuing heroin treatment was also investigated. The people who were prescribed heroin and methadone experienced 23–25 per cent more clinically relevant improvements in their physical, mental, or social condition than persons taking methadone alone. These improvements included better social contacts, less criminality, and less use of cocaine (90 per cent of all the participants had previously been heavy users of cocaine). The follow up study showed that within two months of stopping the treatment more than 80 per cent of the study participants had lost all of these gains. The CCBH study also found that prescribing heroin is relatively safe. Three patients died during the study, which involved the dispensing of heroin 140,000 times, and this is less than half the death rate in methadone programmes. As a result of these findings, CCBH now recommends that combined heroin and methadone treatment should be introduced as part of the addiction care system and that the registration of heroin as a medicine should be promoted along with a medical protocol for prescribing the drug.

No doubt some or all of the policy options considered so far will be unpalatable to some readers because of values they consider to be higher than drug prevention. I, for one would argue that it is worth legalising or at least decriminalising the illicit drug trade in order to cripple organised crime and make it easier to check the spread of HIV by enabling stricter regulation of suppliers' hygiene standards. Others might worry that increasing the price of alcohol and tobacco will, like any other flat tax fall harder on those lower-income earners who do continue to drink and smoke than higher-income earners who do the same. These, and other possible objections, serve to illustrate that public policy inevitably involves a choice between competing social values; and readers must be left to make their own value judgements. One thing is clear, however. The impact of the above policies on the variable of interest to us here – drug-taking behaviour – is indisputable.

The final policy option referred to in Figure 6.3 may at first seem the least contentious. Most people would agree with Grabowski (1986) and with Saunders and Allsop (1991) that there is little point in spending vast sums of public money on drug treatment if clients are released into a climate which not only sanctions, but actively promotes, the use of addictive and mind-altering substances through the popular culture. In recognition of this problem, most Western countries, since the 1980s, have launched ambitious and expensive media health promotion campaigns, intended to reduce the appeal of licit and illicit drug-taking behaviour. Unfortunately, however, there is little to suggest that mass media drug prevention campaigns (by themselves) are capable of effecting any change in drug consumption. Accordingly, there are some who would oppose the aggressive multi-media campaigns (see, for example, Anonymous, 1985; Hansen, 1985) on the grounds that the returns do not justify the cost to other public services. If health promotion is to succeed in reducing the demand for drugs, media campaigns must be complemented by more targeted community interventions.

One example of this is the Stanford Heart Disease Prevention Program (SHDPP) in California (Farquhar *et al.*, 1977; Maccoby *et al.*, 1977; Maccoby and Alexander, 1980; Meyer *et al.*, 1980) which combined mass media and face-to-face instruction. The mass media component took place over two years and informed people that a certain diet would lead to reduction of sugar, salt, saturated fat, cholesterol intake and overall body weight. The public was also informed that cigarette-smoking cessation or reduction and an increase in physical activity would also reduce heart risk. A broad range of media materials were used including over 150 radio and television commercials, several hours of radio and television programming, weekly newspaper columns, billboards, bus posters, and printed material sent by direct mail. The face-to-face component of the intervention used techniques derived from social learning theory and behavioural self-control principles. High-risk individuals were identified through painstaking baseline interview and survey techniques and these people were invited to follow-up interviews with a doctor and 'risk-reduction instructor'. At these interviews, clients were provided with feedback about their risk factors and were issued with an invitation either to a structured risk reduction group or offered the services of a risk-reduction instructor in the home for three months. Treatment included self-monitoring of the target behaviours, charting of progress, and fading of instructional and therapist reinforcement to ensure self-maintenance of new behaviours. Not surprisingly given the level of investment, the SHDPP did succeed in lowering heart risk within the Californian community exposed to the full programme.

Notwithstanding Robinson *et al.*'s (1989) reminder that there is much that can be done at the level of the local community to prevent drug problems, the message of the SHDPP and of health promotion generally is that success does not come cheaply. In the UK, attitudes towards alcohol are increasingly disapprobative, and consumption is declining generally if not yet universally; and smoking, except for teenage girls, is less of a problem all the time (National Campaign Against Drug Abuse, 1992). But these gains have been made only by concerted efforts on the part of governments, health professionals, sporting and cultural bodies and educators. As well, legislative changes have brought an end to smoking in the workplace and on public transport, and have severely restricted the tobacco industry's access to the advertising outlets.

While the social policy options discussed in this section are almost certain to affect relapse rates through their impact on the legal and cultural context of drug use, it could be said that we have begged the fundamental question of how social policy can be influenced. It is worth pointing out in reply that the first step is to recognise that there actually is a connection between prevailing social policy and the behaviour of our individual clients. The next step is to develop informed opinions about what (if any) community-based programme or policy change would be conducive to the maintenance of treatment gains. In the meantime, effective and sensible measures can be taken at the local level through minor but none the less important changes in existing practices and procedures (see Tether and Robinson, 1986; Robinson *et al.*, 1989). For example, providing accurate information about drug effects and how to give up through local organisations and the local media (for example, Rorstad, 1989; Teller, 1989) makes an important local statement. Seeking to influence council decisions about what constitutes a reasonable number of liquor outlets in a municipality (Miller, 1989), implementing an early warning system to head off drunk and disorderly behaviour at public houses (Stevenson, 1989), and promoting alcohol-free public houses (Sangster, 1989) are other local initiatives which have met with a measure of success. Robinson *et al.* (1989) also advocate the promotion of alcohol policy statements in the workplace. An alcohol and work policy is simply an agreement between 'employer and workers' organizations, that a drinking problem is a health problem. It assures employees that those who are identified as having a problem or who themselves come forward for help will not endanger their jobs or their employment rights. It undertakes to assist towards appropriate aid and support' (ibid., p. 78). Assuming such a policy is implemented as intended, it should have the effect of influencing the whole workplace culture. Finally, helping local service organisations to recognise alcohol-related problems and encouraging them to support drug-free entertainment options can also help to promote a culture consistent with relapse prevention at the local level. Moreover, all these interventions are squarely within the mission and mandate of social work.

In this chapter we have looked at interventions aimed at preventing relapse in clients who are trying to break their addictive behaviour. It is most unusual even for specialist drug treatment agencies to engage in the kind of multi-level intervention advocated in this chapter, so it is unreasonable to expect generalist social workers to take responsibility for all the interventions advocated here. Nevertheless, any comprehensive approach to relapse prevention must begin by recognising the complexity of the task involved and the strategies that have some supporting evidence. Generalist social workers have their part to play, as do drug specialists, community workers and policy-makers. The fact that these professions rarely work together may be why relapse rates are so high. Throughout this book, we have placed considerable emphasis on the research evidence. This emphasis is born of a conviction that it is only through basic research and programme evaluation that we will arrive at reliable methods for the treatment and prevention of drug addiction. Thus, before concluding, it is fitting that we spend some time considering the issues involved in evaluating our work.

7

Evaluation

In the seven years or so since the first edition of this book was prepared, the mood among addiction workers has changed considerably. In the earlier edition I claimed that 'an air of pessimism hangs over the field of addictions because of a widespread belief within treatment circles that nothing really works'. The atmosphere is much more sanguine these days, in part because researchers have begun to accept a more realistic definition of success than was the case when Emrick (1974) and others (see, for example, Armor *et al.*, 1978; Polich *et al.*, 1981) declared treatment to be ineffective (see also Chapter 6). More importantly, a number of more recent reviews of the literature have clearly demonstrated the efficacy of treatment over no-treatment and of certain treatment methods over others (Miller *et al.*, 1995; Finney and Monahan, 1996; Carroll, 1998). Among the findings are that social skills training directed at effective interpersonal communication and conflict resolution (see Chapter 5) is superior both to no-treatment and to supportive counselling control groups (Jackson and Oei, 1978; Oei and Jackson, 1980, 1982; Chick *et al.*, 1988; Miller, 1998). Behavioural marital therapy (see Chapter 6) has also proved more effective than individual treatment (McCrady *et al.*, 1986) and various other forms of therapy (Hedberg and Campbell, 1974; O'Farrell *et al.*, 1985), even when the intervention is unilateral (that is, involving only one of the partners) (see Chapters 3 and 6).

The new spirit of optimisim in the addictions field has withstood what many would regard as the discouraging findings of Project MATCH (1997). Project MATCH was a study involving hundreds of drinkers which set out *inter alia* to establish whether some combinations of treatment and client produce better results than others. The sheer size and methodological rigour of the study have led many researchers to eulogise Project MATCH as the most ambitious and definitive treatment study yet conducted in the field of addictions (see, for example, Hall, 1999; Orford, 1999). In this study, participants were randomly assigned to receive either Cognitive Behaviour Therapy (see Chapter 5), Motivational Enhancement Training (see Motivational Interviewing in Chapter 4) or Twelve-Step (Alcoholics Anonymous) Facilitation. Not only did the researchers find very little difference in the effectiveness of the methods overall, but they could find no evidence of any optimal match between client and method. In other words, all methods worked equally well, irrespective of the type of client assigned to them. These findings have reopened the debate about whether the method of treatment matters (for example, Emrick, 1975) and even whether it is treatment at all or factors completely extraneous to treatment that are responsible for change (Orford, 1999). This idea should come as no surprise to readers of this book. Earlier in this book, I argued that clinicians and addiction researchers alike commonly misunderstand the nature of drug dependence (see Chapter 1). Addiction specialists come from reductionist disciplines like psychology and psychiatry that frequently overlook the inherently social dimension of addiction and, as a consequence, look for solutions inside the user's head. But drug dependence is a complex personal, interpersonal, political and cultural phenomenon; it cannot be resolved that easily. In Chapter 2 we outlined a social work perspective on drug addiction and in Chapters 3 and 6 we considered the application of this perspective to prevention. By now it should be reasonable to conclude that drug treatment is unlikely to achieve lasting success unless and until such social interventions are brought into the mainstream of clinical practice and integrated with the more psychotherapeutic methods reviewed in Chapters 3, 4 and 5 of the book. Furthermore, in the absence of relapse-proof treatment techniques, it is essential that practitioners get into the habit of continually re-appraising and re-adjusting their practice, for it is only through careful monitoring that the short-term effectiveness of our interventions can be determined and the longer-term threat of relapse minimised.

The principles of programme evaluation

When planning any kind of intervention, workers make explicit or, more often, implicit decisions about the following issues: (a) what

constitutes success in this intervention? (b) how will I recognise
success when it happens? and (c) how will I know whether success
is due to my intervention or something else? These are also the
fundamental methodological problems involved in programme
evaluation. In somewhat more technical language, the three
research questions identified here relate to the methodological
issues of rationale, measurement and design respectively. While it
is not possible or appropriate in a book of this kind to cover each
of these issues in detail, it is important to conclude by identifying
the techniques and considerations that are relevant. For a more
comprehensive presentation of the science of programme evaluation, the reader is directed to one of the many excellent texts on
the subject (see, for example, Campbell and Stanley, 1963; Cook
and Campbell, 1979; Posavac and Carey, 1985; Herman *et al.*,
1987).

Defining success

Ideally, the questions identified above should be asked and
answered in relation both to instrumental and outcome objectives.
By outcome objective I am referring to the ultimate purpose or
rationale for intervening. Our outcome objective will often be no
more complicated than the modification of drug-taking behaviour
in our client. Sometimes, though, the outcome objective will be to
assist a partner or significant other to cope with the user's behaviour (see Chapter 3), or to bring the user to a point where treatment is seriously contemplated (see Chapters 3 and 4). At still
other times, there may be multiple outcome objectives, such as
improving the marital relationship and reducing drinking or drug-
taking behaviour. Ever since the Rand Report (Armor *et al.*, 1978;
Polich *et al.*, 1981) announced the bad news about relapse rates,
the selection of appropriate outcome criteria has generated intense
debate within the drug treatment literature. Those clinicians who
reject the disease approach to addiction (see Chapter 1) object
that total abstinence need not be the measure of success anyway,
and the conflict surrounding successful non-abstinent treatment
outcome (see Cook, 1985) owes much to Davies's (1962) classic
study which reported that seven out of 93 patients treated in
hospital for alcoholism had managed to control their drinking over

the long term rather than abstain completely. Besides, some researchers would contend (see Emrick and Hansen, 1983) that level of consumption is not as important as quality-of-life measures like physical health, other substance abuse, readmission to treatment, mortality, utilisation of other health care services, legal problems, vocational functioning, improvements in interpersonal relationships, and social/emotional functioning (see, for example, Emrick and Hansen, 1983). For social workers in particular, the best evaluation studies are likely to be those which take this more holistic view of the user's life instead of restricting attention to level of consumption.

What constitutes success in drug prevention work is, therefore, not always as straightforward as one might assume. Furthermore, the evaluator must be clear not only about the precise target of intervention, but also about the length of the follow-up period. As the United States' Surgeon General (1988) noted, short-term success (three to six months) is relatively easy; it is the long haul that is the problem. This has caused Nathan and Skinstad (1987) to recommend that follow-up data be obtained for at least two years after treatment before making a decision about whether or not the intervention has been successful. But strictures such as this will inevitably increase the level of subject attrition and may very well be logistically impossible within generalist social work agencies. It may be that the best most of us can manage is to monitor short-term success in the knowledge that some degree of success in the short-term is likely to be necessary, if not sufficient, for the attainment of long-term success.

In contrast to outcome objectives, an instrumental objective is one which is mainly or entirely striven for in order to facilitate an outcome objective. In the community-reinforcement approach (CRA) (Hunt and Azrin, 1973; Azrin, 1976; Sisson and Azrin, 1989), for example, clients are assisted to find a job under the assumption that employment will counteract excessive drinking. Whereas in some programmes securing work could be a legitimate outcome objective, under CRA employment is instrumental to the primary goal of resolving the addictive behaviour. In the course of any intervention plan there are likely to be multiple instrumental objectives and the success of these must also be monitored if the practitioner is to make inferences about the mechanism(s) responsible for outcome success.

Measuring success

Once criteria for success have been selected, issues of measurement must then be addressed. It can be difficult to convince practitioners that whenever they make judgements of value, even the most qualitative of judgements, they are doing so on the basis of quantity. To assert that a client is 'better', for example, presupposes that we have taken some measure of the quantum of 'goodness' or 'wellness' at Time 1 and readministered the same yardstick at Time 2. We do not avoid the issue if we content ourselves with a statement like 'The client is happy' because while it skirts the comparison between Time 1 and Time 2, 'happy' is not an absolute state and the decision to assign someone to the category of happy people is only possible after we have satisfied ourselves that the individual concerned possesses the requisite qualities to a sufficient degree. It is just as important to recognise that measurement is not an exact science; all measures, from the most precise recordings in physics to the most apparently qualitative judgements in social work, contain error. This situation can be expressed as follows:

$$\text{Observed score} = \text{True score} + \text{Systematic error} + \text{Random error}$$

The above equation conveys that any measure contains three components. The 'true score' refers to that part of the score obtained which actually measures the construct under investigation: the amount of alcohol consumed, the happiness of the client, and so on. 'Systematic error' refers to that component of the score obtained which reflects influences from other constructs besides the one under investigation. For example, our judgement of a person's happiness may be influenced by that person's level of extroversion or desire to please the worker. Thus, to the extent that our measure of happiness is contaminated by such constructs, the score obtained will be distorted by systematic error. The more common term for systematic error within psychometrics is invalidity. Finally, 'random error' reflects non-systematic or capricious influences such as the person's mood on the day or the observer's attention to detail when making observations or administering tests. This random error is more commonly known as unreliability. The objective of any measure, then, is to maximise the 'true' component and minimise the 'error' components of the score. Indeed, any measuring instrument (including the worker's subjective opinion) should meet acceptable standards of reliability and validity if results of the evaluation are to be taken seriously. (For a straightforward introduction to tests of reliability and validity, the reader is directed to Kidder, 1981, ch. 7.)

Attributing success

Having defined what we mean by success and addressed the question of how we can recognise or measure it, we come to the thorny methodological issue of attributing causality. In everyday life, most of us have a tendency to credit ourselves with successes and blame external influences for our failures (see, for example, Forsyth and Schlenker, 1977; Sicoly and Ross, 1977; Snyder *et al.*, 1978; Layden, 1982). This 'attributional bias' is clearly a dangerous phenomenon in professional work because it will almost certainly result in repeating poor practice and, very often, in blaming clients for our own mistakes. If we are to avoid such pitfalls, we need a method for attributing causality objectively. With or without social work intervention, life goes on for our clients, and even the most impoverished of lives is subject to forces other than social work intervention. Any one of these outside influences alone or in combination with other influences may be responsible for treatment outcome.

In their classic essay on experimental design, Campbell and Stanley (1963) identified certain 'threats to internal validity', by which they mean possible alternative explanations for an outcome beside the intervention under investigation. By way of illustration, Table 7.1 lists some of the more important of these threats and indicates when each might apply.

In science, the paradigmatic method for eliminating threats to internal validity is the experiment, and a perfect experiment is one which permits us to conclude unequivocally in favour of a causal connection between an intervention and an outcome. Broadly speaking, the practitioner has two fundamental options when designing an experimental evaluation of their intervention: the between-group experiment (see Campbell and Stanley, 1963) and the single-subject experiment (see Barlow and Hersen, 1984; Barlow *et al.*, 1984). In the between-group method, one whole group of clients is compared before and after, or just after, intervention with another group of subjects who can be assumed to be equivalent or comparable before

the intervention is applied. There are various options for constructing between-group experiments, ranging from so-called 'quasi'
experimental designs, in which it is possible to control only some of the
threats to internal validity, to 'true' experiments in which full or near
full control is possible. However, between-group experimentation of
any kind is very often out of the question for social work practitioners.
It may be ethically objectionable to assign clients to a 'no-treatment'
control group, for instance, or it may be impossible to recruit
sufficient clients with the identical problem so that an identical intervention can be offered to all of them. Even if these problems are
overcome there still remains the worrying fact that between-group
experiments give average results and thereby obscure individual
differences.

***Table* 7.1**   *Threats to internal validity*

Threat	*When applicable*
History	When an effect might be due to extraneous events occurring between the start of intervention and the assessment of outcome
Maturation	When an effect might be due to developmental changes occurring between the start of intervention and the assessment of outcome
Testing	When a test is administered at the beginning and end of intervention, thereby raising the possibility that the first test affected scores on the second test
Instrumentation	When an effect could be due to changes in the measuring instrument itself between the start of treatment and the assessment of outcome. (This is most likely to be the case when the measuring instrument is a person)
Statistical regression	Things in nature tend to drift or 'regress' towards average levels with time. Thus, if the client was at an extreme level to begin with, change could be due to regression to the mean

At the end of the day, a between-group experiment allows us to
conclude only that intervention X 'works' for a hypothetical individual who looks like the arithmetic mean of the intervention group;
and the problem for practitioners is that they deal with real
people, not arithmetic means. Although truistic, this straightforward
assertion is only now starting to be taken seriously by addiction
researchers who are questioning whether between-group experimental method is suitable for the purpose of evaluating intervention.

Krivanek (1988) and Miller (1992) have posited that the between-group approach to evaluation may be responsible for the common finding of no difference between treatment methods in effectiveness. In a nutshell, the argument goes like this: suppose treatment X is effective for person A but not person B, whereas treatment Y is effective for B but not A. It follows that a group containing A and B which is exposed to treatment X will perform identically to a group containing A and B exposed to treatment Y. The conclusion drawn by the researcher is that X and Y are equivalent, but the truth is that the two approaches work and do not work for different people. Although the force of this argument has been seriously weakened by Project MATCH (1997), it is true that the best approach for iden-tifying the optimal combination of client and intervention is the single-subject design (Barlow and Hersen, 1984; Barlow *et al.*, 1984). The essence of single-subject designs is repeated measurement of the individual in the presence and in the absence of intervention. Under the approach, an individual serves as their own control and it becomes theoretically possible to establish whether the interven-tion works for *this person* rather than for the group as a whole.

Political issues in programme evaluation

So far we have dealt with evaluation as if it were purely a scientific exercise. But anyone who has ever undertaken programme evalu-ation knows it is much more than that. Vested interests are at stake, jobs are on the line, funding decisions await and participants some-times disagree about fundamental objectives. In short, programme evaluation is almost always a political as well as a scientific undertaking and the evaluator must be capable of negotiating a way through the delicate issues involved. Some of the most important political considerations are discussed below.

The short lifespan of programme initiatives versus the long lead-time for outcome evaluation

Social problems are rarely solved quickly and, in the case of drug addiction, almost never easily. On the other hand, the policy deci-sions which govern social services often *are* made quickly and expediently. For this reason, policy-makers normally look for short-term results despite the fact that a clear indication of treatment outcome is unlikely to emerge for at least twelve months or so (see Chapter 6). The result is that decisions about the continuation or discontinuation of a programme can be taken without full possession of the facts. Compounding this problem is the pressure for every programme to be successful immediately, even though this is rarely the way that progress occurs. From a scientific point of view, failures can be just as important as successes. Failures tell us a great deal about the hypotheses and procedures that can be eliminated from the universe of possibilities open to the practitioner. As reasonable as this argument may seem, it is likely to fall on deaf ears when policy-makers and bureaucrats are juggling shrinking budgets and deciding on departmental priorities.

Vested interests in technical decisions

An even more fundamental political issue than the pressure for short-term success is the definition of success itself. Vested interests inevitably surround the criteria for success in programme evaluation. For example, policy-makers may consider it vital that a new drug prevention service produce a demonstrable reduction in regional health costs, while the programme providers may be more concerned about the quality of life of their immediate clients. As a result, the seemingly technical matter of selecting dependent variables becomes an inescapably political issue. The evaluator may try to escape the dilemma by accommodating multiple measures of success, but even this is a political decision with political consequences for the programme under investigation.

Client participation

If social programmes are truly designed for the people who use them, it seems only logical that client participation and client feedback should be intrinsic to the evaluation strategy. Clients should be involved in the technical decisions relating to outcome measures and in the ethical and practical considerations surrounding methodology. As well, client feedback will be valuable provided that clients

are given access to the same information as the evaluators themselves. The common practice of merely asking clients what they
thought of the intervention is known to produce unreliable results
unless the clients are provided with the objective data obtained by
the researchers (McCord, 1978). Without this information, subjective
satisfaction ratings tend to be artificially inflated. Knowing this,
evaluators' decisions about how much access clients should be
allowed to data also becomes a political issue.

Getting the report read and utilised

The bookshelves of government ministers and officials are crammed
with dust-covered reports from generations of programme evaluators. Many volumes remain unread and their recommendations
unimplemented. The ultimate fate of an evaluation may not, of
course, be under the researcher's control but there are ways of
writing the report which maximise its practical utility (see also
Posavac and Carey, 1985, ch. 12). For example, policy-makers are
rarely interested in the minutiae of statistical analysis, so forcing the
reader to wade through tables and tests before arriving at a conclusion can act as a disincentive to read and act on the report. It is
often better to confine technical details to an appendix and deal with
the substantive conclusions in a separate section of the report.
Releasing two reports, one for the general public and another for the
backroom boffins, can be another sensible compromise. But however
one goes about it, the general principle must be for the authors to
consider their readership if they expect their recommendations to be
acted on. In addition to the written document, programme evaluators advance their cause if they are able to promote a positive, non-
defensive attitude towards evaluation among programme staff and
policy-makers. Conclusions can be phrased tactfully and negative
findings dealt with constructively. Harsh, unequivocal generalisations
are rarely justified. After all, even the tightest laboratory experiment
should be replicated before acting on its implications. Finally, links
can be built between evaluators and policy-makers by representing
these parties on a steering committee overseeing the research.

Having explored the nature of the presenting problem in Chapter 1,
our approach to social work with addictions is brought to a close by

this chapter on evaluating our effectiveness. In between we developed a model for social work with addictions in Chapter 2 and we saw that an intervention plan capable of taking users right through the stages of change is a complex and exacting task. Chapter 3 dealt with precontemplation: the first of the stages of change. The primary focus at this point was on microsystem interventions because that is normally all the worker has to work with. The user is inaccessible. At the contemplation stage (Chapter 4), our attention shifted to the individual user and intervention at this point was directed at enhancing tentative moves towards change by helping the client weigh up the costs and benefits of the addiction. In Chapter 5 we looked at behavioural self-control strategies for individuals who decide that the time has come to act. As with the contemplation stage, then, the primary focus of intervention at the action stage remained the individual. When we came to the stubborn problem of maintenance in Chapter 6, we broadened our vision again and sought to intervene at multiple levels. Throughout all this work, the adage coined in Chapter 5 continually reemerged: drugs are not just a problem, they are also a solution. Drugs are an accessible and gratifyingly simple solution to pressures of various kinds and if the worker has nothing to offer in exchange, there is no incentive to change and no relief from the rigours of withdrawal. Lasting success requires that drug misusers be convinced that the benefits of change far outweigh the costs, and much of the art of drug prevention boils down to ensuring that this is how the arithmetic comes out when it is performed by users themselves.

References

Aaron, P. and Musto, D. (1981) 'Temperance and prohibition in America: a historical overview', in M. H. Moore and D. R. Gerstein (eds), *Alcohol and Public Policy: Beyond the Shadow of Prohibition*, Washington, DC, National Academy Press.

Addiction Research Foundation (1981) *A Strategy for the Prevention of Alcohol Problems*, Toronto, Addiction Research Foundation.

Alcoholics Anonymous (1939) *Alcoholics Anonymous*, New York, Works Publishing.

Alden, L. (1978) 'Evaluation of a preventive self-management programme for problem drinkers', *Canadian Journal of Behavioural Science*, vol. 10, pp. 258–63.

American Psychiatric Association, Work Group on Substance Use Disorders (1995) 'Practice guidelines for the treatment of patients with substance use disorders: alcohol, cocaine, opioids', *American Journal of Psychiatry*, vol. 152 (Suppl.), pp. 2–59.

Annis, H. M. (1986) 'Is inpatient rehabilitation of the alcoholic cost effective? Con position', *Advances in Alcohol and Substance Abuse*, vol. 5, pp. 175–90.

Annis, H. M. and Davis, C. S. (1986) 'Assessment of expectancies in alcohol dependent clients', in G. A. Marlatt and D. Donovan (eds), *Assessment of Addictive Behaviors*, New York, Guilford Press.

Annis, H. M. and Davis, C. S. (1988) 'Self-efficacy and the prevention of alcoholic relapse: initial findings from a treatment trial', in T. B. Baker and D. S. Cannon (eds), *Assessment and Treatment of Addictive Disorders*, New York, Praeger.

Annis, H. M. and Davis, C. S. (1989) 'Relapse prevention training: a cognitive-behavioral approach based on self-efficacy theory', *Journal of Chemical Dependency*, vol. 2, pp. 81–103.

Anonymous (1985) 'Media campaigns may be worse than a waste of money', *British Medical Journal*, vol. 290, p. 416.

Armor, D., Polich, J. and Stambul, H. (1978) *Alcoholism and Treatment*, New York, Wiley.

Astin, A. (1962) '"Bad habits" and social deviation: a proposed revision of conflict theory', *Journal of Clinical Psychology*, vol. 18, pp. 222–31.

Azrin, N. H. (1976) 'Improvements in the community reinforcement approach to alcoholism', *Behavior Research and Therapy*, vol. 14, pp. 339–48.

Azrin, N. H. and Besalel, V. A. (1980) *Job Club Counselor's Manual*, Baltimore, Md, University Park Press.

Azrin, N. H., Naster, B. J. and Jones, R. (1973) 'Reciprocity counseling: a rapid learning-based procedure for marital counseling', *Behavior Research and Therapy*, vol. 13, pp. 17–27.

Babor, T. F., Ritson, E. B. and Hodgson, R. J. (1986) 'Alcohol-related problems in the primary health care setting: a review of early intervention strategies', *British Journal of Addiction*, vol. 81, pp. 23–46.

Bandura, A. (1977) 'Self-efficacy: toward a unifying theory of behavior change', *Psychological Review*, vol. 84, pp. 191–215.

Bandura, A. (1982) 'Self-efficacy mechanism in human agency', *American Psychologist*, vol. 37, pp. 122–47.

Bandura, A. (1986) *Social Foundations of Thought and Action: A Social Cognitive Theory*, Englewood Cliffs, NJ, Prentice-Hall.

Bandura, A. (1998) 'Health promotion from the perspective of social cognitive theory', *Psychology and Health*, vol. 13, p. 4.

Barber, J. G. (1982) 'Unemployment and helplessness', *Australian Social Work*, vol. 35, pp. 3–10.

Barber, J. G. (1989) 'Microcomputer programs in the prevention of drug and alcohol problems', in B. F. Greyner and N. Solowij (eds), *Cognitive-Behavioural Approaches to the Treatment of Drug and Alcohol Problems*, Sydney, National Drug and Alcohol Research Centre.

Barber, J. G. (1990) 'Computer-assisted drug prevention', *Journal of Substance Abuse Treatment*, vol. 7, pp. 125–31.

Barber, J. G. (1991a) *Beyond Casework*, London, Macmillan.

Barber, J. G. (1991b) 'Microcomputers and prevention of drug abuse', *MD Computing*, vol. 8, pp. 150–5.

Barber, J. G. (1993) 'An application of microcomputer technology to the drug education of prisoners', *Journal of Alcohol and Drug Education*, vol. 38, pp. 14–22.

Barber, J. G. and Crisp, B. R. (1995a) 'Social support and prevention of relapse following treatment for alcohol abuse', *Research on Social Work Practice*, vol. 5, pp. 283–96.

Barber, J. G. and Crisp, B. R. (1995b) 'The Pressures to Change approach to working with the partners of heavy drinkers', *Addiction*, vol. 90, pp. 271–8.

Barber, J. G. and Gilbertson, R. (1996) 'An experimental investigation of a brief unilateral intervention for the partners of heavy drinkers', *Research on Social Work Practice*, vol. 6, pp. 325–36.

Barber, J. G. and Gilbertson, R. (1997) 'Unilateral interventions for women living with heavy drinkers', *Social Work*, vol. 42, pp. 69–78.

Barber, J. G. and Gilbertson, R. (1998) 'Evaluation of a self-help manual for the female partners of heavy drinkers', *Research on Social Work Practice*, vol. 8, pp. 141–51.

Barber, J. G., Bradshaw, R. and Walsh, C. (1989) 'Promoting controlled drinking through television advertising', *Journal of Consulting and Clinical Psychology*, vol. 57, pp. 613–18.

Barber, J. G., Cooper, B. K. and Heather, N. (1991) 'The situational confidence questionnaire (heroin)', *International Journal of the Addictions*, vol. 26, pp. 565–75.

Barber, J. G., Gilbertson, R. and Crisp, B. R. (1995) 'Promoting controlled drinking in a mother by intervening with her daughter', *Families in Society*, vol. 76, pp. 248–53.

Barber, J. G., Crisp, B. R., Ross, M. W., Wodak, A., Miller, M. E. and Gold, J. (1992) 'The social behaviour of injecting drug users', *British Journal of Social Work*, vol. 22, pp. 455–62.

Barlow, D. H. and Hersen, M. (1984) *Single Case Experimental Designs*, New York, Pergamon Press.

Barlow, D. H., Hayes, S. C. and Nelson, R. O. (1984) *The Scientist Practitioner: Research and Accountability in Clinical and Educational Settings*, New York, Pergamon Press.

Bartlett, H. M. (1970) *The Common Base of Social Work Practice*, Washington, DC, National Association of Social Workers.

Beaubrun, M. H. (1977) 'Epidemiological research in the Caribbean context', in B. Rutledge and E. K. Fulton (eds), *International Collaboration: Problems and Opportunities*, Toronto, Addiction Research Foundation.

Beck, A. T., Rush, A. J., Shaw, B. F. and Emery, G. (1979) *Cognitive Therapy for Depression*, New York, Guilford.

Begleiter, H., Porjesz, B., Bihari, B. and Kissin, B. (1984) 'Event-related brain potentials in boys at risk for alcoholism', *Science*, vol. 225, pp. 1493–6.

Benson, H. (1975) *The Relaxation Response*, New York, William Morrow.

Bigelow, G., Liebson, I. A. and Griffiths, R. (1974) 'Alcoholic drinking: suppression by a time-out procedure', *Behaviour Research and Therapy*, vol. 12, pp. 107–15.

Billings, A. G. and Moos, R. H. (1982) 'Work stress and the stress-buffering roles of work and family resources', *Journal of Occupational Behaviour*, vol. 3, pp. 215–32.

Billings, A. G. and Moos, R. H. (1983) 'Psychosocial processes of recovery among alcoholics and their families: implications for clinicians and program evaluator', *Addictive Behaviors*, vol. 8, pp. 205–18.

Billings, A. G., Kessler, M., Gomberg, C. A. and Weiner, S. (1979) 'Marital conflict resolution of alcoholic and nonalcoholic couples during drinking and nondrinking sessions', *Journal of Studies on Alcohol*, vol. 40, pp. 183–95.

Blum, K., Noble, E. P. and Sheridan, P. J. (1990) 'Allelic association of human domaine D_2 receptor gene in alcoholism', *Journal of the American Medical Association*, vol. 263, pp. 2055–60.

Boehm, W. (1958) 'The nature of social work', *Social Work*, vol. 3, pp. 10–19.

Brazier, C. (1984) 'Dealing with dreams', *New Internationalist*, vol. 140, pp. 7–11.

Bromet, E. and Moos, R. H. (1977) 'Environmental resources and the posttreatment functioning of alcoholic patients', *Journal of Health and Social Behavior*, vol. 18, pp. 326–35.

Bromet, E., Moos, R. H., Bliss, F. and Wuthmann, C. (1977) 'Posttreatment functioning of alcoholic patients: its relation to program participation', *Journal of Consulting and Clinical Psychology*, vol. 45, pp. 829–45.

Bronfenbrenner, U. (1979) *The Ecology of Human Development: Experiments by Nature and Design*, Cambridge, Mass., Harvard University Press.

Brown, R. A. (1980) 'Conventional education and controlled drinking education courses with convicted drunken drivers', *Behavior Therapy*, vol. 11, pp. 632–42.

Brown, R., Lichtenstein, E., McIntyre, K. and Harrington-Kostur, J. (1984) 'Effects of nicotine fading and relapse prevention in smoking cessation', *Journal of Consulting and Clinical Psychology*, vol. 52, pp. 307–8.

Brownell, K. D., Marlatt, G. A., Lichtenstein, E. and Wilson, G. T. (1986) 'Understanding and preventing relapse', *American Psychologist*, vol. 7, pp. 65–82.

Brownell, K., Heckerman, C., Westlake, R., Hayes, S. and Monti, P. (1978) 'The effect of couples training and partner cooperativeness in the behavioral treatment of obesity', *Behavior Research and Therapy*, vol. 16, pp. 323–33.

Caddy, G. R. and Lovibond, S. H. (1976) 'Self-regulation and discriminated aversive conditioning in the modification of alcoholics' drinking behavior', *Behavior Therapy*, vol. 7, pp. 223–30.

Campbell, D. T. and Stanley, J. C. (1963) *Experimental and Quasi-Experimental Designs for Research*, Boston, Mass., Houghton Mifflin.

Carkhuff, R. R. and Anthony, W. A. (1979) *The Skills of Helping: An Introduction to Counseling*, Amherst, Mass., Human Resource Development Press.

Carroll, K. M. (1998) 'Treating drug dependence: recent advances and old truths', in W. R. Miller and N. Heather (eds.), *Treating Addictive Behaviors*, 2nd edn, New York, Plenum Press.

Chafetz, M. E. (1961) 'A procedure for establishing therapeutic contact with the alcoholic', *Quarterly Journal of Studies on Alcohol*, vol. 22, pp. 325–8.

Chambliss, C. and Murray, E. J. (1979) 'Cognitive procedures for smoking reduction: symptom attribution versus efficacy attribution', *Cognitive Therapy and Research*, vol. 3, pp. 91–5.

Chaney, E. F. (1989) 'Social skills training', in R. K. Hester and W. R. Miller (eds), *Handbook of Alcoholism Treatment Approaches*, New York, Pergamon Press.

Chaney, E. F., O'Leary, M. R. and Marlatt, G. A. (1978) 'Skill training with alcoholics', *Journal of Consulting and Clinical Psychology*, vol. 46, pp. 1092–104.

Chess, S. B., Neuringer, C. and Goldstein, G. (1971) 'Arousal and field dependence in alcoholics', *Journal of General Psychiatry*, vol. 85, pp. 93–102.

Chick, J., Ritson, B., Connaughton, J., Stewart, A. and Chick, J. (1988) 'Advice versus treatment for alcoholism: a controlled trial', *British Journal of Alcoholism*, vol. 83, pp. 159–70.

Cinciripini, P. M., Lapitsky, L. G., Wallfisch, A., Mace, A., Nezami, E. and Van Vunakis, H. (1994) 'An evaluation of a multicomponent treatment program involving scheduled smoking and relapse prevention procedures: initial findings', *Addictive Behaviors*, vol. 19, pp. 13–22.

Clayton, R. R. (1989) 'Legalization: an idea whose time has not come', *American Behavioral Scientist*, vol. 32, pp. 316–32.

Cloninger, C. R. (1987) 'Neurogenetic adaptive mechanisms in alcoholism', *Science*, vol. 236, pp. 410–16.

Cloninger, C. R. (1991) 'D_2 dopamine receptor gene is associated but not linked with alcoholism', *Journal of the American Medical Association*, vol. 226, pp. 1833–4.

Cohen, S. and Lichtenstein, E. (1990) 'Partner behaviors that support quitting smoking', *Journal of Consulting and Clinical Psychology*, vol. 58, pp. 304–9.

Cohen, M., Liebson, I. A. and Faillace, L. A. (1972) 'A technique for establishing controlled drinking in chronic alcoholics', *Diseases of the Nervous System*, vol. 33, pp. 46–9.

Cohen, M., Liebson, I. A., Faillace, L. A. and Allen, R. P. (1971) 'Moderate drinking by chronic alcoholics', *Journal of Nervous and Mental Disease*, vol. 153, pp. 434–44.

Cohen, S., Lichtenstein, E., Mermelstein, R., Kingsolvers, K., Baer, J. S. and Kamarck, T. W. (1988) 'Social support interventions for smoking cessation', in B. H. Gottleib (ed.), *Marshaling Social Support*, Newbury Park, Calif., Sage.

Colby, S. M., Monti, P. M., Barnett, N. P., Rohsenow, D. J., Damaris, J., Weissman, K., Spirito, A., Woolard, R. H. and Lewander, W. J. (1998) 'Brief motivational interviewing in a hospital setting for adolescent smoking: a preliminary study', *Journal of Consulting and Clinical Psychology*, vol. 66, pp. 574–8.

Colletti, G. and Brownell, K. D. (1982) 'The role of social influence in the etiology and treatment of disease: application to obesity, smoking, and alcoholism', in M. Hersen, R. M. Eisler and P. M. Miller (eds), *Progress in Behavioral Modification*, New York, Academic Press.

Colletti, G. and Supnick, J. A. (1980) 'Continued therapist contact as a maintenance strategy for smoking reduction', *Journal of Consulting and Clinical Psychology*, vol. 48, pp. 665–7.

Compton, B. and Galaway, B. (1984) *Social Work Processes*, Homewood, Ill., Dorsey Press.

Condiotte, M. M. and Lichtenstein, E. (1981) 'Self-efficacy and relapse in smoking cessation programs', *Journal of Consulting and Clinical Psychology*, vol. 49, pp. 648–58.

Cook, D. R. (1985) 'Craftsman versus professional: analysis of the controlled drinking controversy', *Journal of Studies on Alcohol*, vol. 46, pp. 433–42.

Cook, P. J. (1981) 'The effect of liquor taxes on drinking, cirrhosis, and auto accidents', in M. H. Moore and D. R. Gerstein (eds), *Alcohol and Public Policy: Beyond the Shadow of Prohibition*, Washington, DC, National Academy Press.

Cook, T. D. and Campbell, D. T. (1979) *Quasi-Experimentation: Design and Analysis Issues* for *Field Settings*, Boston, Mass., Houghton Mifflin.

Copeland, J., Hall, W., Didcott, P. and Biggs, A. (1992) 'Evaluation of a specialist alcohol and other drug treatment for women: an overview', in J. White (ed.), *Drug Problems in Our Society: Dimensions and Perspectives*, Adelaide, SA, Drug and Alcohol Services Council.

Coppotelli, H. C. and Orleans, C. T. (1985) 'Spouse support for smoking cessation maintenance by women', *Journal of Consulting and Clinical Psychology*, vol. 53, pp. 455–60.

Costello, R. M. (1975) 'Alcoholism treatment and evaluation: in search of methods', *International Journal of the Addictions*, vol. 10, pp. 251–5.

Costello, R. M., Brier, P. and Baillargeon, J. G. (1977) 'Alcoholism treatment programming: historical trends and modern approaches', *Alcoholism: Clinical and Experimental Research*, vol. 1, pp. 311–18.

Crisp, B. R. and Barber, J. G. (1992) 'Drug education at Pentridge Prison: a consumer feedback study', unpublished manuscript.

Cronkite, R. C. and Moos, R. H. (1980) 'Determinants of posttreatment functioning of alcohol patients: a conceptual framework', *Journal of Consulting and Clinical Psychology*, vol. 48, pp. 305–6.

Culbertson, F. M. (1997) Depression and gender: An international review. *American Psychologist*, vol. 52, pp. 25–31.

Cummings, C., Gordon, J. R. and Marlatt, G. A. (1986) 'Relapse: prevention and prediction', in W. R. Miller (ed.), *The Addictive Behaviors*, New York, Pergamon Press.

Dahlgren, L. and Willander, A. (1989) Are special treatment facilities for female alcoholics needed? A controlled 2-year follow-up study from a specialized female unit (EWA) versus a mixed male/female treatment facility. *Alcoholism: Clinical and Experimental Research*, vol. 13, pp. 499–504.

Davidson, R. (1992) 'Prochaska and DiClemente's model of change: a case study?', *British Journal of Addiction*, vol. 87, pp. 821–2.

Davidson, R. (1998) 'The transtheoretical model: a critical overview', in W. R. Miller and N. Heather (eds.), *Treating Addictive Behaviors*, 2nd edn, New York: Plenum Press.

Davies, D. L. (1962) 'Normal drinking in recovered alcohol addicts', *Quarterly Journal of Studies on Alcohol*, vol. 24, pp. 321–32.

De La Cancela, V. (1985) 'Toward a sociocultural psychotherapy for low income ethnic minorities', *Psychotherapy*, vol. 22, pp. 427–33.

DiClemente, C. C. (1981) 'Self-efficacy and smoking cessation maintenance', *Cognitive Therapy and Research*, vol. 5, pp. 15–18.

DiClemente, C. C. and Prochaska, J. O. (1982) 'Self-change and therapy change of smoking behavior: a comparison of processes of change of cessation and maintenance', *Addictive Behavior*, vol. 7, pp. 133–42.

DiClemente, C. C. and Prochaska, J. O. (1998) 'Toward a comprehensive, transtheoretical model of change: stages of change and addictive behaviors', in W. R. Miller and N. Heather (eds), *Treating Addictive Behaviors*, 2nd edn, New York, Plenum Press.

DiClemente, C. C., Prochaska, J. O., Fairhurst, S. K., Velicer, W. F., Velasquez, M. M. and Rossi, J. S. (1991) 'The process of smoking cessation: an analysis of precontemplation, contemplation, and preparation stages of change', *Journal of Consulting and Clinical Psychology*, vol. 59, pp. 295–304.

Djukanovic, B., Milosavcevic, V. and Jovanovic, R. (1976) 'The social life of alcoholics and their wives', *Journal of Studies on Alcohol*, vol. 39, Abstract No. 1141.

Donovan, D. M., Rohsenow, D. J., Schau, E. J. and O'Leary, M. R. (1977) 'Defensive style in alcoholics and nonalcoholics', *Journal of Studies on Alcohol*, vol. 38, pp. 465–70.

Drummond, D. C. and Glautier, S. (1994) 'A controlled trial of cue exposure treatment in alcohol dependence', *Journal of Consulting and Clinical Psychology*, vol. 62, pp. 809–17.

Dubbert, P. M. and Wilson, G. T. (1984) 'Goal-setting and spouse involvement in the treatment of obesity', *Behavior Research and Therapy*, vol. 22, pp. 22–42.

D'Zurilla, T. J. and Goldfried, M. R. (1971) 'Problem solving and behavior modification', *Journal of Abnormal Psychology*, vol. 8, pp. 10–126.

Edwards, G. (1977) 'The Alcohol Dependence Syndrome: usefulness of an idea', in G. Edwards and M. Grant (eds), *Alcoholism: New Knowledge and New Responses*, London, Croom Helm.

Edwards, G. and Gross, M. (1976) 'Alcohol dependence: provisional description of a clinical syndrome', *British Medical Journal*, vol. 1, pp. 1058–61.

Edwards, G., Gross, M. M., Keller, M., Moser, J. and Room, R. (1977a) *Alcohol-Related Disabilities*, Copenhagen, WHO Offset Publication.

Edwards, G., Orford, J., Egert, S., Guthrie, S., Hawker, A., Hensman, C., Mitcheson, M., Oppenheimer, E. and Taylor, C. (1977b) 'Alcoholism: a controlled trial of "treatment" and "advice"', *Journal of Studies on Alcohol*, vol. 38, pp. 1004–31.

Egan, G. (1989) *The Skilled Helper*, Monterey, Calif., Brooks Cole.

Ellis, A., McInerney, J. F., DiGiuseppe, R. and Yeager, R. J. (1988) *Rational-Emotive Therapy with Alcoholics and Substance Abusers*, New York, Pergamon Press.

Eltringham, A. and Barber, J. G. (1990) 'Can microcomputers help the problem drinker?', *Drug and Alcohol Review*, vol. 9, pp. 169–76.

Emrick, C. D. (1974) A review of psychologically oriented treatment of alcoholism: I. The use and interrelationships of outcome criteria and drinking behavior following treatment, *Quarterly Journal of Studies on Alcohol*, vol. 35, pp. 523–49.

Emrick, C. D. and Hansen, J. (1983) Assertions regarding effectiveness of treatment for alcoholism: Fact or fantasy? *American Psychologist*, vol. 38, pp. 1078–88.

Fagerstrom, K. O. (1994) 'Combined use of nicotine replacement products', *Health Values*, vol. 18, pp. 15–20.

Fagerstrom, K. O., Schneider, N. G. and Lunell, E. (1993) 'Effectiveness of nicotine patch and nicotine gum as individual versus combined treatments for tobacco withdrawal symptoms', *Psychopharmacology*, vol. 111, pp. 271–7.

Farid, B., Sherini, M. E. and Raistrick, D. S. (1986) 'Cognitive group therapy for wives of alcoholics', *Drug and Alcohol Dependence*, vol. 4, pp. 349–58.

Farquhar, J. W. *et al.* (1977) 'Community education for cardiovascular health', *Lancet*, June, pp. 1192–5.

Farrell, S. (1985) *Review of National Policy Measures to Prevent Alcohol-Related Problems*, Geneva, World Health Organisation.

Farren, C. K. and Tipton, K. F. (1999) 'Trait markers for alcoholism: clinical utility', *Alcohol and Alcoholism*, vol. 34, pp. 649–65.

Festinger, L. (1964) *Conflict, Decision and Dissonance*, Stanford, Calif., Stanford University Press.

Finestone, H. (1964) 'Cats, kicks and color', in H. Becker (ed.), *The Other Side*, New York, Free Press.

Finkelstein, N. (1994) 'Treatment issues for alcohol- and drug-dependent pregnant and parenting women', *Health Social Work*, vol. 19, pp. 7–15.

Finney, J. W. and Monahan, S. C. (1996) 'The cost-effectiveness of treatment for alcoholism: a second approximation', *Journal of Studies on Alcohol*, vol. 57, pp. 229–43.

Finney, J. W. and Moos, R. H. (1981) 'Characteristics and prognoses of alcoholics who became moderate drinkers and abstainers after treatment', *Journal of Studies on Alcohol*, vol. 42, pp. 94–105.

Fiore, M. C., Smith, S. S., Jorenby, D. E. and Baker, T. B. (1994) 'The effectiveness of the nicotine patch for smoking cessation: a meta-analysis', *Journal of the American Medical Association*, vol. 271, pp. 1940–7.

Fleming, M. E., Barry, K. L., Manwell, L. B., Johnson, K. and London, R. (1997) 'Brief physician advice for problem alcohol drinkers: a randomized controlled trial in community-based care'. *Journal of the American Medical Association*, vol. 277, pp. 1039–45.

Forcier, M. W., Kurtz, N. R., Parent, D. G. and Corrigan, M. D. (1986) 'Deterrence of drunk driving in Massachusetts: criminal justice system impacts', *International Journal of the Addictions*, vol. 21, pp. 119–22.

Foroud, T. and Li, T. K. (1999) 'Genetics of alcoholism: a review of recent studies in human and animal models', *American Journal of Addictions*, vol. 8, pp. 261–78.

Forsyth, D. and Schlenker, B. (1977) 'Attributing the causes of group performance: effects of performance quality, task importance and future testing', *Journal of Personality*, vol. 45, pp. 220–36.

Foy, D. W., Nunn, B. L. and Rychtarick, R. G. (1984) 'Broad spectrum behavioral treatment for chronic alcoholics: effects of training controlled drinking skills', *Journal of Consulting and Clinical Psychology*, vol. 52, pp. 218–30.

Franken, I. H. A., de Haan, H. A., van der Meer, C. W., Haffmans, P. M. J. and Hendricks, V. M. (1999) 'Cue reactivity and effects of cue exposure in abstinent drug users', *Journal of Substance Abuse Treatment*, vol. 16, pp. 81–5.

Fraser, M. and Kohlert, N. (1988) 'Substance abuse and public policy', *Social Service Review*, March, pp. 103–26.

George, W. (1989) 'Marlatt and Gordon's relapse prevention model: a cognitive-behavioral approach to understanding and preventing relapse', *Journal of Chemical Dependence Treatment*, vol. 2, pp. 125–52.

Germain, C. B. and Gitterman, A. (1980) *The Life Model of Social Work Practice*, New York, Columbia University Press.

Goldfried, M. R. and Davison, G. C. (1976) *Clinical Behavior Therapy*, New York, Holt, Rinehart & Winston.

Goldfried, M. R. and Robins, C. (1982) 'On the facilitation of self-efficacy', *Cognitive Therapy and Research*, vol. 6, pp. 361–80.

Goldstein, A. (1994) *Addiction: From Biology to Drug Policy*, New York, Freeman.

Goldstein, H. (1973) *Social Work Practice: a Unitary Approach*, Columbia, University of South Carolina Press.

Goodwin, D. W., Schulsinger, F. and Hermansen, L. (1973) 'Alcohol problems in adoptees raised apart from alcoholic biological parents', *Archives of General Psychiatry*, vol. 28, pp. 238–43.

Gormally, J., Rardin, D. and Black, S. (1980) 'Correlates of successful response to a behavioral weight control clinic', *Journal of Counseling Psychology*, vol. 27, pp. 179–91.

Gorwood, P., Batel, P., Gouya, L., Courtois, F., Feingold, J. and Ades, J. (2000) 'Reappraisal of the association between the DRD2 gene, alcoholism and addiction', *European Psychiatry*, vol. 15, pp. 90–6.

Grabowski, J. (1986) 'Acquisition, maintenance, cessation and reacquisition: an overview and behavioral perspective of relapse to tobacco use', in F. Tims and C. Leukefeld (eds), *Relapse and Recovery in Drug Abuse*, National Institute on Drug Abuse Research Monograph 72, Rockville, Maryland, Department of Health and Human Services.

Greenwald, A. F. and Bartmeier, L. H. (1963) 'Psychiatric discharges against medical advice', *Archives of General Psychiatry*, vol. 8, pp. 117–19.

Grichting, W. L. and Barber, J. G. (1986) *The Drug Offensive at Work in North Queensland*, Townsville, James Cook University Press.

Grichting, W. L. and Barber, J. G. (1988) 'Fighting drug abuse in Australia', *International Journal of the Addictions*, vol. 23, pp. 491–507.

Griffin, M. L., Weiss, R. D., Mirin, S. M. and Lange, U. (1989) 'A comparison of male and female cocaine abusers', *Archives of General Psychiatry*, vol. 46, pp. 122–6.

Haaga, D. A. F. and Stewart, B. L. (1992) 'Self-efficacy for recovery from a lapse after smoking cessation', *Journal of Consulting and Clinical Psychology*, vol. 60, pp. 24–8.

Hajek, P. (1996) 'Current issues in behavioral and pharmacological approaches to smoking cessation', *Addictive Behaviors*, vol. 21, pp. 699–707.

Hall, W. (1999) 'Patient matching treatment for alcohol dependence: is the null hypothesis still alive and well?', *Addiction*, vol. 94, pp. 52–4.

Hamburg, S. (1975) 'Behavior therapy in alcoholism: a critical review of broad-spectrum approaches', *Journal of Studies on Alcohol*, vol. 36, pp. 69–87.

Hamilton, S. B. and Bornstein, P. H. (1976) Broad-spectrum behavioral approach to smoking cessation: effects of social support and paraprofessional training on the maintenance of treatment effects', *Journal of Consulting and Clinical Psychology*, vol. 4, pp. 598–600.

Handmaker, N. S., Miller, W. R. and Manicke, M. (1999) 'Findings of a pilot study of motivational interviewing with pregnant drinkers', *Journal of Studies on Alcohol*, vol. 60, pp. 285–7.

Hansen, A. (1985) 'Will the government's mass media campaign on drugs work?', *British Medical Journal*, vol. 290, pp. 1054–5.

Harper, R. and Hardy, S. (2000) 'An evaluation of motivational interviewing as a method of intervention with clients in a probation setting', *British Journal of Social Work*, vol. 30, pp. 393–400.

Hartman, A. (1970) 'To think about the unthinkable', *Social Casework*, vol. 51, pp. 467–74.

Heather, N. (1986) 'Change without therapists: the use of self-help manuals by problem drinkers', in W. R. Miller and N. Heather (eds), *Treating Addictive Behaviors: Processes of Change*, New York, Plenum Press.

Heather, N. (1987) 'DRAMS for problem-drinkers: the potential of a brief intervention by general practitioners and some evidence of its effectiveness', in T. Stockwell and S. Clement (eds), *Helping the Problem Drinker: New Initiatives in Community Care*, London, Croom Helm.

Heather, N. (1989) 'Brief intervention strategies', in R. K. Hester and W. R. Miller (eds), *Handbook of Alcoholism Treatment Approaches: Effective Alternatives*, New York, Pergamon Press.

Heather, N. (1992) 'Addictive disorders are essentially motivational problems', *British Journal of Addiction*, vol. 8, pp. 825–35.

Heather, N. and Robertson, I. (1983) *Controlled Drinking*, London, Methuen.

Heather, N. and Robertson, I. (1985) *Problem Drinking: The New Approach*, Harmondsworth, Middlesex, Penguin.

Heather, N., Robertson, I., MacPherson, B., Allsop, S. *et al.* (1987) Effectiveness of a controlled drinking self-help manual: One-year follow-up results. *British Journal of Clinical Psychology*, vol. 26, pp. 279–87.

Heather, N. and Tebbutt, J. (1990) *The Effectiveness of Treatment for Drug and Alcohol Problems*, National Campaign Against Drug Abuse Monograph No. 11, Canberra, Australian Government Publishing Service.

Heather, N., Gold, R. and Rollnick, S. (1991) *Readiness to Change Questionnaire: User Manual*, Sydney, National Drug and Alcohol Research Centre.

Heather, N., Tebbutt, J. and Greeley, J. (1993) 'Alcohol cue exposure directed at a goal of moderate drinking'. *Journal of Behaviour Therapy and Experimental Psychiatry*, vol. 24, pp. 187–95.

Heather, N., Whitton, B. and Robertson, I. (1986) 'Evaluation of a self-help manual for media recruited problem drinkers: six month follow-up results', *British Journal of Clinical Psychology*, vol. 25, pp. 19–34.

Heather, N., Brodie, J., Wale, S., Wilkinson, G., Luce, A., Webb, E. and McCarthy, S. (2000) 'A randomized controlled trial of moderation-oriented cue exposure', *Journal of Studies on Alcohol*, vol. 61, pp. 561–70.

Hedberg, A. G. and Campbell, L. M. (1974) 'A comparison of four behavioral treatment approaches to alcoholism', *Journal of Behavior Therapy and Experimental Psychology*, vol. 5, pp. 251–6.

Heilizer, F. (1964) 'Conflict models, alcohol, and drinking patterns', *Journal of Psychology*, vol. 57, pp. 43–5.

Hepple, J. and Robson, P. (1996) 'The effect of caffeine on cue exposure responses in ex-smokers', *Addiction*, vol. 91, pp. 269–73.

Herman, J. L., Morris, J. L. and Fitz-Gibbon, C. T. (1987) *The Program Evaluation Kit*, Vols 1–9, Newbury Park, Calif., Sage.

Hester, R. K. and Miller, W. R. (1989) 'Self-control training', in R. K. Hester and W. R. Miller (eds), *Handbook of Alcoholism Treatment Approaches*, New York, Pergamon Press.

Hill, S. Y. (1998) 'Alternative strategies for uncovering genes, contributing to alcoholism: unpredictable findings in a genetic wonderland', *Alcohol*, vol. 16, pp. 53–9.

Horgen, K. B. and Brownell, K. D. (1998) 'Policy change as a means for reducing the prevalence and impact of alcoholism, smoking, and obesity', in W. R. Miller and N. Heather (eds), *Treating Addictive Behaviors*, 2nd edn, New York, Plenum Press.

Horn, D. (1972) 'Determinants of change', in G. Richardson (ed.), *The Second World Conference on Smoking and Health*, London, Pitman Medical.

Horn, J. L., Wanberg, K. W. and Foster, F. M. (1987) *The Alcohol Use Inventory*, Minneapolis, Minn., National Computer Systems.

Hubbard, R. and Marsden, M. (1986) 'Relapse to use of heroin, cocaine and other drugs in the first year after treatment', *NIDA Research Monograph*, vol. 2, pp. 15–166.

Hunt, G. M. and Azrin, N. H. (1973) 'A community-reinforcement approach to alcoholism', *Behavior Research and Therapy*, vol. 11, pp. 91–104.

Israel, Y., Hollander, O., Sanchez-Craig, M., Booker, S., Mitifir, V., Gingrich, F. L. and Rankin, J. G. (1996) 'Screening for problem drinking and counseling by the primary care physician–nurse team', *Alcoholism: Clinical and Experimental Research*, vol. 20, pp. 1443–50.

Ivey, A. E. (1983) *Intentional Interviewing and Counseling*, Monterey, Calif., Brooks Cole.

Jackson, P. and Oei, T. P. S. (1978) 'Social skills training and cognitive restructuring with alcoholics', *Drug and Alcohol Dependence*, vol. 3, pp. 369–74.

Jacobson, G. A. (1989) 'A comprehensive approach to pretreatment evaluation: I. Detection, assessment and diagnosis of alcoholism', in R. K. Hester and W. R. Miller (eds), *Handbook of Alcoholism Treatment Approaches: Effective Alternatives*, New York, Pergamon Press.

Janchill, M. P. (1969) 'Systems concepts in casework theory and practice', *Social Casework*, vol. 50, pp. 740–82.

Janis, I. L. (1959) 'Decisional conflicts: a theoretical analysis', *Journal of Conflict Resolution*, vol. 3, pp. 6–27.

Janis, I. L. (1983) 'The role of social support in adherence to stressful decisions', *American Psychologist*, vol. 38, pp. 143–60.

Janis, I. L. and Hoffman, D. (1970) 'Facilitating effects of daily contact between partners who make decisions to cut down on smoking', *Journal of Personality and Social Psychology*, vol. 1, pp. 25–35.

Janis, I. L. and Mann, L. (1968) 'A conflict theory approach to attitude change and decision making', in A. Greenwald, T. Brock and T. Ostrom (eds), *Psychological Foundations of Attitudes*, New York, Academic Press.

Janis, I. L. and Mann, L. (1977) *Decision Making: A Psychological Analysis of Conflict, Choice and Commitment*, New York, Free Press.

Janis, I. L. and Rodin, J. (1979) 'Attribution, control and decision-making: social psychology and health care', in G. Stone, F. Cohen and N. Adler (eds), *Health Psychology: A Handbook: Theories, Applications and Challenges of a Psychological Approach to the Health Care System*, San Francisco, Jossey-Bass.

Jansen, A. (1998) 'A learning model of binge eating: cue reactivity and cue exposure', *Behaviour Research and Therapy*, vol. 36, pp. 257–72.

Jellinek, E. M. (1952) 'Phases of alcohol addiction', *Quarterly Journal of Studies on Alcohol*, vol. 7, pp. 1–88.

Jellinek, E. M. (1960) *The Disease Concert of Alcoholism*, New Haven, Conn., Hillhouse Press.

Johnson, V. E. (1973) *I'll Quit Tomorrow*, New York, Harper.

Johnson, V. E. (1986) *Intervention: How to Help Those Who Don't Want Help*, Minneapolis, Minn., Johnson Institute.

Jonah, B. A. and Wilson, R. J. (1983) 'Improving the effectiveness of drink-driving enforcement through increased efficiency', *Accident Analysis and Prevention*, vol. 15, pp. 463–81.

Jones, A. C. (1985) 'Psychological functioning in blacks', *Psychotherapy*, vol. 22, pp. 362–9.

Jones, E. E. and Nisbett, R. F. (1971) *The Actor and Observers: Divergent Perceptions of the Causes of Behavior*, New York, General Learning Press.

Julien, R. M. (2000) *A Primer of Drug Action*, 9th edn, Houndmills, Palgrave.

Jurd, S. M. (1992) 'Why alcoholism is a disease', *Medical Journal of Australia*, vol. 156, pp. 215–17.

Kalin, R., McClelland, D. and Kahn, M. (1965) 'The effects of male social drinking on fantasy', *Journal of Personality and Social Psychology*, vol. 1, pp. 441–52.

Kanfer, F. H. (1979) 'Self-management: strategies and tactics', in A. P. Goldstein and F. H. Kanfer (eds), *Maximizing Treatment Gains: Transfer Enhancement in Psychotherapy*, New York, Academic Press.

Kanfer, F. H. (1988) 'Implications of a self-regulation model of therapy for treatment of addictive behaviors', in W. R. Miller and N. Heather (eds), *Treating Addictive Behaviors: Processes of Change*, New York, Plenum Press.

Kanfer, F. H. and Grimm, L. G. (1980) 'Managing clinical change: a process model of therapy', *Behavior Modification*, vol. 4, pp. 419–44.

Karpman, S. (1968) 'Fairy tales and script drama analysis', *Transactional Analysis Bulletin*, vol. 7, pp. 39–43.

Kendell, R. E. (1983) 'Effect of economic changes on Scottish drinking habits, 1978–1982', *British Journal of Addiction*, vol. 9, pp. 319–25.

Kidder, L. H. (1981) *Research Methods in Social Relations*, New York, Holt, Rinehart & Winston.

Killen, J. D., Maccoby, N. and Taylor, C. B. (1984) 'Nicotine gum and self-regulation training in smoking relapse prevention', *Behavior Therapy*, vol. 15, pp. 234–48.

Kissin, B., Platz, A. and Su, W. H. (1971) 'Selective factors in treatment choice and outcome in alcoholics', in N. K. Mello and J. H. Mendelson (eds), *Recent Advances in Studies on Alcoholism*, Washington, DC, US Government Printing Office.

Kristenson, H. (1983) *Studies on Alcohol Related Disabilities in a Medical Intervention*, 2nd edn, Malmo, Sweden, University of Lund.

Kristenson, H., Ohlin, H., Hulten-Nosslin, M., Trell, E. and Hood, B. (1983) 'Identification and intervention of heavy drinking in middle-aged men: results and follow-up of 24:60 months of long-term study with randomized controls', *Journal of Alcoholism: Clinical and Experimental Research*, vol. 20, pp. 203–9.

Krivanek, J. A. (1982) *Drug Problems, People Problems: Causes, Treatment and Prevention*, Sydney, Allen & Unwin.

Krivanek, J. A. (1988) *Addictions*, Sydney, Allen & Unwin.

Layden, M. A. (1982) 'Attributional style therapy', in C. Antaki and C. Brewin (eds), *Attributions and Psychological Change*, London, Academic Press.

Leake, G. J. and King, A. S. (1977) 'Effect of counselor expectations on alcoholic recovery', *Alcohol Health and Research World*, vol. 1, pp. 16–22.

Lee, M., Lee, S. and Kwak, D. I. (1997) 'No association between the dopamine D-sub-2 receptor gene and Korean alcoholism', *Psychiatric Genetics*, vol. 7, pp. 93–5.

Lennings, C. J. (2000) 'Harm minimisation or abstinence: an evaluation of current policies and practices in the treatment and control of intravenous drug using groups in Australia', *Disability and Rehabilitation: An International Multidisciplinary Journal*, vol. 22, pp. 57–64.

Leu, R. E. (1975) 'What can economists contribute?', in M. Grant (ed.), *Economics and Alcohol: Consumption and Controls*, London, Croom Helm.

Levine, H. G. (1978) 'The discovery of addiction: changing conceptions of habitual drunkenness in America', *Journal of Studies on Alcohol*, vol. 39, pp. 143–74.

Lewit, E. M. and Coate, D. (1983) 'The potential for using excise taxes to reduce smoking', *Journal of Health Economics*, vol. 1, pp. 121–45.

Lichtenstein, E. (1982) 'The smoking problem: a behavioral perspective', *Journal of Consulting and Clinical Psychology*, vol. 50, pp. 804–19.

Lichtenstein, E., Glasgow, R. E. and Abrams, D. (1986) 'Social support in smoking cessation: in search of effective interventions', *Behavior Therapy*, vol. 1, pp. 607–19.

Lieberman, M. A., Yalom, I. D. and Miles, M. B. (1973) *Encounter Groups: First Facts*, New York, Basic Books.

Lu, R. B., Ko, H. C., Chang, F. M., Castiglione, C. M. *et al.* (1996) 'No association between alcoholism and multiple polymorphisms at the dopamine D2 receptor gene (DRD2) in three distinct Taiwanese populations', *Biological Psychiatry*, vol. 39, pp. 419–29.

McAllister, I., Moore, R. and Makkai, T. (1991) *Drugs in Australian Society: Patterns, Attitudes and Policies*, Melbourne, Longman Cheshire.

MacAndrew, C. and Edgerton, R. B. (1969) *Drunken Comportment: A Social Explanation*, Chicago, Ill., Aldine.

McClearn, G. (1981) 'Genetic studies in animals', *Alcoholism: Clinical and Experimental Research*, vol. 5, pp. 447–8.

Maccoby, N. and Alexander, J. (1980) 'Use of media in lifestyle programs', in P. O. Davidson and S. M. Davidson (eds), *Behavioral Medicine: Changing Health Lifestyles*, New York, Brunner/Mazel.

Maccoby, N., Farquhar, J. W., Wood, P. and Alexander, J. K. (1977) 'Reducing the risk of cardiovascular disease: effects of a community based campaign on knowledge and behavior', *Journal of Community Health*, vol. 3, pp. 100–14.

McConnaughy, E. A., Prochaska, J. O. and Velicer, C. C. (1983) 'Stages of change in psychotherapy: measurement and sample profiles', *Psychotherapy: Theory, Research and Practice*, vol. 20, pp. 368–75.

McCord, J. (1978) 'A thirty-year followup of treatment effects', *American Psychologist*, vol. 33, pp. 284–9.

McCrady, B. S. (1988) 'The family in the change process', in W. R. Miller and N. Heather (eds), *Treating Addictive Behaviors: Processes of Change*, New York, Plenum Press.

McCrady, B. S., Noel, N. E., Abrams, D. B., Stout, R. L., Nelson, H. F. and Hay, W. M. (1986) 'Comparative effectiveness of three types of spouse involvement in outpatient behavioral alcoholism treatment', *Journal of Studies on Alcohol*, vol. 47, pp. 459–67.

MacDonald, J. G. (1987) 'Predictors of treatment outcome for alcoholic women', *International Journal of the Addictions*, vol. 22, pp. 235–48.

MacDonald, L. (1965) '"Physchopathology" of narcotics addiction: a new point of view', in E. Harmes (ed.), *Drug Addiction in Youth*, New York, Pergamon Press.

McIntyre, K. O., Lichtenstein, E. and Mermelstein, R. J. (1983) 'Self-efficacy and relapse in smoking cessation: a replication and extension', *Journal of Consulting and Clinical Psychology*, vol. 51, pp. 632–3.

McIntyre-Kingsolver, K., Lichtenstein, E. and Mermelstein, R. J. (1986) 'Spouse training in a multicomponent smoking cessation program', *Behavior Therapy*, vol. 17, pp. 67–74.

Mackay, P. W., Donovan, D. M. and Marlatt, G. A. (1991) 'Cognitive behavioral approaches to alcohol abuse', in R. J. Frances and S. I. Miller (eds), *Clinical Textbook of Addictive Disorders*, New York, Guilford Press.

MacKinnon, D. P. and Woodward, J. A. (1986) 'The impact of raising the minimum drinking age on driver fatalities', *International Journal of the Addictions*, vol. 21, pp. 1331–8.

McLellan, A. T., Arndt, I. O., Metzger, D. S., Woody, G. E. and O'Brien, C. P. (1993) 'The effects of psychosocial services in substance abuse treatment', *Journal of the American Medical Association*, vol. 269, pp. 1953–9.

Mahoney, M. J. (1974) 'Self-reward and self-monitoring techniques for weight control', *Behavior Therapy*, vol. 5, pp. 48–57.

Manson, M. P. and Lerner, A. (1962) *The Marriage Adjustment Inventory*, Los Angeles, Western Psychological Services.

Marlatt, G. A. and Gordon, J. R. (1980) 'Determinants of relapse: implications for the maintenance of behavioral change', in P. Davidson and S. Davidson (eds), *Behavioral Medicine: Changing Health Lifestyles*, New York, Brunner/Mazel.

Marlatt, G. A. and Gordon, J. (eds) (1985) *Relapse Prevention: Maintenance Strategies in the Treatment of Addictive Behaviors*, New York, Guilford Press.

Marlatt, G., Demming, B. and Reid, J. (1973) 'Loss of control drinking in alcoholics: an experimental analogue', *Journal of Abnormal Psychology*, vol. 81, pp. 233–41.

Marlott, J. M. Glasgow, R. E., O'Neil, H. K. and Klesges, R. C. (1984) 'Co-worker social support in a worksite smoking control program', *Journal of Applied Behavior Analysis*, vol. 1, pp. 485–95.

Marsh, J. and Miller, N. (1985) 'Female clients in substance abuse treatment', *International Journal of the Addictions*, vol. 20, pp. 995–1019.

Martino, S., Carroll, K. M., O'Malley, S. S and Rounsaville, B. J. (2000) 'Motivational interviewing with psychiatrically ill substance abusing patients', *American Journal on Addictions*, vol. 9, pp. 88–91.

Mattick, R. P. and Jarvis, T. J. (eds) (1992) *An Outline for the Management of Alcohol Problems: Quality Assurance Project*, Sydney, National Drug Abuse Research Centre.

Mattick, R. P., Bell, J., Daws, L. C., White, J. M. *et al.* (1997) *Review of the Evidence on the Effectiveness of Antagonists in Managing Opioid Dependence*, University of New South Wales, Sydney, National Drug and Alcohol Research Centre.

Mello, N. and Mendelson, J. (1978) 'Behavioral pharmacology of alcohol, heroin and marijuana use', in J. Fishman (ed.), *The Bases of Addiction*, Berlin, Dahlem Konferenzen.

Mermelstein, R. J., Cohen, S., Lichtenstein, E., Baer, J. and Kamarck, T. (1986) 'Social support and smoking cessation and maintenance', *Journal of Consulting and Clinical Psychology*, vol. 54, pp. 444–53.

Merton, R. K. (1957) *Social Theory and Social Structure*, Glencoe, Ill., Free Press.

Meyer, A. J., Nash, J. D., McAlister, A. L., Maccoby, N. and Farquhar, J. W. (1980) 'Skills training in a cardiovascular health education', *Journal of Consulting and Clinical Psychology*, vol. 48, pp. 129–42.

Miller, B. (1989) 'A licensing forum', in D. Robinson, P. Tether and J. Teller (eds) (1989) *Local Action of Alcohol Problems*, London, Routledge.

Miller, P. M., Hersen, M., Eisler, R. M. and Watts, J. G. (1974) 'Contingent reinforcement of lowered blood/alcohol levels in an outpatient chronic alcoholic', *Behaviour Research and Therapy*, vol. 12, pp. 261–3.

Miller, W. R. (1977) 'Behavioral self-control training in the treatment of problem drinkers', in R. B. Stuart (ed.), *Behavioral Self-Management: Strategies, Techniques and Outcomes*, New York, Bruner/Mazel.

Miller, W. R. (1978) 'Behavioural treatment of problem drinkers: a comparative outcome study of three controlled drinking therapies', *Journal of Consulting and Clinical Psychology*, vol. 46, pp. 74–86.

Miller, W. R. (1982) 'The effectiveness of treatment for substance abuse', *Journal of Substance Abuse Treatment*, vol. 9, pp. 93–102.

Miller, W. R. (1983) 'Motivational interviewing with problem drinkers', *Behavioral Psychotherapy*, vol. 11, pp. 147–72.

Miller, W. R. (1985) 'Motivation for treatment: a review with special emphasis on alcoholism', *Psychological Bulletin*, vol. 98, pp. 84–107.

Miller, W. R. (1987) 'The treatment of alcohol problems: what works?', unpublished manuscript.

Miller, W. R. (1989) 'Increasing motivation for change', in R. K. Hester and W. R. Miller (eds), *Handbook of Alcoholism Treatment Approaches: Effective Alternatives*, Elmsford, NY: Pergamon Press.

Miller, W. R. (1991) 'What motivates people to change?', in W. R. Miller and S. Rollnick (eds), *Motivational Interviewing: Preparing People to Change Addictive Behavior*, New York, Guilford Press.

Miller, W. R. (1993) 'The evolution of treatment for alcohol problems: from the 1940s to the 1980s', in Addiction Research Foundation, *The 40th Anniversary Lecture Series*, Toronto, Addiction Research Foundation.

Miller, W. R. (1998) 'Enhancing motivation for change', in W. R. Miller and N. Heather (eds), *Treating Addictive Behaviors*, 2nd edn, New York, Plenum Press.

Miller, W. R. and Heather, N. (1988) (eds) *Treating Addictive Behaviors: Processes of Change*, New York, Plenum Press.

Miller, W. R. and Hester, R. K. (1986) 'Treating the problem drinker: modern approaches', in W. R. Miller (ed.), *The Addictive Behaviors*, New York, Pergamon Press.

Miller, W. R. and Hester, R. K. (1988) 'Matching problem drinkers to optimal treatments', in W. R. Miller and N. Heather (eds), *Treating Addictive Behaviors: Processes of Change*, New York, Plenum Press.

Miller, W. R. and Marlatt, G. A. (1987) *Comprehensive Drinker Profile Manual Supplement*, Odessa, Fla, Psychological Assessment Resources.

Miller, W. R. and Meyers, R. J. (1999) 'The community-reinforcement approach', *Alcohol Research and Health*, vol. 23, pp. 116–21.

Miller, W. R. and Munoz, R. F. (1976) *How to Control Your Drinking*, Englewood Cliffs, NJ, Prentice-Hall.

Miller, W. R. and Rollnick, S. (eds) (1991) *Motivational Interviewing: Preparing People to Change Addictive Behavior*, New York, Guilford Press.

Miller, W. R. and Taylor, C. A. (1980) 'Relative effectiveness of bibliotherapy, individual and group self-control training in the treatment of problem drinkers', *Addictive Behaviors*, vol. 15, pp. 13–24.

Miller, W. R., Gribskov, C. J. and Mortell, R. L. (1981a) 'Effectiveness of a self-control manual with and without therapist contact', *International Journal of the Addictions*, vol. 16, pp. 1247–54.

Miller, W. R., Meyers, R. J. and Tonigan, J. S. (1999) 'Engaging the unmotivated in treatment for alcohol problems: a comparison of three strategies for intervention through family members', *Journal of Consulting and Clinical Psychology*, vol. 67, pp. 688–97.

Miller, W. R., Pechacek, R. F. and Hamburg, S. (1981b) 'Group behaviour therapy for problem drinkers', *International Journal of the Addictions*, vol. 16, pp. 827–37.

Miller, W. R., Sovereign, R. G. and Krege, B. (1988) 'Motivational interviewing with problem drinkers: II. The Drinker's Check-up as a preventive intervention', *Behavioural Psychotherapy*, vol. 16, pp. 251–68.

Miller, W. R., Taylor, C. A. and West, J. C. (1980) 'Focused versus broad-spectrum behavior therapy for problem drinkers', *Journal of Consulting and Clinical Psychology*, vol. 48, pp. 590–601.

Miller, W. R., Andrews, N. R., Wilbourne, P. and Bennett, M. E. (1998) 'A wealth of alternatives: effective treatments for alcohol problems', in W. R. Miller and N. Heather (eds), *Treating Addictive Behaviors*, 2nd edn, New York, Plenum Press.

Miller, W. R., Brown, J. M., Simpson, T. L., Handmaker, N. S., Bien, T. H., Luckie, L. F., Montgomery, H. A., Hester, R. K. and Tonigan, J. S. (1995) 'What works? A methodological analysis of the alcohol treatment outcome literature', in R. K. Hester and W. R. Miller (eds), *Handbook of Alcoholism Treatment Approaches: Effective Alternatives*, 2nd edn, Boston, Mass., Allyn & Bacon.

Milmoe, S., Rosenthal, R., Blane, H. T., Chafetz, M. E. and Wolf, I. (1967) 'The doctor's voice: postdictor of successful referral of alcoholic patients', *Journal of Abnormal Psychology*, vol. 72, pp. 78–84.

Monti, P. M., Abrams, D. B., Kadden, R. M. and Cooney, N. L. (1989) *Treating Alcohol Dependence: A Coping Skills Guide*, New York, Guilford Press.

Monti, P. M., Rohsenow, D. J., Rubonis, A. V., Niaura, R. S., Sirota, A. D., Colby, S. M., Goddard, P. and Abrams, D. B. (1993) 'Cue exposure with coping skills treatment for male alcoholics: a preliminary investigation', *Journal of Consulting and Clinical Psychology*, vol. 61, pp. 1011–19.

Moore, M. H. and Gerstein, D. R. (1981) 'Regulating the supply of alcoholic beverages', in M. H. Moore and D. R. Gerstein (eds), *Alcohol and Public Policy: Beyond the Shadow of Prohibition*, Washington, DC, National Academy Press.

Moos, R. H. and Billings, A. G. (1983) 'Conceptualizing and measuring coping resources and processes', in L. Goldberg and S. Breznitz (eds), *Handbook of Stress: Theoretical and Clinical Aspects*, New York, Macmillan.

Moos, R. H., Finney, J. W. and Gamble, W. (1982) 'The process of recovery from alcoholism: II. Comparing spouses of alcoholic patients and spouses of matched community controls', *Journal of Studies on Alcohol*, vol. 43, pp. 888–909.

Moras K. (1998) 'Behavioral therapies for female drug users: an efficacy-focused review', in C. L. Wetherington and A. B. Roman (eds), *Drug Addiction Research and the Health of Women*, Rockville, Md, National Institute on Drug Abuse.

Morgan, P. (1988) 'Power, politics and public health: the political power of the alcohol beverage industry', *Journal of Public Health Policy*, vol. 9, pp. 177–97.

Murphy, J. K., Williamson, D. A., Buxton, A. E., Moody, S. C., Absher, N. and Warner, M. (1982) 'The long-term effects of spouse involvement upon weight loss and maintenance', *Behavior Therapy*, vol. 13, pp. 681–93.

Murray, J. B. (1989) 'Psychologists and alcoholic women', *Psychological Reports*, vol. 64, pp. 627–44.

Nathan, P. E. and Skinstad, A. H. (1987) 'Outcomes of treatment for alcohol problems: current methods, problems, and results', *Journal of Consulting and Clinical Psychology*, vol. 55, pp. 332–40.

National Campaign Against Drug Abuse (1992) *Statistical Update: Number 17*, Canberra, Department of Health, Housing and Community Services.

National Institute on Drug Abuse (1999) 'Treatment methods for women', NIDA Infofax #13562, Maryland.

New Internationalist (1984) 'Dealing with dreams', no. 140, October.

Niaura, R., Rohsenow, D., Binkoff, J., Monti, P., Pedraza, M. and Abrams, D. B. (1988) 'The relevance of cue reactivity to understanding alcohol and smoking relapse', *Journal of Abnormal Psychology*, vol. 2, pp. 133–52.

Oei, T. P. S. and Jackson, P. (1980) 'Long-term effects of group and individual social skills training with alcoholics', *Addictive Behaviors*, vol. 5, pp. 129–36.

Oei, T. P. S. and Jackson, P. (1982) 'Social skills and cognitive behavioral approaches to the treatment of problem drinking', *Journal of Studies on Alcohol*, vol. 43, pp. 532–47.

O'Farrell, T. J. and Cowles, K. S. (1989) 'Marital family therapy', in R. K. Hester and W. R. Miller (eds), *Handbook of Alcoholism Treatment Approaches: Effective Alternatives*, New York, Pergamon Press.

O'Farrell, T. J., Cutter, H. S. G. and Floyd, F J. (1985) 'Evaluating behavioral marital therapy for male alcoholics: effects on marital adjustment and communication before to after treatment', *Behavior Therapy*, vol. 16, pp. 147–67.

Orford, J. (1985) *Excessive Appetites: A Psychological View of Addictions*, New York, John Wiley.

Orford, J. (1999) 'Future research directions: a commentary on Project MATCH', *Addiction*, vol. 94, pp. 62–6.

Orford, J. and Edwards, G. (1977) *Alcoholism: A Comparison of Treatment and Advice, with a Study of the Influence of Marriage*, London, Oxford University Press.

Orford, J. and Guthrie, S. (1976) 'Coping behaviour used by wives of alcoholics: a preliminary investigation', in G. Edwards, M. A. H. Russell, D. Hawks and M. MacCafferty (eds), *Alcohol Dependence and Smoking Behaviour*, London, Saxon House.

Orford, J., Guthrie, S., Nicholls, P., Oppenheimer, E., Egert, S. and Hensman, C. (1975) 'The cohesiveness of alcoholism-complicated marriages and its influence on treatment outcome', *British Journal of Psychiatry*, vol. 36, pp. 1254–67.

Orleans, T. C., Schoenbach, V. J., Wagner, E. H., Quade, D., Salmon, M. A., Pearson, D. C., Fiedler, J., Porter, C. Q. and Kaplan, B. H. (1991) 'Self-help quit smoking interventions: effects of self-help materials, social support instruction, and telephone counseling', *Journal of Consulting and Clinical Psychology*, vol. 59, pp. 439–48.

Parker, M. W., Winstead, D. K. and Willi, F. J. (1979) 'Patient autonomy in alcohol rehabilitation: I. Literature review', *International Journal of the Addictions*, vol. 14, pp. 1015–22.

Pendery, M. L., Maltzman, I. M. and West, L. J. (1982) 'Controlled drinking by alcoholics? New findings and a reevaluation of a major affirmative study', *Science*, vol. 217, pp. 169–75.

Pincus, A. and Minahan, A. (1973) *Social Work Practice: Method and Model*, Itasca, Ill., Peacock Publishers.

Pliner, P. and Cappell, H. (1974) 'Modification of affective consequences of alcohol: a comparison of social and solitary drinking', *Journal of Abnormal Psychology*, vol. 83, pp. 418–25.

Polich, J. M., Armor, D. J. and Braiker, H. B. (1981) *The Course of Alcoholism: Four Years After Treatment*, New York, Wiley.

Polich, M. J., Ellickson, P. L., Reuter, P. and Kahan, J. P. (1984) *Strategies for Controlling Adolescent Drug Use*, Santa Monica, Calif., Rand Corporation.

Pomerleau, O. F. (1984) 'Reinforcing properties of nicotine: smoking and induced vospressin and beta-endorphin release, antioception and anxiety reduction', *Pavlovian Journal of Biological Science*, vol. 19, p. 107.

Porterfield, K. M. (1992) *Teenage Perspectives: Focus on Addiction*, Oxford, ABC-CLIO.

Posavac, E. J. and Carey, R. G. (1985) *Program Evaluation: Methods and Case Studies*, 2nd edn, Englewood Cliffs, NJ, Prentice-Hall.

President's Commission on Organized Crime (1986) *American's Habit: Drug Abuse, Drug Trafficking; and Organized Crime*, Washington, DC, Government Printing Office.

Prochaska, J. O. (1979) *Systems of Psychotherapy: A Transtheoretical Analysis*, Homewood, Ill., Dorsey Press.

Prochaska, J. O. and DiClemente, C. C. (1982), 'Transtheoretical therapy: toward a more integrative model of change', *Psychotherapy: Theory, Research and Practice*, vol. 19, pp. 276–8.

Prochaska, J. O. and DiClemente, C. C. (1983) 'Stages and processes of self-change of smoking: toward an integrative model of change', *Journal of Consulting and Clinical Psychology*, vol. 51, pp. 390–5.

Prochaska, J. O. and DiClemente, C. C. (1984) *The Transtheoretical Approach: Crossing the Traditional Boundaries of Therapy*, Homewood, Ill., Dow Jones/Irwin.

Prochaska, J. O. and DiClemente, C. C. (1988) 'Toward a comprehensive model of change', in W. R. Miller and N. Heather (eds), *Treating Addictive Behaviors*, New York, Plenum Press.

Prochaska, J. O. and DiClemente, C. C. (1992) 'Criticisms and concerns of the transtheoretical model in light of recent research', *British Journal of Addiction*, vol. 87, pp. 825–35.

Prochaska, J. O. and Velicer, W. F. (1997) 'The transtheoretical model of health behavior change', *American Journal of Health Promotion*, vol. 12, pp. 38–48.

Prochaska, J. O., DiClemente, C. C. and Norcross, J. C. (1992) 'In search of how people change: applications to addictive behaviors', *American Psychologist*, vol. 47, pp. 1102–14.

Prochaska, J. O., Crimi, P., Lapsanski, D., Martel, L. and Reid, P. (1982) 'Self-change processes, self-efficacy and self-concept in relapse and maintenance of cessation of smoking', *Psychological Reports*, vol. 51, pp. 983–90.

Prochaska, J. O. Diclemente, C. C. and Norcross, J. C. (1997) 'In search of how people change: Applications to addictive behaviors', in G. A. Marlatt and G. R. VandenBos (eds), *Addictive Behaviors: Readings on Etiology, Prevention, and Treatment*. Washington, DC: American Psychological Association. pp. 671–96.

Prochaska, J. O., Velicer, W. F., Guadagnoli, E., Rossi, J. S. and DiClemente, C. C. (1991) 'Patterns of change: dynamic typology applied to smoking cessation', *Multivariate Behavioral Research*, vol. 26, pp. 83–107.

Project MATCH Research Group (1997) 'Matching alcoholism treatment to client heterogeneity: Project MATCH posttreatment drinking outcome', *Journal of Studies on Alcohol*, vol. 58, pp. 7–29.

Project MATCH Research Group (1998) 'Project MATCH secondary a priori hypotheses', *Addiction*, vol. 92, pp. 1671–98.

Raistrick, D. and Davidson, R. (1985) *Alcoholism and Drug Addiction*, London, Churchill Livingstone.

Rankin, H., Hodgson, R. and Stockwell, T. (1983) 'Cue exposure and response prevention with alcoholics: a controlled trial', *Behaviour Research and Therapy*, vol. 21, pp. 435–46.

Raynes, A. E. and Patch, V. D. (1971) 'Distinguishing features of patients who discharge themselves from psychiatric wards', *Comprehensive Psychiatry*, vol. 12, pp. 43–9.

Reed, B. G. (1982) 'Intervention strategies for drug-dependent women: an introduction', in G. M. Beschner, B. G. Reed and J. Mondanaro (eds), *Treatment Services for Drug Dependent Women*, Rockville, Md, National Institute on Drug Abuse.

Reed, B. G. (1987) 'Developing women-sensitive drug dependence services: why so difficult?', *Journal of Psychoactive Drugs*, vol. 19, pp. 151–64.

Reed, D. S. (1981) 'Reducing the costs of drinking and driving', in M. H. Moore and D. R. Gerstein (eds), *Alcohol and Public Policy: Beyond the Shadow of Prohibition*, Washington, DC, National Academy Press.

Risk Prevalence Study (1990) *Risk Factor Study Survey No. 3, 1989*, Canberra, National Heart Foundation and Australian Institute of Health.

Ritson, B. (1968) The prognosis of alcohol addicts treated by a specialized unit. *British Journal of Psychiatry*, vol. 114, pp. 1019–29.

Ritson, B. (1986) 'The merits of simple intervention', in W. R. Miller and N. Heather (eds), *Treating Addictive Behaviors: Processes of Change*, New York, Plenum Press.

Robertson, I. and Heather, N. (1985) *So You Want To Cut Down Your Drinking?*, Edinburgh, Scottish Health Education Group.

Robins, L. N. and Ratcliff, K. S. (1979) 'Continuation of antisocial behavior into adulthood', *International Journal of Mental Health*, vol. 7, pp. 96–116.

Robinson, D., Tether, P. and Teller, J. (eds) (1989) *Local Action on Alcohol Problems*, London, Routledge.

Rodriguez, M. R. P. and Lichtenstein, E. (1977) 'Dyadic interaction for the control of smoking', University of Oregon, Eugene, unpublished manuscript.

Rogers, C. R. (1951) *Client-centred Therapy*, Boston, Mass., Houghton Mifflin.

Rogers, C. R., Deckner, C. W. and Mewborn, C. R. (1978) 'An expectancy value theory approach to the long-term modification of smoking behavior', *Journal of Clinical Psychology*, vol. 34, pp. 562–6.

Rollnick, S. Heather, N. and Bell A. (1992) 'Negotiating behaviour change in medical settings: the development of brief motivational interviewing', *Journal of Mental Health*, vol. 1, pp. 25–37.

Room, R. (1973) 'The social psychology of dependence', in World Health Organisation, *The Epidemiology of Drug Dependence*, Copenhagen, WHO.

Rorstad, D. (1989) 'Relations with the local media', in D. Robinson, P. Tether and J. Teller (eds), *Local Action of Alcohol Problems*, London, Routledge.

Rosenberg, C. M., Gerrein, J. R., Manohar, V. and Liftik, J. (1976) 'Evaluation of training of alcoholism counselors', *Journal of Studies on Alcohol*, vol. 37, pp. 1236–46.

Ross, L. H. (1982) *Deterring the Drinking Driver*, Lexington, Mass., Lexington Books.

Rubin, J. L. (1979) 'Shifting perspectives on the Alcoholism Temperance Movement: 1940–1955', *Journal of Studies on Alcohol*, vol. 40, pp. 376–85.

Russell, M. A. H., Wilson, C., Taylor, C. and Baker, C. (1979) 'Effects of general practitioners' advice against smoking', *British Medical Journal*, vol. 2, pp. 231–5.

Sadava, S. W. (1975) 'Research approaches in illicit drug use: a critical review', *Genetic Psychology Monographs*, vol. 91, pp. 3–59.

Sanchez-Craig, M. (1990) 'Brief didactic treatment for alcohol and drug-related problems: an approach based on client choice', *British Journal of Addiction*, vol. 85, pp. 169–77.

Sanchez-Craig, M. and Lei, H. (1986) 'Disadvantages of imposing the goal of abstinence on problem drinkers: an empirical study', *British Journal of Addiction*, vol. 81, pp. 505–12.

Sanchez-Craig, M., Wilkinson, D. A. and Walker, K. (1987) 'Theory and methods for secondary prevention of alcohol problems: a cognitively based approach', in W. M. Cox (ed.), *Treatment and Prevention of Alcohol Problems*, Orlando, Fla, Academic Press.

Sangster, D. (1989) 'The Parrot and the Palm idea', in D. Robinson, P. Tether and J. Teller (eds) (1989), *Local Action of Alcohol Problems*, London, Routledge.

Saunders, B. and Allsop, S. (1991) 'Alcohol problems and relapse: can the clinic combat the community?', *Journal of Community and Applied Social Psychology*, vol. 1, pp. 213–21.

Schacter, S. (1982) 'Recidivism and self cure of smoking and obesity', *American Psychologist*, vol. 37, pp. 436–44.

Schuckitt, M. A. (1981) 'The genetics of alcoholism', *Alcoholism: Clinical and Experimental Research*, vol. 5, pp. 439–40.

Schuckitt, M. A. (1999) 'New findings in the genetics of alcoholism', *Journal of the American Medical Association*, vol. 281, pp. 1875–6.

Schuckitt, M. A. and Gold, E. O. (1988) 'A simultaneous evolution of multiple markers of ethanol/placebo challenges', *Archives of General Psychiatry*, vol. 45, pp. 211–16.

Seeley, J. R. (1960) 'Death by cirrhosis and the price of beverage alcohol', *Canadian Medical Association Journal*, vol. 83, pp. 1361–3.

Selzer, M. L., Vinokur, A. and Van Rooijen, L. (1975) 'Self-administered Short Michigan Alcoholism Screening Test (SMAST)', *Journal of Studies on Alcohol*, vol. 36, pp. 117–26.

Shaw, S. (1979) 'A critique of the concept of the Alcohol Dependence Syndrome', *British Journal of Addiction*, vol. 74, pp. 339–48.

Shiffman, S. (1987) 'Maintenance and relapse: coping with temptation', in T. Nirenberg (ed.), *Advances in the Treatment of Addictive Behaviors*, NJ: Ablex.

Shiffman, S. and Wills, T. A. (eds) (1985) *Coping and Substance Use*, Orlando, Fla, Academic Press.

Sicoly, F. and Ross, M. (1977) 'Facilitation of ego-biased attributions by means of self-serving observer feedback', *Journal of Personality and Social Psychology*, vol. 35, pp. 734–41.

Sisson, R. W. and Azrin, N. H. (1986) 'Family-member involvement to initiate and promote treatment of problem drinkers', *Journal of Behavior Therapy and Experimental Psychiatry*, vol. 17, pp. 15–21.

Sisson, R. W. and Azrin, N. H. (1989) 'The community reinforcement approach', in R. K. Hester and W. R. Miller (eds), *Handbook of Alcoholism Treatment Approaches: Effective Alternatives*, New York, Pergamon Press.

Sitharthan, T., Sitharthan, G., Hough, M. J. and Kavanagh, D. J. (1997) 'Cue exposure in moderation drinking: a comparison with cognitive-behavior therapy', *Journal of Consulting and Clinical Psychology*, vol. 65, pp. 878–82.

Skinner, B. F. (1953) *Science and Human Behavior*, New York, Macmillan.

Skinner, B. F. (1966) 'Operant behavior', in W. K. Honig (ed.), *Operant Behavior. Areas of Research and Application*, New York, Appleton-Century-Croft.

Skinner, H. A. and Allen, B. A. (1983) 'Differential assessment of alcoholism', *Journal of Studies on Alcohol*, vol. 44, pp. 852–62.

Snyder, M., Stephan, W. and Rosenfield, D. (1978) 'Attributional egotism', in J. Harvey, W. Ickes and R. Kidd (eds), *New Directions in Attributional Research*, Vol. 2, Hillsdale, NJ, Erlbaum.

Sobell, L. C. and Sobell, M. B. (1986) 'Can you do without alcohol abusers' self-reports?', *Behavior Therapy*, vol. 9, pp. 141–6.

Sobell, M. B. and Sobell, L. C. (1973) 'Individualized behavior therapy for alcoholics', *Behavior Therapy*, vol. 4, pp. 49–72.

Sokolow, L., Welte, J., Hynes, G. and Lyons, J. (1980) 'Treatment-related differences between female/male alcoholics', *Journal of Addiction and Health*, vol. 1, pp. 42–56.

Solomon, R. L. (1977) 'An opponent process theory of acquired motivation: the affective dynamics of addiction', in J. D. Maser and M. E. P. Seligman (eds), *Psychopathology: Experimental Models*, San Francisco, Freeman.

Solomon, R. L. and Corbitt, J. D. (1974) 'An opponent-process theory of motivation: I. Temporal dynamics of affect', *Psychological Review*, vol. 81, pp. 119–45.

Stein, I. D. (1974) *Systems Theory, Science and Social Work*, Metuchen, NJ, Scarecrow Press.

Steinglass, P., Weiner, S. and Mendelson, J. H. (1971) 'In-hospital treatment of alcoholic couples', paper presented at the Annual Meeting of the American Psychiatric Association, Anaheim, Calif.

Stevenson, J. A. (1989) '"Pub Watch": an early warning scheme', in D. Robinson, P. Tether and J. Teller (eds), *Local Action of Alcohol Problems*, London, Routledge.

Stimson, G. V. and Ogbourne, A. C. (1970) 'Survey of addicts prescribed heroin at London clinics', *Lancet*, 30 May, pp. 1163–6.

Strain, E. C., Bigelow, G. E., Liebson, L. A. and Stitzer, M. L. (1999) 'Moderate- vs high-dose methadone in the treatment of opioid dependence: a randomized trial', *Journal of the American Medical Association*, vol. 281, pp. 1000–5.

Strain, E. C., Stitzer, M. L., Liebson, I. A. and Bigelow, G. E. (1994) 'Comparison of buprenorphine and methadone in the treatment of opioid dependence', *American Journal of Psychiatry*, vol. 151, pp. 1025–30.

Strean, H. (1971) *Social Casework: Theories in Action*, Metuchen, NJ, Scarecrow Press.

Stunkard, A. J., Sorensen, T. I. A., Hanis, C., Teasdale, T. W., Chakraboratory, R., Schull, W. J. and Shulsinger, F. (1986) 'An adoption study of human obesity', *New England Journal of Medicine*, vol. 314, pp. 193–8.

Sue, D. W. (1975) 'Asian Americans: social–psychological forces affecting their life styles', in S. Picou and R. Campbell (eds), *Career Behavior of Special Groups*, Columbus, Ohio, Charles E. Merrill.

Supnick, J. A. and Colletti, G. (1984) 'Relapse coping and problem solving behavior following treatment for smoking', *Addictive Behaviors*, vol. 9, pp. 401–4.

Surgeon General (1988) *The Health Consequences of Smoking: Nicotine Addiction. A Report of the Surgeon General*, Rockville, Md, US Department of Health and Human Services.

Sutton, S. (2001) 'Back to the drawing board: a review of applications of the transtheoretical model to substance use', *Addiction*, vol. 96, pp. 175–86.

Swanson, A. J., Pantalon, M. V. and Cohen, K. R. (1999) 'Motivational interviewing and treatment adherence among psychiatric and dually diagnosed patients', *Journal of Nervous and Mental Disease*, vol. 187, pp. 630–5.

Symes, B. A. and Nicki, R. M. (1997) 'A preliminary consideration of cue-exposure, response-prevention treatment for pathological gambling behaviour: two case studies', *Journal of Gambling Studies*, vol. 13, pp. 145–57.

Tabakoff, B. and Hoffman, P. L. (1988) 'Neurochemical effects of alcohol', in Frances, R. J. and Miller, S. I. (eds) *Clinical Textbook of Addictive Disorders*, New York, NY: The Guilford Press.

Tai, B. and Blaine, J. (1997) *Naltrexone: An Antagonist Therapy for Heroin Addiction*. Bethesda, Md, National Institute on Drug Abuse.

Teller, J. (1989) 'Sensible drinking: leaflets for target groups', in D. Robinson, P. Tether and J. Teller (eds), *Local Action of Alcohol Problems*, London, Routledge.

Tether, P. and Robinson, D. (1986) *Preventing Alcohol Problems: A Guide to Local Action*, London, Tavistock.

Thornton, C. C., Gottheil, E., Gellens, H. K. and Alterman, A. I. (1977) 'Voluntary versus involuntary abstinence in the treatment of alcoholics', *Journal of Studies on Alcohol*, vol. 38, pp. 1740–8.

Tober, G. (1991) 'Helping the precontemplator', in R. Davidson, S. Rollnick and I. MacEwan (eds), *Counselling the Problem Drinker*, London, Tavistock/Routledge.

Treadway, D. C. (1989) *Before It's Too Late: Working with Substance Abuse in the Family*, New York, Norton.

Tuchfeld, B. S. (1981) 'Spontaneous remission in alcoholics: empirical observation and theoretical implications', *Journal of Studies on Alcohol*, vol. 42, pp. 626–41.

Tucker, B. M. (1982) 'Social support and coping: applications for the study of female drug abuse', *Journal of Social Issues*, vol. 38, pp. 117–37.

Vaillant, G. E. (1983) *The Natural History of Alcoholism*, Cambridge, Mass., Harvard University Press.

Vaillant, G. E. and Milofsky, E. S. (1982) 'Natural history of male alcoholism', *Archives of General Psychiatry*, vol. 39, pp. 127–33.

Valle, S. K. (1981) 'Interpersonal functioning of alcoholism counsellors and treatment outcome', *Journal of Studies on Alcohol*, vol. 42, pp. 783–90.

van den Brink, W., Hendriks, V. M., Blanken, P., Huijsman, I. A. and van Ree, J. M. (2002) *Medical Co-prescription of Heroin: Two Randomized Controlled Trials*, Utrecht, Central Committee on the Treatment of Heroin Addicts (CCBH).

Vickery, A. (1974) 'A systems approach to social work intervention: its uses for work with individuals and families', *British Journal of Social Work*, vol. 4, pp. 389–403.

Vogler, R. E., Weissbach, T. A., Compton, J. V. and Martin, G. T. (1977) 'Integrated behavior change techniques for problem drinkers in the community', *Journal of Consulting and Clinical Psychology*, vol. 45, pp. 267–79.

Vontress, C. E. (1971) 'Racial differences: impediments to rapport', *Journal of Counseling Psychology*, vol. 24, pp. 420–9.

Wallack, L. M. and Barrows, D. C. (1981) *Preventing Alcohol Problems in California: Evaluation of the Three Year 'Winners' Program*, San Francisco: California Department of Alcohol and Drug Problems.

Wallen, J. (1992) 'A comparison of male and female clients in sub-stance abuse treatment', *Journal of Substance Abuse Treatment*, vol. 9, pp. 243–8.

Ward, J., Mattick, R. P. and Hall, W. (1998) *Methadone Maintenance Treatment and Other Opioid Replacement Therapies*, University of New South Wales, Sydney, National Drug and Alcohol Research Centre.

Weiner, B. (1978) *Theories of Motivation: From Mechanism to Cognition*, Chicago, Ill., Rand McNally.

Weingardt, K. R. and Marlatt, G. A. (1998) 'Sustaining change: helping those who are still using', in W. R. Miller and N. Heather (eds), *Treating Addictive Behaviors*, 2nd edn, New York, Plenum Press.

Westerberg, V. S. (1998) What predicts success? in W. R. Miller and Heather, N. (eds), *Treating Addictive Behaviors* 2nd edn, New York, NY: Plenum Press.

Whipple, S. C., Parker, E. S. and Noble, E. P. (1988) 'An atypical neuro-cognitive profile in alcoholic fathers and their sons', *Journal of Studies on Alcohol*, vol. 49, pp. 240–4.

Wikler, A. (1965) 'Conditioning factors in opiate addiction and relapse', in D. M. Wilner and G. G. Kassebaum (eds), *Narcotics*, New York, McGraw-Hill.

Wilson G. T. (1985) 'Psycological prognostic factors in the treatment of obesity', in J. Hirsch and T. B. Van Itallie (eds), *Recent Advances in Obesity Research*, vol. 4, pp. 301–11, London, Libbey.

Wilson, G. T. and Brownell, K. D. (1980) 'Behavior therapy for obesity: an evaluation of treatment outcome', *Advances in Behaviour Research and Therapy*, vol. 3, pp. 49–86.

Wisotsky, S. (1983) 'Exposing the war on cocaine: the futility and destructiveness of prohibition', *Wisconsin Law Review*, vol. 6, pp. 1305–1426.

World Health Organisation (1969) *Sixteenth Report of the WHO Expert Committee on Drug Dependence*, WHO Technical Report Series, No. 407, Geneva, WHO.

World Health Organisation (1977) *International Classification of Disease*, 9th revision, Geneva, WHO.

World Health Organisation (1981) 'Nomenclature and classification of drug and alcohol-related problems', *Bulletin of the World Health Organisation*, vol. 59, pp. 225–42.

Worting, C. E. and Schmeling, D. (1976) 'Agenda-setting effects of drug abuse public service ads', *Journalism Quarterly*, vol. 53, pp. 743–6.

Yahne, C. E. and Miller, W. R. (1999) 'Enhancing motivation for treatment and change', in B. S. McCrady and E. E. Epstein (eds), *Addictions: A Comprehensive Guidebook*, New York, Oxford University Press.

Index